Praise for *Military Gadgets*

"*Military Gadgets* is a wide-ranging but concise overview of the high-tech stuff that's come into service over the last decade and things that will come on-line over the next dozen years. This is the most useful single-volume reference in this area that I've seen. Evans manages to be insightful and informative, and succeeds in providing a broad overview without getting thin or shallow. Emphasis is on cutting-edge thinking and technology. I can tell you where my copy of *Military Gadgets* will be kept: close at hand in the studio for emergency consultation, held ready to help me convince my listeners that I am omniscient."

—Tom Wisker, host of "Weaponry,"
WBAI Radio, New York City

"Nick Evans has done marvelously well the tedious and thorough task of collecting information from a variety of sources to allow us to understand and appreciate military gadgets without getting lost in a forest of excess complexity. This book is recommended to all, from the general public, the military practitioner, to the political decision maker. With *Military Gadgets*, one can very quickly acquaint oneself with very complex military systems."

—Professor Xavier K. Maruyama,
Naval Postgraduate School

Military Gadgets

How Advanced Technology Is Transforming Today's Battlefield . . . and Tomorrow's

FT Prentice Hall
FINANCIAL TIMES

In an increasingly competitive world, it is quality
of thinking that gives an edge—an idea that opens new
doors, a technique that solves a problem, or an insight
that simply helps make sense of it all.

We work with leading authors in the various arenas
of business and finance to bring cutting-edge thinking
and best learning practice to a global market.

It is our goal to create world-class print publications
and electronic products that give readers
knowledge and understanding which can then be
applied, whether studying or at work.

To find out more about our business
products, you can visit us at www.ft-ph.com

Pearson
Education

Military Gadgets

How Advanced Technology Is Transforming Today's Battlefield . . . and Tomorrow's

Nicholas D. Evans

FINANCIAL TIMES

An Imprint of PEARSON EDUCATION
Upper Saddle River, NJ • New York • London • San Francisco • Toronto • Sydney
Tokyo • Singapore • Hong Kong • Cape Town • Madrid
Paris • Milan • Munich • Amsterdam
www.ft-ph.com

Library of Congress Cataloging-in-Publication Data

Evans, Nicholas D.

  Military gadgets : how advanced technology is transforming today's battlefield-- and tomorrow's / Nicholas D. Evans.

  p. cm.

  Includes index.

  ISBN 0-13-144021-7

  1. United States--Armed Forces--Weapons systems. 2. Military art and science--Effect of technological innovations on--United States. 3. Naval art and science--Effect of technological innovations on--United States. 4. Aeronautics, Military--Effects of technological innovations on--United States. I. Title.

UF503.E94 2003
355.8--dc22   2003049514

Editorial/production supervision: *Donna Cullen-Dolce*
Cover design director: *Jerry Votta*
Cover design: *Nina Scuderi*
Interior design: *Meg VanArsdale*
Manufacturing buyer: *Alexis Heydt-Long*
Executive editor: *Jim Boyd*
Editorial assistant: *Linda Ramagnano*
Marketing manager: *Laura Bulcher*

© 2004 Pearson Education, Inc.
Publishing as Financial Times Prentice Hall
Upper Saddle River, New Jersey 07458

Financial Times Prentice Hall offers excellent discounts on this book when ordered in quantity for bulk purchases or special sales. For more information, please contact: U.S. Corporate and Government Sales, 1-800-382-3419, corpsales@pearsontechgroup.com. For sales outside of the U.S., please contact: International Sales, 1-317-581-3793, international@pearsontechgroup.com.

Phraselator is a trademark of VoxTec. All other company and product names mentioned herein are the trademarks or registered trademarks of their respective owners.

Printed in the United States of America

Second Printing

ISBN 0-13-144021-7

Pearson Education Ltd.
Pearson Education Australia Pty, Limited
Pearson Education Singapore, Pte. Ltd.
Pearson Education North Asia Ltd.
Pearson Education Canada, Ltd.
Pearson Educación de Mexico, S.A. de C.V.
Pearson Education—Japan
Pearson Education Malaysia, Pte. Lt

This book is dedicated to the men and women of the U.S. and allied armed forces who have dedicated their lives to the pursuit of freedom. Every day they help to make the world a safer place by protecting our homelands and helping bring support and stability to regions of conflict and areas of need around the globe.

Contents

Preface   xiii

Acknowledgments   xix

Part I: Today's Battlefield   1

1   Air Warfare   7

B-1B Lancer   10
B-2 Spirit   12
B-52 Stratofortress   15
AV-8B Harrier II Plus (Harrier "Jump Jet")   17
F-117A Nighthawk   20
Merlin HM Mk-1 Helicopter   23
AH-64D Apache Longbow   25
E-3 Sentry (AWACS)   29
E-8C Joint STARS   32
RQ-1 Predator   34
RQ-4A Global Hawk   37
Defense Satellite Communications System   39
Military Strategic and Tactical Relay System   42
Navstar Global Positioning System   44
PAVE PAWS Radar System   46
Ground-Based Electro-Optical Deep Space Surveillance   48
Evolved Expendable Launch Vehicle (EELV)   50

2   Ground Warfare   55

M1A1 Abrams   57
M2A3 and M3A3 Bradley Fighting Vehicle System   60
Challenger 2 Main Battle Tank   62
Warrior Fighting Vehicle   65
Night Vision Goggles (AN/PVS-7)   67
Joint Service Lightweight Integrated Suit Technology   70
M40/42 Chemical Biological Protective Masks   72
Marine Corps Combat Identification Program   74
Force XXI Battle Command Brigade and Below   76
Tactical Internet   79

3   Munitions   83

GBU-28/GBU-37 "Bunker Buster"   86
BLU-114/B "Blackout Bomb"   88
BLU-82/B "Daisy Cutter"   90
Massive Ordnance Air Blast Bomb   92
AGM-114B/K/M/N Hellfire   94
AIM-9 Sidewinder   96
Joint Direct Attack Munition   98
AGM-154 Joint Standoff Weapon   101
Patriot Advanced Capability-3   104
Tomahawk Cruise Missile   106
LGM-30 Minuteman III   109
LG-118A Peacekeeper   113
Trident Fleet Ballistic Missile   115

4   Naval Warfare 119

Nimitz-Class Aircraft Carrier   121
Aegis Weapons System   124
Ticonderoga-Class Cruisers   127
Arleigh Burke-Class Destroyers   130
Attack Submarines (SSN)   134
Fleet Ballistic Missile Submarines (SSBN)   139
Guided-Missile Submarines (SSGN)   142
Sea Shadow (IX 529)   144

Part II: Tomorrow's Battlefield 147

5 Air Warfare 153

F-35 Joint Strike Fighter 155
F-22 Raptor 158
RAH-66 Comanche 161
V-22 Osprey 164
X-45A Unmanned Combat Air Vehicle 167
Unmanned Combat Armed Rotorcraft 170
Organic Air Vehicle 172
Hummingbird Warrior 175
Micro Air Vehicle 176
X-43A Hypersonic Flight 179

6 Ground Warfare 183

Future Combat Systems 186
Unmanned Ground Combat Vehicle 188
Objective Force Warrior 191
Future Warrior 194
Terrorism Information Awareness 197
Human Identification at a Distance 200
Evidence Extraction and Link Discovery 202
Babylon 204
Brain Machine Interfaces 207

7 Munitions 211

Affordable Moving Surface Target Engagement 213
Self-Healing Minefield 215
Airborne Laser 218
Electromagnetic Pulse 221

8 Naval Warfare 225

CVN 21 Future Aircraft Carrier 227
DD(X) Land Attack Destroyer 229
CG(X) Cruiser 232
Littoral Combat Ship 234
Virginia-Class Submarine 237
Long-Term Mine Reconnaissance System 240

Glossary   243

References and Web Sites   253

Index   255

Preface

As members of the general public, much of what we know about modern warfare and the day-to-day status of recent conflicts around the world has been fed to us via the media in terms of newspaper articles, radio broadcasts, and live television coverage. The television coverage, in particular, has provided us with real-time images and insights into the very lives and activities of our allied forces, the enemies they have battled, and the citizens they have liberated via the last resort of war. We have been provided with a barrage of information into all aspects of these conflicts: the diplomatic stories, the economic stories, the human stories, and the military stories. During these times, we have been bombarded with a nightly parade of armchair generals and analysts talking in military parlance about strategy, weapons, and tactics, often using unintelligible acronyms for new military capabilities that we know little about. We've also witnessed the postwar peacekeeping efforts and have come to realize that peacekeeping is often as hazardous—and sometimes more so—than the battle itself.

Military Gadgets is written with the goal of providing an overview of some of the current and future advanced technologies in use by our armed services today and under development in our research labs. It covers the capabilities of our allied forces, with an emphasis on the United States, as well as some of the capabilities in place with the British forces.

If you've ever wondered how your tax dollars are being spent, this book should help to provide some insights into some of the large-scale, multi-million-, and even multi-billion-dollar programs within the President's budget and funded by the Department of Defense. In fact, the fiscal year 2004 budget for the Department of Defense requested $380 billion for three key areas: winning the global war on terrorism, sustaining near-term force readiness through high-quality people and forces, and transforming the U.S. military and defense establishment. These transformation investments are the subject of this book and include programs such as missile defense; satellite communications; information technology; precision-guided munitions; chemical and biological defense; unmanned aerial, ground, and underwater vehicles; the actual warfighter himself or herself; and general transformation programs within the U.S. Army, Navy, and Air Force. Many of these are recent initiatives that aim to bring totally new systems and capabilities to bear upon the military arsenal and the war on terrorism. Others investments are upgrade programs and service life extensions designed to keep our legacy equipment working in the near term and better suited to meet our needs as we undergo this transformation.

Just as news coverage of war has moved from weekly updates on the cinema screen during World War II to real-time video from reporters on the battlefield during Operation Iraqi Freedom and beyond, so, too, has our military equipment transformed from massive machinery and overwhelming force toward a more networked, real-time, agile, precision force. Some of the key concepts include network-centric warfare; a system-of-systems approach; battlespace dominance; and global reach, global power. These are all concepts from the much-talked-about revolution in military affairs, or RMA, that is changing today's military.

In recent years, this transformation of the military has been occurring so rapidly that even today's military equipment and systems can seem like science fiction. Today, we have missile defense systems that can take down enemy missiles with the speed and accuracy equivalent to a bullet hitting another bullet in mid-flight; we have precision-guided munitions that can hit a target area the size of a soccer field from a distance of over 15 miles; and we have record-breaking unmanned aerial vehicles (UAVs) that can perform intelligence, surveillance, and reconnaissance missions completely autonomously while flying at up to 65,000 feet with the ability to cross entire oceans. Rather than science fiction, however, these systems exemplify the above mentioned concepts of a system of systems, battlespace dominance, and global reach, global power.

If we look at some of the future technologies for the battlefield, the truth becomes even more like science fiction. Today, United States tax dollars are funding various Defense Advanced Research Projects Agency (DARPA) initiatives, such as hypersonic flight, exoskeletons for human performance augmentation, self-healing minefields as an alternative to anti-personnel mines, brain machine interfaces, high-power fiber lasers, human identification at a distance, micro-air vehicles, morphing aircraft structures, and terrorism information awareness. While today's military technologies exemplify the transformation initiatives over the last decade or two and up to recent years, current research activities will exemplify the transformation of the military, both in this decade and well beyond the next.

The aim of this book is to provide some insights into these and many other military systems and initiatives by providing a common-language description of their features, background, and usage scenarios. The book is divided into two major sections: *Today's Battlefield* and *Tomorrow's Battlefield*. Within each section are chapters specific to air warfare, ground warfare, munitions, and naval warfare.

Today's Battlefield

In the *Today's Battlefield* coverage, the air warfare section includes not only advanced manned aircraft such as the B-2 Spirit and F-117 Nighthawk, but also UAVs such as the Predator and Global Hawk, space-based systems such as the Defense Satellite Communications System (DSCS) and Milstar communications and relay satellites, the

Navstar Global Positioning System (GPS), the PAVE PAWS radar system, deep space surveillance systems such as Ground-Based Electro-Optical Deep Space Surveillance (GEODSS), and new satellite launch systems such as the Evolved Expendable Launch Vehicle (EELV).

The ground warfare section includes a combination of the latest tanks and armored vehicles, such as the M1A1 Abrams and M2 Bradley, the Challenger 2 and Warrior within the British Army, as well as the latest in night vision equipment, chemical and biological protective suits and masks, Marine Corps friend-or-foe identification systems, and digitized battlefield systems such as the Tactical Internet and Force XXI Battle Command Brigade and Below (FBCB2). These systems provide the latest in lethality, survivability, and network-centric warfare.

The section on munitions focuses on a range of traditional and smart weapons systems, such as the Bunker Buster, Blackout Bomb, Massive Ordnance Air Blast (MOAB), Hellfire missile, Joint Direct Attack Munition (JDAM), Joint Standoff Weapon (JSOW), Patriot Advanced Capability PAC-3, and Tactical Tomahawk, as well as our legacy of submarine-launched ballistic missiles (SLBMs) and intercontinental ballistic missiles (ICBMs). These systems span the historical range of mission requirements from the Cold War days of the nuclear deterrent to present-day special mission, precision strike, and ballistic missile defense requirements.

Finally, the section on naval warfare focuses on the traditional fleet of aircraft carriers, cruisers, and destroyers, such as the latest Nimitz-class carrier, the USS *Ronald Reagan* (CVN 76), the Ticonderoga-class cruisers, and the Arleigh Burke-class destroyers. It also takes a look at our advanced weapons capabilities, such as the Aegis Weapons System, our various attack submarines, ballistic-missile submarines, guided-missile submarines, and experimental stealth ships, such as the *Sea Shadow*.

Tomorrow's Battlefield

In the *Tomorrow's Battlefield* coverage, we take a look at advanced technologies and platforms that have not yet entered service but will do so in a timeframe ranging from next year out to 2025. The air warfare section includes discussion of the latest manned fighter projects, such as the F-35 Joint Strike Fighter and F-22 Raptor, plus the latest programs for unmanned flight, such as the X-45 unmanned combat air vehicle (UCAV), unmanned combat armed rotorcraft (UCAR), and the Hummingbird Warrior. The section also looks at how technologies such as hypersonic flight will enable operational weapons to fly at fives times the speed of sound.

The ground warfare section takes a look at the U.S. Army's Objective Force initiatives, including the Future Combat Systems and Objective Force Warrior programs, plus a look at the information technology initiatives, such as Terrorism Information Awareness (TIA), Human Identification at a Distance (HumanID), Babylon, and even Brain Machine Interfaces. The section also looks out to 2025 to see how the U.S. Army Soldier Systems Center at Natick, Massachusetts is conceptualizing the future soldier in its Future Warrior concept.

The section on munitions focuses on challenges such as engaging evasive, moving targets with the Affordable Moving Surface Target Engagement (AMSTE) program; new intelligent minefields such as the Self-Healing Minefield, which can help reduce casualties to personnel; and new weapons systems such as the Airborne Laser (ABL), which can defend the United States, our troops overseas, and our allies against the threats of short- and long-range ballistic missiles.

Finally, the section on naval warfare takes a look at the next-generation Navy fleet, including carriers, surface combatants, submarines, and unmanned underwater vehicles (UUVs). Coverage includes a look at the CVN 21 future carrier; the future surface combatants; including the CG(X) cruiser, DD(X) destroyer, and the Littoral Combat Ship (LCS); plus the most advanced submarine in the world, the Virginia class. The UUV that is studied is the Long-Term Mine Reconnaissance System (LMRS), which is set to enter initial operational capability in 2004.

Aim of This Book

From a sheer content perspective, the depth and breadth of these military weapon systems is so large that many books could be and have been written on several of the individual weapons systems themselves or on the topic of transformation within the military. The sheer number and complexity of systems in use within the military is staggering, as are the number of defense contractors and their market capitalizations, and the total amount of ongoing investment within the industry.

The focus of *Military Gadgets*, therefore, is not to be a complete reference of all military weapons in service today and those to come, but to focus on some of the most advanced-technology weapons systems and platforms that are in service now and that may well be in service in the future.

The book aims to take the most interesting and exciting advanced technology platforms, both large and small, and explore them within the context of the transformation of the military. These systems are examples of how our military has been transforming itself in recent years, as it has done in times past, and how it will continue to transform itself in the years to come in order to meet the changing landscape of modern warfare and the global war on terrorism. The topic of transformation within the military is discussed in each chapter so that the evolution of these weapons systems and their current technological direction can be understood in this higher context of military affairs. Those who favor the doctrine of a "revolution in military affairs" and a transformation of the military can point to some of the weapons systems in this book as a way to chart the progress of the military in achieving the various milestones along the way toward this transformation while maintaining and supporting the legacy systems that are important for the present day.

Transformation of the military is an ongoing process—a journey, rather than a destination. This book aims to demonstrate some of the current advanced technology success stories on today's battlefield and some of the ones to come on the battlefield of tomorrow.

Acknowledgments

I owe a great deal of thanks to the civilians, military personnel, science and technology organizations, and commercial defense contractors that have inspired me in the world of military gadgets and the transformation of the military—some old friends and many new acquaintances, who have expressed interest and enthusiasm for this project and have provided their insights, kind advice, and permissions.

In particular, I'd like to thank (in alphabetical order by service and company) Kate Roberts (Alvis Vickers, Ltd.); Ann Beach, Marta Newhart and Greg Thon (Boeing); Jan Walker (DARPA); Scott Lusk (Lockheed Martin); Brooks McKinney (Northrop Grumman); Jennifer Allen (Raytheon); Jean-Louis "Dutch" De Gay and Jerry Whitaker (U.S. Army SBCCOM Natick Soldier Center); Bruce Zielsdorf (U.S. Army, Public Affairs Office), Cecil Green (U.S. Army, Fort Hood Public Affairs Office), Major Philip Smith (U.S. Army, Deputy PAO for 1st Cavalry Division) and Major Alphonso L. Gamble (U.S. Army,

Force Integration Officer 1st Cavalry Division); LT Kathy Sandoz, (USN, Deputy Director of Public Affairs, Navy Office of Information, East); and Maria Zacharias (USN, Public Affairs Specialist, Naval Sea Systems Command).

I'd like to thank Jim Boyd, Executive Editor at Financial Times Prentice Hall, for his interest in bringing this idea to fruition and for his wise advice and support every step of the way. I'd also like to thank Donna Cullen-Dolce and Jerry Votta for their great work and dedication on the production side.

Finally, I'd like to thank my wife, Michele, and my sons, Andrew and David, for their patience with me and for allowing me to take family time on evenings and weekends in order to put this book together. Without your encouragement and support, this book would not have been possible.

Readers who would like to correspond with the author can contact him at *ndevans@emergingfoundations.com.*

I

Today's Battlefield

T oday's battlefield may seem like a strange place to begin a discussion of the transformation of the military. Especially when we often think of transformational initiatives as occurring within research and development programs that are not yet in operational service. Today's battlefield is vitally important, however, because it demonstrates the current, highly advanced operating capabilities of the military and some of the key transformations of the prior decades—and even recent transformations—that have made their way into active service.

Over hundreds of years, the military has continually transformed itself in order to maintain its superiority and preparedness against a wide variety of threats. Rather than a one-time event, transformation has been a basic operating principle of warfare and has been in effect since the ages of the bow and arrow. Some of the major transformational capabilities over history have included the development of the first "iron-clad" ships, the rifle, jet engine, aircraft carriers, stealth fighters, unmanned aerial vehicles, precision-guided munitions, the Internet, and network-centric warfare. Each of these technological advances has transformed the way that wars have been fought and have provided their inventors with a decided advantage of overwhelming force or capability. In some cases, they have also opened new vulnerabilities that can be exploited via asymmetric warfare.

Transformation is not limited to technology, of course. It is also about human initiative and leadership to find new solutions to ever-changing battlefield, peacekeeping, and defense situations. Even legacy technology or methods can be applied in new ways and combinations in order to achieve a transformational capability and effect. Donald Rumsfeld, Secretary of Defense for the United States Defense Department, gave an example during the recent conflict in Afghanistan after the September 11 terrorist attacks on America. In an address on "21st-Century Transformation" made to the National Defense University in early 2002, he spoke of how the Special Forces involved in the attack on Mazar-e-Sharif used a combination of laser-guided weapons, 40-year-old B-52 bombers, and men on horseback to combat Taliban and al Qaeda fighters in what was deemed as the first cavalry attack of the 21st century. A transformational capability, therefore, is not limited to advanced technologies. It can include the integration of both new and old capabilities and techniques to achieve its desired effect.

The other point to note about transformation is that not all new technology can create transformational effects. Some of it may not even be appropriate for routine military needs, due to limited practicality, high complexity, or cost. An example from over a century ago was the Moncrieff counterweight disappearing gun (Figure P1–1) used by the British. The gun was designed by Captain Colin Scott Moncrieff in 1858 and was approved for use in 1871 for British defenses around naval ports such as Plymouth, Devon, in the southwest of England. Although it had an innovative design that allowed the gun to pivot above and below the parapet of a gun emplacement for its own safety and concealment, the cost of the weapon made it unsuitable for widespread military use. The last gun of its kind was dismantled in 1900. Another factor was that at the time, soldiers were considered expendable, so there was limited incentive to invest heavily in defending gun positions beyond the basic armaments of the forts.

Figure P1–1   The Moncrieff counterweight disappearing gun. (*Source:* Photo by Nick Evans, Courtesy of Crownhill Fort)

Another example of an innovation that did not have staying power was the A1E1 heavy tank, named the *Independent* (Figure P1–2). This was an experimental tank built by the British in 1926 and comprising five rotating turrets so that the turrets could be operated independently on the battlefield. The project was abandoned as too expensive and never entered service. It did, however, influence the Russian T-35 tank, which saw operational service but had problems of its own. The T-35 had one main turret, four smaller turrets, and a crew of 11. The obvious difficulty lay in the ability for the tank commander to relay fire control, or firing, instructions to his gunners in such a multi-turreted vehicle.

Although various weapons designs were aimed at transforming the battlefield, there was also experimentation with the actual techniques of battle. In World War II, the Germans used a technique called *Blitzkrieg*, German for "lightning war," in order to conduct rapid, highly mobile, coordinated attacks on parts of enemy lines and also for broader invasions. The technique used a combination of fast-moving tanks and mobilized infantry and artillery, together with coordinated dive bombers. This transformation in how war was fought came in contrast to the trench warfare of World War I, where troops would be stuck for months with limited advances on either

Figure P1–2   The A1E1 *Independent* heavy tank. (*Source*: Photo by Nick Evans, Courtesy of the Tank Museum, Bovington)

side and a hostile "no man's land" separating the two sides. The Blitzkrieg placed the tank in an aggressive, forward position instead of being in an infantry support role; it also used air power to "soften up" targets ahead of the high-speed ground attack. The first use of the Blitzkrieg was in September 1939 during the German invasion of Poland, and it later included France and Russia. Later, this term was shortened to *the Blitz* and used to describe the German air raids over England.

In more recent years, the military has continually transformed itself in order to meet the requirements of the Cold War, the various conflicts in the Middle East, and now the global war on terrorism. Transformation today is as important, if not more so, than it ever has been in order to keep up with the ever-changing threat. The new threat is now harder to determine and prepare against. It can occur at anytime, anyplace, anywhere. Today's military has a tremendous challenge, now and in the years to come: to prepare to fight wars against the unknown, the uncertain, and the unexpected.

The good news is that today's military has taken the lessons learned from prior conflicts, together with the forward-looking initiative of its leaders, and has continually transformed itself to be able to take on enemies and defeat them with its unique projection of military power. Even before the terrorist attacks of September 11, the Department of Defense had decided to move away from the "two major theatre war" concept for force sizing and to prepare a future defense strategy comprised of the following six transformational goals:

1. Protect bases of operation at home and abroad, and defeat the threat of chemical, biological, radiological, nuclear, and high-yield explosive (CBRNE) weapons
2. Assure information systems in the face of attack and conduct effective information operations
3. Project and sustain U.S. forces in distant anti-access and area-denial environments
4. Deny enemies sanctuary by providing persistent surveillance, tracking, and rapid engagement
5. Enhance the capability and survivability of space systems
6. Leverage information technology and innovative concepts to develop interoperable joint command, control, communications, computers, intelligence, surveillance, and reconnaissance (Joint C4ISR)

The Quadrennial Defense Review of 2001, which contained these six transformational goals, also stressed the need for robust research and development efforts in order to achieve these objectives. It called for an increase in funding for science and technology (S&T) programs to a level of 3 percent of Department of Defense spending per year and for increased collaboration between private research and the government.

Because transformation is an ongoing process and needs to be balanced with sustaining current legacy forces to tackle current threats, the recapitalization of certain legacy forces is vital. Many parts of the services, especially Air Force aircraft and some of the Naval fleet, are advancing in age. The Defense Department is, therefore, selectively replacing, upgrading, and extending the life of some of these assets to prevent them from becoming operationally and technologically obsolete. Because of this, it is fitting when discussing today's battlefield that we also explore some of the legacy equipment, often a decade or more old, in addition to the newer arrivals on the scene.

As we learned from the attack on Mazar-e-Sharif, the combination of these capabilities, both old and new, can enable transformational advantage when tackling present-day threats. Transformation is also an evolution, rather than a revolution, and something that it is hoped this book will illustrate by discussing the wealth of advanced technologies, as well as some legacy assets that can aid us on this path.

1

Air Warfare

I n terms of air warfare, a powerful array of bombers, fighters, helicopters, surveillance aircraft, unmanned aerial vehicles, communications satellites, early warning systems, and space launch vehicles are all part of the current air and space inventory within the U.S. Air Force—the world's most powerful air and space force.

Many of these aircraft, such as the B-2 bomber, the F-117A fighter, and the RQ-1 Predator, are instantly familiar visually from their striking appearance and from the numerous stories in the media. The E-3A Sentry, known as AWACS, and the E-8C Joint Surveillance Target Attack Radar System, known as Joint STARS, are also well recognizable names, although the details of their mission and capabilities are often less well understood.

Along with these easily recognizable weapons and systems, there are also some lesser known technologies that are highly advanced in their capabilities. For example, the Merlin HM Mk-1 helicopter used by the British Royal Navy is a new and advanced anti-surface ship and anti-submarine helicopter. It can seek and destroy enemy submarines with a combination of radar, active sonar that is actually lowered into the water, acoustic processors, and homing torpedoes. Unmanned aerial vehicles have advanced considerably, as well. Operational unmanned aerial vehicles include the Predator, Hunter, Shadow, and Pioneer. Even developmental systems, such as the Global Hawk, have recently been placed into action. The RQ-4A Global Hawk has actually set a world endurance record for an unmanned aerial vehicle. In April 2001, it flew over 7,500 miles across the Pacific Ocean to Australia completely autonomously with no "man-in-the-loop" control required.

Moving to space, the Ground-Based Electro-Optical Deep Space Surveillance (GEODSS) system can detect and track objects as small as a basketball more than 20,000 miles in space. The PAVE PAWS radar system has a range of 3,000 nautical miles and maintains a surveillance net focused between 3 and 10 degrees above the horizontal, looking for incoming submarine-launched ballistic missiles (SLBMs) and inter-continental ballistic missiles (ICBMs). The PAVE PAWS is perhaps a reminder of the Cold War but a strategic capability that may protect us in the future.

It is, therefore, fitting to explore some of the current technologies of the U.S. Air Force, which have outstanding and record-breaking capabilities, before we start to look out further onto the horizon for the technologies of the future. Equipped with this knowledge, we will be able to realize how advanced air warfare has become over the last several decades, the importance of our assets in space, and how the dominance of air and space can play a critical part in modern warfare.

Today, the systems of the U.S. Air Force are not only highly evolved but they are also taking unique approaches toward partnering with industry in order to reduce costs of operation. An example is the Evolved Expendable Launch Vehicle (EELV), which is a space lift modernization program. The program will reduce the costs of launching Air Force satellites into space by over 25 percent and will save a projected $6 billion in launch costs between 2002 and 2020. EELV has already seen its first successful mission for the U.S. Air Force with the launch of a Defense Satellite Communications System (DSCS) payload in early 2003, using a Boeing Delta IV launch vehicle from Cape Canaveral Air Force Station in Florida.

On today's battlefield, the technologies and personnel of the Air Force play a vital role in several key areas. They can perform intelligence, surveillance, and reconnaissance to monitor activities that may signal hostile intentions, such as the buildup of troops and equipment near country boundaries, terrorist communications, or incoming missile threats. As Operation Desert Storm, Operation Iraqi Freedom, and other campaigns have shown, they can also provide a powerful strike capability to effectively win the war before the ground battle begins. Although an air war may not spell victory by itself and the ground forces are usually needed to oust invading forces or to overthrow dangerous regimes, the air campaign can serve to decapitate the command and control infrastructure so that the enemy has less ability to retaliate.

Freedom of access to space is also vitally important. Much of today's network-centric warfare is enabled by powerful satellite systems, such as DSCS and Military Strategic and Tactical Relay (Milstar), used to relay secure, jam-resistant transmissions around the world from our submarines and ships to high-priority military users, such as commanders on the ground or back at headquarters. Space is a vital asset for the military to maintain global communications and to ensure accurate global positioning via the well-known Navstar Global Positioning System (GPS) satellites. These satellites not only help civilian users of GPS data in finding their way on land and at sea with resolutions up to 3 meters in accuracy, but they also help the military in keeping track of the positions of friendly and enemy ground forces and in targeting precision munitions along with other navigation systems, such as inertial guidance.

This chapter contains coverage of a number of assets used in both air and space. These and many others form the basis of the Air Force core competencies of air and space superiority, global attack, rapid global mobility, precision engagement, information superiority, and agile combat support.

B-1B Lancer

The B-1B Lancer is the U.S. Air Force's long-range, multi-role bomber capable of intercontinental missions delivering precision and non-precision weapons without the need for refueling. This $200 million-plus aircraft can fly at supersonic speeds in excess of 900 miles per hour (mph) and was originally deployed in 1985. The crew of four includes an aircraft commander, copilot, offensive systems officer, and defensive systems officer. The B1-B is powered by four General Electric turbofan engines with afterburners. It has been used in combat in support of Operation Desert Fox, Operation Allied Force, and Operation Iraqi Freedom. It has moveable wings and a low-radar cross-section, and has set a number of world records for speed, payload, and distance.

Features

The B-1B features a variety of offensive and defensive avionics (aviation electronics), which allow it to penetrate enemy airspace and conduct missions with increased survivability. The offensive measures include a radar system that utilizes synthetic aperture radar with 3-meter accuracy, ground-moving target indicator and terrain-following radar modes, a GPS and Inertial Navigation System (INS), an avionics control unit, a Doppler radar, and a radar altimeter. All these offensive features allow B-1B crews to conduct their missions without the need for ground-based navigation aids.

The B-1Bs defensive avionics include electronic and other forms of counter-measures that can detect and respond to enemy radar systems and missiles. Electronic jamming is applied to counter enemy radar detection, and expendable chaff and flares can be used to counter heat-seeking missiles approaching from the rear. Towed decoy, systems such as the ALE-50 or the ALE-55, can also be used to provide protection against radio frequency (RF) threats. The radar signature of the aircraft is also reduced to just 1 percent of that of the B-52, due to its shape and radar-absorption materials.

The three internal bays of the B-1B can incorporate up to 84 Mk-82 general-purpose bombs or Mk-62 naval mines, 30 Cluster Bomb Units (CBUs), 24 Joint Direct Attack Munitions (JDAMs), 30 Wind-

Figure 1–1   B-1B Lancer. (*Source:* Boeing)

Corrected Munition Dispensers (WCMDs), 12 Joint Standoff Weapons (JSOWs), or 24 Joint Air-to-Surface Standoff Missiles (JASSMs).

Background

The B-1B (Figure 1–1) is a modified B-1A that includes upgrades for its offensive and defensive avionics, as well as weapons payload, range, and speed. The first B-1B, *The Star of Abilene*, was delivered to Dyess Air Force Base (AFB) in Texas in June 1985. Dyess AFB is home to the 9th Bomb Wing of the U.S. Air Force and holds 39 of the B-1B bombers manufactured between 1985 and 1988. Other AFBs for the B-1B include Ellsworth AFB in South Dakota and Mountain Home AFB in Idaho.

The B-1B was originally used as a nuclear weapons carrier during the Cold War and was modified to carry conventional weapons as part of the Conventional Mission Upgrade Program (CMUP) in 1993. Since 1993, this upgrade program has added capabilities for Mk-82 non-precision 500-pound bombs, CBUs, an ALE-50 repeater decoy system, JDAM weapons systems, anti-jam radios, plus JSOW and JASSM weapons for increased standoff capability.

Facts

Type: Long-range, multi-role, heavy bomber
Contractor: Boeing, North America (formerly Rockwell International, North American Aircraft)
Operations Air Frame and Integration: Offensive avionics, Boeing Military Airplane; defensive avionics, AIL Division
Length: 146 feet (44.5 meters)
Wingspan: 137 feet (41.8 meters) extended forward, 79 feet (24.1 meters) swept aft
Height: 34 feet (10.4 meters)
Weight: Empty, approximately 190,000 pounds (86,183 kilograms)
Maximum Takeoff Weight: 477,000 pounds (216,634 kilograms)
Powerplant: 4 General Electric F-101-GE-102 turbofan engines with afterburners
Thrust: 30,000-plus pounds with afterburner per engine
Speed: 900-plus mph (Mach 1.2 at sea level)
Range: Intercontinental, unrefueled
Ceiling: More than 30,000 feet (9,144 meters)
Armament: 3 internal weapons bays can accommodate up to 84 Mk-82 general-purpose bombs or Mk-62 naval mines, 30 CBU-87/89 cluster munitions or CBU-97 Sensor Fused Weapons, and up to 24 GBU-31 JDAM GPS-guided bombs or Mk-84 general-purpose bombs
Crew: 4 (aircraft commander, copilot, offensive systems officer, and defensive systems officer)
Date Deployed: June 1985
Unit Cost: $283.1 million (fiscal 98 constant dollars)
Inventory: Active force, 72; ANG, 18; Reserve, 0

Source: U.S. Air Force

B-2 Spirit

The B-2 Spirit is a multi-role, long-range bomber operated by the U.S. Air Force that can deliver conventional or nuclear weapons and penetrate deep into enemy defenses, due to its advanced stealth technology. Its stealth technology includes reduced signatures for infrared, acoustic, electromagnetic, visual, and radar observation, making it hard for enemy defensive systems to detect and engage.

The B-2 was first revealed to the public in 1988 and has a unit cost in excess of $1 billion. The crew consists of two pilots, compared with the four of the B-1B. The two crew members include a pilot who sits on the left and a mission commander who sits on the right. The active inventory of the B-2 is 21 aircraft, all of which are operated out of Whiteman AFB in Missouri, home to the 509th Bomb Wing. The B-2 is manufactured by Northrop Grumman as the prime contractor and has seen operations in Operation Allied Force, Operation Enduring Freedom, and Operation Iraqi Freedom.

Features

The B-2 flies at high subsonic speeds, compared with the supersonic flight of the B-1B. Its ceiling, however, is 50,000 feet, compared with the B-1B's 30,000 feet. In terms of payload, it can attack eight times as many targets as the F-117A and has a capability for 40,000 pounds of munitions. Conventional unguided weapons on board the B-2 may include Mk-84 2,000-pound general-purpose bombs, Mk-82 500-pound bombs, CBU-87/B 1,000-pound Combined Effects Munitions, CBU-89 1000-pound anti-tank and anti-personnel mines, or CBU-97 1,000-pound Sensor Fuzed Weapons for attacking armor. Conventional precision weapons on board the B-2 may include the GBU 27, JDAMs, JSOWs, and Tri-Service Standoff Attack Missiles (TSSAMs).

The range of the B-2 is 6,000 nautical miles without refueling and 10,000 miles with one refueling. It is powered by four General Electric engines, and it has a length of 69 feet and a wingspan of 172 feet. The stealth coatings on the wings of the B-2 need to be protected from rain and humidity when on the ground, so it is typical for the Air Force to use portable, air-conditioned hangars to protect them when refueling on land or when temporarily forward-deployed.

Background

The B-2 (Figure 1–2) development program started in 1981. Originally, the Air Force planned to have 132 operational aircraft in sup-

Figure 1–2   B-2 Spirit. (*Source:* U.S. Air Force)

port of Cold War strategic bombing requirements, but this number was later reduced to 21 as the need for nuclear bombing capabilities declined and the B-2 was repurposed for conventional weapons. The aircraft first entered the operational fleet at Whiteman AFB on December 17, 1993. It has been employed during Operation Allied Force and Operation Enduring Freedom, where it flew round trips to Kosovo and Afghanistan from its home base. During Operation Iraqi Freedom, some of the planes were forward-deployed to Diego Garcia Island in the Indian Ocean closer to Iraq and were based outside the U.S. for the first time in their history. Another forward-deployment base is now RAF Fairford in Gloucestershire in the United Kingdom. During Iraqi Freedom, B-2 crews would also launch from Whiteman AFB and make 37-hour round trips to Baghdad and back.

Facts

Type: Multi-role heavy bomber
Contractor: Northrop Grumman
Contractor Team: Boeing Military Airplanes, General Electric Aircraft Engine Group, and Hughes Training, Link Division

Length: 69 feet (20.9 meters)

Height: 17 feet (5.1 meters)

Wingspan: 172 feet (52.12 meters)

Takeoff Weight (Typical): 336,500 pounds (152,635 kilograms)

Power plant: 4 General Electric F-118-GE-100 engines

Thrust: 17,300 pounds each engine

Speed: High subsonic

Ceiling: 50,000 feet (15,152 meters)

Range: Intercontinental, unrefueled

Armament: Conventional or nuclear weapons

Payload: 40,000 pounds (18,144 kilograms)

Crew: 2 pilots

Unit Cost: Approximately $1.157 billion (fiscal 98 constant dollars)

Date Deployed: December 1993

Inventory: Active force, 21 (1 test); ANG, 0; Reserve, 0

Source: U.S. Air Force

B-52 Stratofortress

Like the B-1B and B-2, the B-52 is a multi-role, long-range heavy bomber. It is capable of carrying nuclear or conventional ordnance and has a ceiling of 50,000 feet and a speed of 650 mph. The Boeing-manufactured aircraft is considered the backbone of the strategic bombers in the U.S. Air Force and has been in service since 1955. It is kept updated with the latest technologies, including refined electronic defensive and offensive systems, more powerful Pratt & Whitney turbofan engines, and low-altitude capabilities. It has proven its worth during many operations, including most recently, Operation Desert Storm, Operation Enduring Freedom, and Operation Iraqi Freedom. During Desert Storm, the aircraft dropped 40 percent of all weapons dropped by coalition forces. At the time of the aircraft's 50th anniversary on April 12, 2002, it had also dropped nearly 35 percent of ordnance during Operation Enduring Freedom.

Features

The B-52 has a crew of five that includes an aircraft commander, pilot, radar navigator, navigator, and electronic warfare officer. It is powered by eight Pratt & Whitney turbofan engines and has a length of 159 feet and a wingspan of 185 feet. In terms of ordnance, it is the most capable of all the strategic bombers and can carry up to 70,000 pounds of payload internally or attached to its external pylons. Typical ordnance employed includes gravity bombs, cluster bombs, precision-guided missiles, and JDAMs. Its range is 8,800 miles. Perhaps the most amazing feature of the B-52 is its longevity. Having been introduced into service in 1955, it has been a part of almost all major military operations since that time and is projected to continue in service past 2040 through a Boeing service life extension program.

Background

The origin of the B-52 (Figure 1–3) dates back to 1946 when the U.S. Army Air Force issued a requirement for a new, long-range heavy bomber. In the same year, Boeing was awarded an engineering study and preliminary design contract for the B-52. A total of 744 B-52 bombers were built by Boeing, including the XB-52 and YB-52 test models, at its plants in Wichita and Seattle up until October 1962. Today, the inventory is maintained by the U.S. Air Force's Air Combat Command and the Air Force Reserves. Air Combat Command has a total of 94 B-52H models in service today, which are based at Barksdale AFB in Louisiana. During the first Gulf War, B-52s conducted round trip sorties from Barksdale to Iraq and back during 35-hour nonstop missions.

Facts

Type: Heavy bomber
Contractor: Boeing Military Airplane Co.
Length: 159 feet, 4 inches (48.5 meters)
Height: 40 feet, 8 inches (12.4 meters)
Wingspan: 185 feet (56.4 meters)
Powerplant: 8 Pratt & Whitney engines TF33-P-3/103 turbofan

Figure 1–3   B-52 Stratofortress. (*Source:* U.S. Air Force)

Thrust: Each engine up to 17,000 pounds
Speed: 650 mph (Mach 0.86)
Ceiling: 50,000 feet (15,151.5 meters)
Weight: Approximately 185,000 pounds empty (83,250 kilograms)
Maximum Takeoff Weight: 488,000 pounds (219,600 kilograms)
Range: Unrefueled 8,800 miles (7,652 nautical miles)
Armament: Approximately 70,000 pounds (31,500 kilograms) mixed ordnance: bombs, mines, and missiles. (Modified to carry air-launched cruise missiles, Harpoon anti-ship, and Have Nap missiles.)
Crew: 5 (aircraft commander, pilot, radar navigator, navigator, and electronic warfare officer)
Accommodations: 6 ejection seats
Unit Cost: $53.4 million (fiscal 98 constant dollars)
Date Deployed: February 1955
Inventory: Active force, 85; ANG, 0; Reserve, 9

Source: U.S. Air Force

AV-8B Harrier II Plus (Harrier "Jump Jet")

The AV-8B Harrier II Plus is known to many as the *Harrier Jump Jet*, which originated in the 1960s. This latest incarnation is used by the U.S. Marine Corps to attack and destroy both surface and air targets and for close air support of ground troops. It is characterized by its vertical and short take-off and landing (V/STOL) capability, which enables it to take off and land with minimal runway requirements. The aircraft achieves this by using four rotating nozzles that can direct the airflow from its single Rolls Royce Pegasus turbofan engine either downward or horizontally. To take off, the aircraft directs the nozzles downward; to gain forward speed, the nozzles are rotated through 90 degrees to their horizontal position.

In addition to being in service with the U.S. Marine Corps, the aircraft is also used by the Spanish and Italian Navy and the British Royal Air Force. The British aircraft is designated the Harrier GR7 and has RAF-specific modifications to its navigation and defensive systems, as well as additional underwing pylons for carrying Sidewinder air-to-air missiles.

Features

In addition to its unique V/STOL capability, the Harrier is also capable of carrying a variety of air-to-air and air-to-surface munitions. These may include the Sidewinder, Maverick, Advanced Medium-Range Air-to-Air Missile (AMRAAM), laser-guided bombs, cluster bombs, and precision-guided weapons systems such as JDAM. The aircraft also has a 25-mm rapid-fire Gatling gun. Its maximum speed is approximately 661 mph, and its range is 1,600 miles.

Pilots keep the aircraft stable during initial hover by using "puffers," which are built into the wingtips. These puffers direct small amounts of additional air flow from the engine so that the plane can fine-tune its balance to complement the lift being generated by the nozzles.

Background

The Harrier II Plus (Figure 1–4) was developed as part of a three-nation agreement between the United States, Spain, and Italy. The first production aircraft was delivered in November 1983 and was manufactured by Boeing, BAE SYSTEMS, and Rolls Royce. The U.S. Marine Corps received its first aircraft in July 1993. In the United Kingdom, the first flight of the Harrier GR7 was in 1989, with deliveries to RAF squadrons beginning in 1990. British deployments of

Figure 1–4   AV-8B Harrier II Plus. (*Source*: Boeing)

Harriers have included NATO and United Nations operations in Bosnia, Serbia, and in the Persian Gulf. The British Royal Navy has its own version of the Harrier, the Sea Harrier. As part of a move toward a Joint Force Harrier, the Royal Navy will be retiring the Sea Harrier by 2006 and replacing it with the GR7 and its successor, the GR9.

During Operation Desert Storm, the Harrier was the first Marine Corps tactical strike platform to arrive within the theater. The aircraft flew over 3,380 sorties and maintained a mission capable rate of over 90 percent. It has also seen service in Operation Southern Watch, Operation Allied Force, and Operation Enduring Freedom.

Facts

Type: Attack and destroy surface targets under day and night visual conditions
Contractor: McDonnell Douglas
Length: 46.3 feet (14.11 meters)
Wingspan: 30.3 feet (9.24 meters)
Propulsion: Rolls Royce F402-RR-408 turbofan engine
Thrust: F402-44-408: 23,400 pounds

Armament: Mk-82 series 500-pound bombs, Mk-83 series 1,000-pound bombs, GBU-12 500-pound laser-guided bombs, GBU-16 1000-pound laser-guided bombs, AGM-65F IR Maverick missiles, AGM-65E Laser Maverick missiles, CBU-99 cluster munitions, AIM-9M sidewinders, Lightening II targeting POD to deliver GBU-12 and GBU-16 bombs with pinpoint accuracy.
Crew: 1
Date Deployed: January 12, 1985; AV-8BII (Plus) introduced in June 1993
Unit Replacement Cost: $23.7 million

Source: U.S. Marine Corps

F-117A Nighthawk

The F-117A Nighthawk is a single-seat, subsonic stealth fighter that is used as a tactical, precision strike aircraft within heavily defended airspace. It was the world's first operational aircraft to exploit low-observable stealth technology. Its stealth design gives it a radar cross-section equivalent to a large bird to help it evade enemy radar and deliver its payload of munitions. Manufactured by Lockheed Martin as a "Skunk Works" project, the aircraft achieved initial operational capability in 1983 and has seen combat in Operation Just Cause in Panama, Operation Desert Storm, Operation Allied Force, and several other missions.

Features

The main feature of the F-117A Nighthawk that differentiates it from most other aircraft is its heavy use of stealth technology. The highly angular shape of the aircraft, combined with other stealth techniques, means that it has a very low radar signature that approximates 0.01 square meters in cross-section, equivalent to a large bird. This means that not only is it hard to detect, but it is also not detected until it is within a few miles of any tracking radar system, giving an adversary less time to react.

Due to the faceting of the aircraft, most electromagnetic energy from radar is reflected at angles other than that of the arriving signal and, therefore, never returned to the tracking radar. The radar signature is also minimized through the use of radar-absorbent materials coated onto the plane's surface. Additionally, weapons are carried on swing-down trapezes within an internal weapons bay to avoid radar reflection from the externally carried munitions of conventional aircraft. The heat signature of the aircraft, another detectable feature, is reduced by mixing cold air with the exhaust gases and passing them through slots between the wings and the tail.

The aircraft is a single-seater, which is unusual for an attack aircraft, due to the requirements for navigation and mission planning that are typically carried out by two or more pilots. It is powered by two General Electric F404 turbofan engines and features quadruple redundant fly-by-wire flight controls. Pilot workload is reduced by an advanced digital avionics suite that includes support for navigation and attack systems and automated mission planning. Air refueling means that the aircraft has a practically unlimited range and can operate long-duration missions from U.S. air bases, in addition to being forward-deployed when necessary.

Background

The origin of the F-117A (Figure 1–5) was the "Have Blue" project in 1973. This project was launched to study the creation of stealth combat aircraft with little or no radar signature. The "Have Blue" research aircraft were first flown in Area 51 in Nevada in 1977. The production decision on the F-117A was made in 1978, and it was just 31 months later that the first flight of the F-117A occurred in June 1981. The aircraft was not announced publicly until 1988 and remained a secret for many years. Nighthawk production ran between 1982 and 1990, and a total of 65 were produced by Lockheed Aeronautical Systems Company.

During Operation Desert Storm, the Nighthawk flew over 1,300 sorties and was the only U.S. or coalition aircraft to strike targets in downtown Baghdad. Nighthawks also led the first allied air strike against Yugoslavia in March 1999 during NATO's Operation Allied Force.

Although the Nighthawk dates back several decades from the present day, it has made a significant impact on the transformation of the military in terms of low-observable stealth technology and has provided considerable advantage for modern day air warfare. Its pre-

Figure 1–5   117A Nighthawk. (*Source:* Lockheed Martin)

cision strike and stealth capabilities enable it to penetrate highly defended airspace and conduct first-strike missions against high-value targets, such as enemy radar and command bunkers.

Facts

Type: Fighter/attack
Contractor: Lockheed Aeronautical Systems
Length: 63 feet, 9 inches (19.4 meters)
Height: 12 feet, 9.5 inches (3.9 meters)
Weight: 52,500 pounds (23,625 kilograms)
Wingspan: 43 feet, 4 inches (13.2 meters)
Powerplant: 2 General Electric F404 nonafterburning engines
Speed: High subsonic
Range: Unlimited with air refueling
Armament: Internal weapons carriage
Unit Cost: $45 million
Crew: 1
Date Deployed: 1982
Inventory: Active force, 55; ANG, 0; Reserve, 0

Source: U.S. Air Force

Merlin HM Mk-1 Helicopter

The Merlin HM Mk-1 is an anti-surface-ship and anti-submarine helicopter in use by the British Royal Navy. It features a state-of-the-art, integrated mission system that gives it an independent capability to search for, locate, and attack enemy targets, such as submarines.

Features

In addition to anti-surface-ship and anti-submarine warfare, the Merlin is required to perform secondary roles, including search and rescue, troop support, vertical replenishment, and casualty evacuation as a replacement for the Sea King HAS Mk-6 helicopter. The Merlin, which is a derivative of the EH101 helicopter, operates from Royal Navy Invincible-class aircraft carriers and Type-23 frigates. It is tasked with carrying an array of sensors, electronics, and weapons over long distances as part of its mission. This includes operating day and night and in high sea states.

The helicopter has a dual redundant flight control system and is operated by a crew of three: pilot, observer, and air crewman. Autopilot functionality enables the pilot to fly most of the mission in a hands-off mode as necessary. Sensors and weapons systems include a Marconi Blue Kestrel radar, Thomson-Marconi active "dunking" sonar, GEC Marconi AQS 903 acoustic processor, and homing torpedoes. The radar is mounted underneath the helicopter cockpit in a flat circular dome and is capable of full 360-degree operation. All crew members have access to management computers and tactical displays onboard the aircraft.

During a mission, a common technique is for the Merlins to operate in pairs. One aircraft performs the search function with radar and sonar while the second is used to deploy the torpedoes, once the target has been located. The active "dunking" sonar is lowered into the water from the Merlin and is used to enhance submarine detection range. The torpedoes are dropped via parachute, and once in the water, they detach from the parachute, arm themselves, and actively steer toward their target.

Stationed at Royal Naval Air Station (RNAS) Culdrose in Cornwall, United Kingdom, there are a total of 44 aircraft in active service.

Lockheed Martin serves as the prime contractor with EH Industries, the company formed by Agusta of Italy and GKN Westland in the United Kingdom as the subcontractor for the aircraft portion of the overall mission system.

Two other capabilities that support the operations of the Merlin include the Merlin Training System (MTS) and the Merlin Support and Spares Availability System (MSSAS). MTS is based at RNAS Culdrose, Cornwall and features a Weapon System Trainer, Mechanical System Trainer, various subsystem trainers, computer-based training, and air crew trainers. The air crew trainers feature cockpit simulators with visual displays that can be coupled together for full mission situations across air crews to be rehearsed. The MSSAS program is used to supply spares to the Merlin helicopters for the first five years of the helicopters' operational use. It also serves to model and forecast the demand for spares and for service in order to improve understanding of aircraft demands over time.

Background

The Merlin (Figure 1–6) is one of the most technically advanced aircraft in the Fleet Air Arm—the air component of the British Royal Navy. The Merlin contract was awarded in 1991 and called for the delivery of 44 aircraft by 2002. The first flight by a production Merlin occurred on December 6, 1995, and the first mission system-fitted Merlin flew in January 1997. The first aircraft was delivered to the Royal Navy in December 1998 and the final aircraft in December 2002.

In June 2003, the British Ministry of Defense, Defense Procurement Agency, announced the selection of Lockheed Martin UK Ltd. as the preferred contractor to perform a two-year, 18-million-pound assessment on possible upgrades for the Merlin Mk-1. These changes will be made as a result of operational experience from the Gulf and from technology advances since the aircraft was first conceived. Included in these possible upgrades are enhancements to improve the utility and versatility of the aircraft, particularly in the area of surface surveillance.

Figure 1–6 Merlin. (*Source*: Lockheed Martin)

Facts

Type: Anti-submarine warfare

Contractor: Lockheed Martin

Length: 22.9 meters

Rotor Diameter: 18.6 meters

Maximum Weight: 14,600 kilograms

Powerplant: 3 Rolls Royce Turbomeca freepower turbines

Maximum Speed: 167 knots

Weapons: 4 homing torpedoes or depth charges

Radius of Operation: Over 200 nautical miles

Crew: 1 pilot, 1 observer, 1 air crewman

Service: Royal Navy (RNAS Culdrose, Cornwall, United Kingdom)

Date Deployed: March 1999 (12 aircraft)

Total Program Cost: 4.65 billion (U.K. pounds)

Source: Royal Navy, Lockheed Martin

AH-64D Apache Longbow

The AH-64D Apache Longbow is the U.S. Army's multi-role combat helicopter. It is the next generation of the AH-64A Apache and is equipped with fully integrated avionics and weapons plus communications upgrades that allow it to communicate with the Army's Tactical Internet. The Longbow designation means that it is equipped with a millimeter wave fire control radar (FCR) for target detection and classification, in addition to other upgrades that help it to keep pace with the Army's transformation to the Objective Force.

Features

The Apache Longbow is a twin-engine, four-bladed helicopter that is designed to operate in day, night, and adverse weather conditions and provide aerial weapons delivery to engage armored targets, primarily tanks, and other enemy targets, such as air defense radar systems. It is manned by a pilot in the elevated rear seat and a copilot gunner (CPG) in the front seat of the helicopter.

In terms of armament, the Apache Longbow can carry AGM-114 Hellfire anti-tank missiles, AGM-122 Sidearm anti-radar missiles, AIM-9 Sidewinder air-to-air missiles, 70-mm folding-fin aerial rockets, and an M230 33-mm gun. A typical payload is 16 Hellfire missiles, 76 70-mm rockets, or a combination of both. The configurations vary according to mission type, which can include combat, multi-role, close support and ground support.

The FCR is easily visible mounted above the four blades of main rotor head of the helicopter, and its technical functionality makes the Apache Longbow the most advanced combat helicopter in the world. Using this system, the helicopter is able to detect and classify more than 128 targets (stationary or mobile), prioritize the most important 16 targets, and initiate a fire-and-forget attack using its Hellfire missiles or other armaments in under one minute for the entire operation. At the same time, it can also transmit images and target location information to other aircraft or ground forces.

The Longbow is a good example of how the Army's capabilities can be transformed by taking proven platforms, such as the AH-64A, and modernizing them with planned upgrades, such as support for the Tactical Internet and improved fire control systems. These planned upgrades enable the Apache to be a part of the Objective Force by supporting digital communication of real-time battlefield information to air and ground forces.

Other innovative upgrades include a new blade fold system that can reduce the time it takes to deploy the aircraft into combat anywhere around the world after it has been transported via cargo planes, such as the C-5. The blade fold system means that the blades remain attached to the aircraft while in transit, can be quickly reassembled for flight, and do not have to be removed, as was done previously. This also saves space, allows six helicopters to be transported on a C-5, and even eliminates the need for additional planes to haul special reassembly equipment.

Background

The AH-64A Apache went into production in the early 1980s, and the first helicopter entered U.S. Army service in 1984. For over a decade, the AH-64A was recognized as the most advanced combat-proven helicopter in the world and has played a role in most modern day conflicts.

Manufactured by Boeing in Mesa, California, the production of the Apache transitioned from the AH-64A to the newer AH-64D (Figure 1–7) in 1997. The first AH-64D Apache was introduced to the public in June 1998 at Fort Hood in Texas, and the first fully equipped unit was fielded in November of the same year.

In total, over 1,300 Apaches have been delivered to customers around the world, and Boeing expects to have delivered over 2,000 worldwide by the end of the decade. International customers for the Longbow include Egypt, Israel, Japan, Kuwait, The Netherlands, the Republic of Singapore, and the United Kingdom. In the United Kingdom, the Longbow is designated as AH Mk1 by the British Army.

During Operation Iraqi Freedom, Apaches destroyed between 40 and 50 Iraqi tanks, personnel carriers, air defense guns, artillery systems, and armed vehicles, according to the U.S. Army. Prior to and during the previous Gulf War, Apaches were credited with playing a major role in the liberation of Kuwait by destroying enemy radar sites, then destroying more than 500 tanks during Operation Desert

Figure 1–7   AH-64D Apache Longbow. (*Source*: Boeing)

Storm. The Apache Longbow is expected to be a crucial part of the U.S. Army inventory until the year 2025 or beyond.

Facts

Type: Multi-role combat helicopter
Contractor: Boeing
Length: 58.17 feet (17.73 meters)
Height: 16.25 feet (4.95 meters)
Wingspan: 17.15 feet (5.227 meters)
Combat Mission Speed: 167 mph
Combat Range: 300 miles
Combat Endurance: 2.5 hours
Mission Weight: 16,600 pounds
Armament: Hellfire missiles, 2.75-inch rockets, and 30-mm chain gun
Crew: 2 (pilot and copilot gunner)
First Flight: September 30, 1975
First Entered Service: AH-64A (1984), AH-64D (1998)

Source: U.S. Army, Boeing

E-3 Sentry (AWACS)

The E-3 Sentry is the premier air battle command and control aircraft in the world today. It is an airborne warning and control system (AWACS) that provides surveillance, command, control, and communications for the U.S., NATO, and other allied forces, such as the United Kingdom, France, and Saudi Arabia.

Features

The AWACS is based on a modified Boeing 707/320 commercial airliner frame and is distinguished by the rotating radar dome, measuring 30 feet in diameter and 6 feet in thickness, called a *radome*, mounted 14 feet above the fuselage by two vertical struts. The equipment within the radome performs surveillance over land or water with a range of up to 375 kilometers. The radar can be combined with a friend-or-foe identification system to detect, identify, and track low-flying aircraft and even surface ships. Because it is airborne and mobile, this radar system has the potential for greater survivability during a conflict than do ground-based radars and is also not subject to ground clutter returns that decrease the signal-to-noise ratio for ground-based radar.

The AWACS includes computer subsystems on board that can collect and interpret data in real time and present the information via computer display equipment to the crew. This information provides them with a detailed view of the battlefield in terms of the position and track of both friendly and enemy ships and aircraft, and can be relayed to command and control centers on the ground or on board other AWACS. Information from AWACS can also be forwarded to the President of the United States and the Secretary of Defense in times of crisis.

The crew consists of a flight crew of four, including two pilots, a navigator, and a flight engineer, plus a mission crew of 13 to 19 specialists. The aircraft can fly for 8 hours without refueling and can be refueled via a probe or boom system in the forward fuselage.

Missions for the AWACS can include air defense for the boundaries of U.S. and NATO countries, as well as a variety of air-to-ground operations. The air-to-ground operations include surveillance work for the U.S. Customs Service and gathering information required for interdiction, reconnaissance, airlift, and close-air support for ground forces.

Background

The AWACS (Figure 1–8) was originally developed for use during the Cold War but has recently proven its continued value during the recent Gulf conflicts and elsewhere. The first E-3s were delivered to the 552nd Airborne Warning and Control Wing in March 1977. This is now the 552nd Air Control Wing, Tinker AFB, Oklahoma and serves as the main base for the E-3 with 28 aircraft in inventory. The total inventory for the U.S. Air Force is 33, which includes aircraft at Tinker AFB plus others in Alaska and Japan.

NATO acquired its E-3s in January 1982 with the last one delivered in 1985. The United Kingdom acquired the E-3 as its airborne early warning platform instead of the Nimrod AEW 3, which had experienced delays in its in-service date.

During Operation Desert Storm, E-3s flew more than 400 missions for a total of more than 5,000 hours of on-station flight time. In this role, they supported more than 120,000 coalition sorties and provided time-critical information in support of 38 of 40 air-to-air kills recorded during the conflict.

Facts

Type: Airborne surveillance, command, control, and communications
Contractor: Boeing
Length: 145 feet, 6 inches (44 meters)
Wingspan: 130 feet, 10 inches (39.7 meters)
Height: 41 feet, 4 inches (12.5 meters)
Rotodome: 30 feet in diameter (9.1 meters), 6 feet in thickness (1.8 meters), mounted 11 feet (3.33 meters) above fuselage
Powerplant: 4 Pratt & Whitney TF33-PW-100A turbofan engines
Thrust: 21,000 pounds (9,450 kilograms) each engine
Speed: Optimum cruise 360 mph (Mach 0.48)
Ceiling: Above 29,000 feet (8,788 meters)
Maximum Takeoff Weight: 347,000 pounds (156,150 kilograms)
Endurance: More than 8 hours (unrefueled)

Figure 1–8 E-3 Sentry. (*Source:* U.S. Air Force, Photo by Master Sgt. Dave Ahlschwede)

Crew: Flight crew of 4 plus mission crew of 13–19 specialists (mission crew size varies according to mission)
Date Deployed: March 1977
Inventory: Active force, 33; Reserve, 0; Guard, 0
Unit Cost: $123.4 million (fiscal 98 constant dollars)

Source: U.S. Air Force

E-8C Joint STARS

The E-8C Joint Surveillance Target Attack Radar System (Joint STARS) is an airborne battle management and command and control platform that provides ground surveillance information, including targeting information for fixed and mobile enemy targets to ground and air theater commanders. The real-time information from Joint STARS can help to improve battlefield awareness and provide targeting information to friendly firepower, including aircraft, surface ships, and field artillery.

Features

Like AWACS, the Joint STARS aircraft is based on a modified Boeing 707-300 series aircraft that is modified to support a radar system plus various communications and operations and control subsystems. It differs externally by having the radar system mounted underneath the fuselage in a canoe-shaped radome measuring 40 feet in length, compared with the more prominent, top-mounted, circular radome on the AWACS.

Joint STARS also differs from AWACS in that it is dedicated to air-to-ground surveillance and focuses on the wide area surveillance, moving target indicator (MTI), and fixed target indicator (FTI) target classification and synthetic aperture radar within its radar operating modes. This means it can provide targeting data on fixed assets, such as airfields, buildings, bridges, power plants, and other critical infrastructure elements, as well as mobile assets such as tanks, armored vehicles, and even mobile missile launchers. It can also be used during peacekeeping operations to help monitor ground force movements. With so many enemy capabilities going mobile in order to evade attack, the ground moving target indicators on Joint STARS are also being incorporated into other newer platforms, such as unmanned aerial vehicles.

The side-looking, phased-array antenna of the radar has a 120-degree field of view and can be used to locate, classify, and track ground targets at distances of more than 250 kilometers. The data is presented in graphic or tabular format to operators on board the aircraft on video screens.

Figure 1-9 Joint STARS. (*Source:* Northrop Grumman)

Crew for the Joint STARS consists of 4 flight crew members plus 15 Air Force and 3 Army specialists but varies according to mission. For long-endurance missions with airborne refueling, this crew can be approximately doubled up to 6 flight crew members and 28 operators, for a total crew of 34. Refueling can extend the range from approximately 9 hours to 20 hours.

Background

The Joint STARS (Figure 1-9) program originated with two separate Army and Air Force programs that were merged in 1982, with the Air Force as the lead service. In September 1985, Northrop Grumman was awarded the contract to produce two Joint STARS aircraft. These aircraft were deployed in 1991 during Operation Desert Storm, flying 49 combat sorties, even while they were still in development.

After the Gulf War, the first aircraft was formally placed in service with the 93rd Air Control Wing in June 1996 and was later deployed in support of Operation Joint Endeavor. Joint STARS aircraft were also used during Operation Allied Force, Operation Enduring Freedom, and Operation Iraqi Freedom.

Facts

Type: Airborne battle management
Contractor: Northrop Grumman
Length: 152 feet, 11 inches (46.6 meters)
Height: 42 feet, 6 inches (13 meters)
Wingspan: 145 feet, 9 inches (44.4 meters)
Powerplant: 4 Pratt & Whitney TF33-102C engines
Thrust: 19,200 pounds each engine
Speed: Optimum orbit speed 390–510 knots (Mach 0.52–0.65)
Ceiling: 42,000 feet (12,802 meters)
Maximum Takeoff Weight: 336,000 pounds (152,409 kilograms)
Range: 9 hours (unrefueled)
Crew: Flight crew of 4 plus 15 Air Force and 3 Army specialists (crew size varies according to mission)
Date Deployed: 1996
Inventory: Active force, 13 (16 to be delivered to Air Force by 2004); ANG, 0; Reserve, 0
Unit Cost: $244.4 million (fiscal 98 constant dollars)

Source: U.S. Air Force

RQ-1 Predator

The RQ-1 Predator is a medium-altitude, long-endurance, unmanned aerial vehicle (UAV). It performs reconnaissance and surveillance missions; it is also capable of engaging enemy targets using precision-guided Hellfire missiles. The Predator is an entire system that is comprised of four aircraft and their sensors, a Ground Control Station (GCS), a Predator Primary Satellite Link (PPSL), and 55 associated personnel. It performs a vital role by undertaking missions in moderate-risk environments that can be dangerous for manned aircraft, due to the threat of enemy air defenses or to contamination from chemical or biological weapons. The intelligence it gathers in terms of live video imagery helps to support ground troops by giving them a view of target locations prior to engaging. Its laser designator can help to direct missile strikes launched from either the Predator itself or from other tactical aircraft.

Features

The Predator can fly at up to 25,000 feet and has a range of 400 nautical miles. Its cruising speed is around 84 mph, and it is powered by a rear-mounted propeller driven by a Rotax 914 four-cylinder engine producing just over 100 horsepower.

The system is operated by a pilot stationed on the ground who flies the unmanned Predator with a joystick or on autopilot from within the Ground Control Station housed in a small, mobile van. The pilot is able to view a live video image from the aircraft's onboard television camera mounted on the nose, and a sensor operator is also able to view events on the ground. During missions, the Predator can track and follow fast-moving vehicles and other localized events within its relatively narrow field of view and can use laser-guided Hellfire missiles to destroy enemy armored vehicles or other targets.

The Predator communications with the GCS include either a direct line-of-sight data link or a satellite data link for over-the-horizon control. The equipment carried in the bottom turret of the aircraft can provide live video, stills, and radar imagery both day and night and in all weather conditions. The data captured by the Predator can be transmitted in real time to commanders around the world using its satellite data links. These data links provide 1.5-megabytes per second (Mbps) downstream and 0.064-Mbps upstream data rates, meaning that the downstream link from the aircraft to the ground can transmit data at about the speed of a conventional broadband Internet connection.

Background

The first Predator flew in July 1994 as part of the Department of Defense's Advanced Concept Technology Demonstration (ACTD) program. The original contract for ten aircraft was awarded to General Atomics Aeronautical Systems of San Diego, California six months earlier.

The system entered production in August 1997 and made history on February 21, 2001, when it became the first unmanned aerial vehicle to launch a live missile. On that date, it completed tests in Nevada

Figure 1–10 RQ-1 Predator. (*Source:* General Atomics)

and successfully struck an unmanned Army tank using a laser-guided Lockheed Martin AGM-114 Hellfire anti-tank missile.

The Predator (Figure 1–10) is operated by the 11th and 15th reconnaissance squadrons at Indian Springs Air Force Auxiliary Field in Nevada and has seen combat action in the Balkans, Southeast Asia, the Persian Gulf, Yemen, Afghanistan, and Iraq. In Yemen, the Predator was used by the CIA to kill six al Qaeda suspects in November 2002.

Due to its low speed and medium-altitude flight, the Predator is susceptible to attack from the ground. In fact, nearly half of the Air Force's fleet were reported to have been shot down between the time the aircraft entered service and early 2003. However, this hasn't slowed down the appetite for these systems, and approximately two per month are expected to be delivered to the U.S. Air Force during 2003. During Operation Iraqi Freedom, Predators were used extensively to attack a variety of targets, including air defense batteries, missile launchers, radars, and TV satellite communications dishes, as well as for multiple reconnaissance missions.

Facts

Type: Airborne surveillance reconnaissance and target acquisition
Contractor: General Atomics Aeronautical
Length: 27 feet (8.22 meters)
Height: 6.9 feet (2.1 meters)

Weight: 1,130 pounds (512 kilograms) empty, maximum takeoff weight 2,250 pounds (1,020 kilograms)
Wingspan: 48.7 feet (14.8 meters)
Powerplant: Rotax 914 four-cylinder engine producing 101 horsepower
Speed: Cruise speed around 84 mph (70 knots), up to 135 mph
Range: up to 400 nautical miles (454 miles)
Ceiling: up to 25,000 feet (7,620 meters)
Fuel Capacity: 665 pounds (100 gallons)
Payload: 450 pounds (204 kilograms)
System Cost: $40 million (1997 dollars)
Inventory: Active force, 48; ANG, 0; Reserve, 0

Source: U.S. Air Force

RQ-4A Global Hawk

The RQ-4A Global Hawk is a high-altitude, long-endurance UAV that provides the U.S. Air Force with near-real-time, high-resolution images from intelligence, surveillance, and reconnaissance missions. The Global Hawk program is managed by the U.S. Air Force's Aeronautical Systems Center at Wright-Patterson AFB, Ohio.

Features

The Global Hawk is currently the most sophisticated UAV in military service. It is powered by a jet engine, compared with the Rotax 914 four-cylinder engine of the RQ-1 Predator, and is capable of flying for over 36 hours and traveling 13,500 nautical miles. In fact, the aircraft set the world record for the longest distance traveled by a UAV when it traveled nonstop from Edwards AFB across the Pacific Ocean to Australia between April 22 and 23, 2001 as part of an interoperability test between the U.S. and Australian military services.

The Global Hawk is completely autonomous, meaning that it does not require a human on the ground to control it. It is fully capable of flying an entire mission, including taking off, traveling to a target destination, remaining on station over the target for up to 24 hours, then returning to base using preloaded mission flight plans. Global Hawk "pilots" on the ground, however, are capable of communicating with the aircraft and can adjust mission parameters as necessary via its satellite and direct line-of-sight data links with the ground.

The aircraft can fly at up to 65,000 feet at speeds of up to 400 mph. During a typical mission, it can survey a geographic area the size of the state of Illinois within 24 hours. It has a cloud-penetrating synthetic aperture radar, ground moving target indicator, and electro-optical and infrared sensors for capturing images. The infrared sensors can even detect the cold spots where aircraft have recently been positioned on a runway, thus cooling the concrete. An integral part of the Global Hawk system is the Global Hawk Ground Segment, which is developed by Raytheon. This Ground Segment includes systems for the Launch and Recovery Element (LRE), the Mission Control Element (MCE), and related ground communication equipment. The Ground Segment also relays the imagery to tactical commanders in near real-time.

The benefits of a system such as Global Hawk are that it is a safer way to perform intelligence, surveillance, and reconnaissance missions and can operate for longer durations than can human pilots. Additionally, the crew members on the ground can change their work shifts, safe in the knowledge that the Global Hawk is executing its preloaded mission plan.

Background

The Global Hawk (Figure 1–11) was originally part of a Defense Advanced Research Projects Agency (DARPA) initiative called the *High-Altitude Endurance UAV program*, with Air Force, Navy, and Army participation, and was unveiled to the public in February 1997. Global Hawk entered the engineering, manufacturing, and development phase of formal defense system acquisition in March 2001. In June 2002, it had clocked up over 1,000 combat flight hours in support of Operation Enduring Freedom.

Facts

Type: High-altitude, long-endurance unmanned aerial reconnaissance system
Contractor: Northrop Grumman

Figure 1–11   RQ-4A Global Hawk. (*Source:* U.S. Air Force)

Length: 44 feet, 4 inches
Height: 15 feet, 2 inches
Wingspan: 116 feet, 2 inches
Ferry Range: 13,500 nautical miles
Endurance: 35+ hours
Maximum Altitude: 65,000+ feet
Takeoff Gross Weight: 25,600 pounds
Payload: 2,000 pounds
Sensors: Synthetic Aperture Radar and Electro-Optical/Infrared

Source: Northrop Grumman and Federation of American Scientists (FAS)

Defense Satellite Communications System

The DSCS is the backbone of the U.S. military's global satellite communications, providing secure voice and data communications that are nuclear-hardened and have anti-jamming capabilities. The DSCS supports all Department of Defense branches of service, as well as other special users, such as NATO and the United Kingdom, and is operated by the U.S. Air Force Space Command. Its main mission is to provide secure communications between commanders at multiple locations and troops in the field.

Features

The DSCS satellites communicate on six channels in the super-high-frequency (SHF) range. They also have a special-purpose single channel that can be used by the President of the United States to communicate with nuclear forces. The satellites orbit is a geostationary orbit, meaning that they stay in a fixed position over a specific area on Earth. They operate at an altitude of over 22,000 miles and have an operational life expectancy of 10 years.

The constellation of DSCS satellites over the Earth consists of five primary satellites in operation at any one time to achieve full coverage around the globe. These five coverage areas are the East Pacific (EPAC), West Atlantic (WLANT), East Atlantic (ELANT), Indian Ocean (IO), and the West Pacific (WPAC). Additional satellites are maintained in geostationary orbit to provide reserve capability in the event that any of the other primary satellites fail.

Background

The roots of the DSCS (Figure 1–12) date back to 1966 when the Department of Defense inaugurated the Initial Defense Communications Satellite Program. In 1971, this program was renamed, and the first of the DSCS Block II satellites was launched. The first DSCS III satellite was launched in October 1982. Lockheed Martin Missiles & Space is the primary contractor and has produced 14 DSCS satellites.

The MILSATCOM Joint Program Office of the Space and Missile Systems Center (SMC), Los Angeles AFB, California is responsible for development, acquisition, and sustainment of the DSCS Space Segment.

DSCS was used throughout Operation Desert Storm and as the primary communications link for U.S. forces in Bosnia.

Facts

Type: Worldwide, long-haul communications
Contractor: Lockheed Martin Missiles & Space

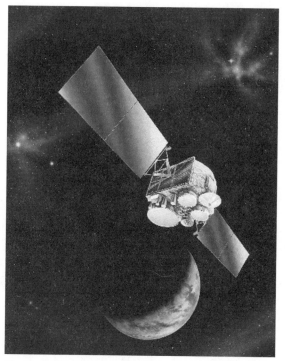

Figure 1–12   DSCS satellite. (*Source:* Lockheed Martin)

Dimensions: Rectangular body is 6 feet long (1.8 meters), 6 feet high (1.8 meters), and 7 feet wide (2.1 meters); 38-foot span (11.5 meters) with solar arrays deployed
Weight: 2,716 pounds (1,232 kilograms)
Orbit Altitude: 22,230 miles (35,887 kilometers)
Powerplant: Solar arrays generating average of 1,500 watts
Launch Vehicle: Atlas II, later the evolved expendable launch vehicle
Capability: Up to 200 Mbps
Survivability: Nuclear tested
Unit Cost: $200 million
Inventory: 4

Source: U.S. Air Force, MILSATCOM

Military Strategic and Tactical Relay System

Milstar is the Department of Defense's most advanced satellite communications system. Like the DSCS, its mission is to provide secure, jam-resistant communications to high-priority military users across the various services.

Milstar also functions as an intelligent switchboard in the sky by connecting ground communications terminals with each other and by linking with other Milstar satellites as necessary. It has been likened to the "FedEx of communications systems," due to its robustness, high reliability, and low probability of interception or detection by the enemy.

Features

Like the DSCS satellites, Milstar satellites are placed in geostationary orbit over 22,000 miles above the Earth's surface. They have a life expectancy of ten years and weigh approximately 10,000 pounds.

The satellites carry low data rate (LDR) and medium data rate (MDR) payloads, meaning that the amount of data that can be transmitted is generally less than the high data rate capability of the DSCS satellites. The LDR communications can carry 75–2,400 bits per second (bps) of voice and data over 192 channels in the Extremely High Frequency (EHF) range. This transmission speed is equivalent to some of the earlier computer modems prior to today's faster modems. The MDR communications can transmit between 4,800 bps and 1.544 Mbps of voice and data over 32 channels. This is closer to the broadband connections that we are familiar with in the home or office.

The entire Milstar system is comprised of the satellites, terminals for ground users, and mission control. The terminals can provide encrypted voice, video, data, Teletype, and facsimile communications and can be used for uploading instructions to cruise missiles in real-time. The "switchboard in the sky" concept of performing processing and routing on board the satellite means that land-based relay stations are not required. This helps enhance the low probability of interception for these critical communications.

Figure 1–13   Milstar satellite. (*Source:* Lockheed Martin)

Background

The unit cost of the Milstar (Figure 1–13) satellites is approximately $800 million. The first two satellites were launched in 1994 and 1995 aboard Titan IV-Centaur boosters built by Lockheed Martin. These initial satellites carried the LDR payload. The next three satellites to be launched carried the MDR payload and completed the operational Milstar satellite configuration.

Like the DSCS program, the MILSATCOM Joint Program Office, Space and Missile System Center, Los Angeles AFB is responsible for acquiring and sustaining the Milstar satellite program.

Facts

Type: Survivable global military communications system
Primary Contractor: Lockheed Martin Missiles & Space
Weight: About 10,000 pounds (4,536 kilograms)
Orbit Altitude: 22,250 nautical miles (inclined geostationary orbit)
Powerplant: Solar panels generating 8,000 watts

Payload:
>> LDR communications (voice, data, Teletype, and facsimile) at 75–2,400 bps (Block I and II)
>> MDR communications (video, voice, data, Teletype, facsimile) at 4,800 bps to 1.544 Mbps (Block II only)

First Launch: February 7, 1994
Launch Vehicle: Titan IVB/Centaur upper stage
Unit Cost: $800 million

Source: U.S. Air Force, MILSATCOM

Navstar Global Positioning System

The Navstar GPS is a constellation of satellites that provides precise navigation data to military, commercial, and civilian users worldwide. GPS is a system capable of providing three-dimensional position information, together with extremely accurate velocity and time information, 24 hours a day, continuously, in real-time and in all weather conditions. The system is operated and controlled by the 50th Space Wing's 2nd Space Operations Squadron, Schriever AFB, Colorado.

Features

The Navstar radio-positioning system consists of a 24-satellite constellation, with each satellite orbiting the Earth every 12 hours. The satellites continuously emit navigation signals on two different frequencies named *L1* and *L2*. In addition to the satellites themselves, the system also comprises a worldwide satellite control network and the GPS receivers. The control network includes a Master Control Station plus five monitor stations and four ground antennas located around the world.

In terms of accuracy, the system can provide three-dimensional positional information to within a few feet, time to within a millionth of a second, and velocity to within a fraction of a mile per hour. Receivers can be used in aircraft, ships, land vehicles, and handheld devices (handheld devices are becoming available to the general public for $100 or even less). The applications for GPS positioning range from all aspects of the military, such as basic navigation, aerial refueling, and missile guidance, to many civilian uses, such as hiking, shipping, and even driving directions.

GPS positioning works by taking four or more simultaneous distance measurements to determine the position of a receiver at a certain point in time. The two different frequencies used by Navstar enable corrections to be made for distortion effects in the Earth's atmosphere. The accuracy of these systems is due to the precise time keeping within the satellites. They use atomic clocks with a margin of error of approximately 1 second every 300,000 years.

Background

The concept of GPS got its start during the "race to space" in the 1950s between the United States and the Soviet Union, when scientists at John Hopkins University studied how to use satellite-based radio signals for accurate positioning of U.S. Navy ships and submarines. The U.S. Air Force initiated a program in the mid-1960s using the same principles but applied it to moving vehicles on land or in the air. In 1973, these two programs were combined, and the Navigation Technology Program was formed, which later evolved into Navstar.

There have been four generations of Navstar satellites (Figure 1–14) in orbit: Blocks I, II, IIA, and IIR. The Block I satellites were first launched in 1978 and were used to test space-based navigation principles. The current constellation is comprised of the Blocks II, IIA, and IIR satellites, which were launched beginning in 1989.

To date, the cost to the U.S. Air Force for developing and procuring GPS satellites has been $6.3 billion, not including the cost for end-user military receivers or satellite launch costs. Although this is a large figure, it is estimated that the worldwide commercial market for GPS equipment and applications will be over $50 billion by 2010.

Facts

Type: Precise navigation, timing, and velocity information worldwide

Contractor: Blocks I and II/IIA, Rockwell International (Boeing North American); Block IIR, Lockheed Martin; Block IIF, Boeing North American

Figure 1–14   Navstar GPS satellite. (*Source:* Boeing)

Weight: Block IIA, 3,670 pounds (1,816 kilograms); Block IIR, 4,480 pounds (2,217 kilograms)
Height: Block IIA, 136 inches (3.4 meters); Block IIR, 70 inches (1.7 meters)
Width (includes wingspan): Block IIA, 208.6 inches (5.3 meters); Block IIR, 449 inches (11.4 meters)
Powerplant: Solar panels generating 800 watts
Design Life: Blocks II/IIA, 7.5 years; Block IIR, 10 years
Date of First Launch: 1978
Launch Vehicle: Delta II
Date Constellation Operational: July 1995 (at full operational capacity)

Source: U.S. Air Force

PAVE PAWS Radar System

The PAVE PAWS is an Air Force Space Command radar system that provides missile early warning and space surveillance. It is operated by the 21st Space Wing Squadrons and is used primarily to detect and track submarine-launched ballistic missiles (SLBMs) and intercontinental ballistic missiles (ICBMs) aimed at the United States and Canada. The PAVE PAWS sites are located at Beale AFB in California, Cape Cod Air Force Station in Massachusetts, and Clear Air Force

Station in Alaska. The term *PAWS* stands for Phased-Array Warning System, whereas *PAVE* is simply an Air Force program name.

Features

PAVE PAWS differs from a traditional radar system because it doesn't need to be physically aimed at a target. The entire radar system is mounted on two sides of a 32-meter-high building with three sides. Because each side has a field of view of 120 degrees, the total field of view of the system is 240 degrees. The pulsed radio frequency signals from the radar can be directed electronically by controlling the phase of the incoming and outgoing signals. The beam can be quickly directed in many directions and can track multiple objects at any one time in case of a massive ICBM attack. The information from the PAVE PAWS systems is sent to the U.S. Strategic Command's Missile Warning and Space Control Centers at the Cheyenne Mountain Air Station in Colorado.

In terms of elevation, the radar beam is typically focused at elevations between 3 and 10 degrees above the horizontal during what is known as its "surveillance fence." The 3-degree elevation helps to keep it clear of the local area, which could be subjected to environmental microwave radiation without this clearance. Beyond the surveillance fence, the radar can aim between 3 and 85 degrees from the horizontal. The detection range of the radar is 3,000 nautical miles, or 5,556 kilometers.

Background

PAVE PAWS (Figure 1–15) started as a Request for Proposal in June 1975 and was put into operation in April 1980. The operating sites have changed over the years, due to consolidation after the end of the Cold War. Over the years, some concern has been expressed over the environmental and public safety aspects of these systems and Web sites, such as pavepaws.org, which provides information and monthly updates as to the results of various studies of these hypothesized risks.

Facts

Peak Power: 1,792 active elements at 325 watts = 582.4 kilowatts (kW)
Duty Factor: 25 percent (11 percent search, 14 percent track)

Figure 1–15   PAVE PAWS early warning radar system. (*Source:* U.S. Air Force Space Command)

Average Power: 145.6 kW
Effective Transmit Gain: 37.92 decibels (dB)
Active Radar Diameter: 22.1 meters
Frequency: 420–450 megahertz (MHz)
Radar Detection Range: 5,556 kilometers (3,000 nautical miles)
Wavelength: 0.69 meters at 435 MHz
Sidelobes: –20 dB (first), –30 dB (second), –38 dB (root mean square)
Face Tilt: 20 degrees
Number of Faces: 2
3-dB Beam Width: 2.2 degrees

Source: FAS

Ground-Based Electro-Optical Deep Space Surveillance

Ground-based Electro-Optical Deep Space Surveillance (GEODSS) sites are assigned to Air Force Space Command and have the task of tracking objects within deep space in orbits between 3,000 and 22,000 miles from the Earth. The sites track everything from active satellites to "space junk" and can track items as small as a basketball from 20,000 miles away. The primary mission of the GEODSS sites is to detect, track, and identify all space objects within this area of coverage. Satellite information is provided to the Space Control Center at Cheyenne Mountain AFB, Colorado within seconds of detection.

Features

There are three GEODSS sites worldwide, which are located at Socorro, New Mexico, Maui, Hawaii, and Diego Garcia, British Indian Ocean Territories. The sites use three technologies to perform their task: a telescope, low-light-level television cameras, and computers. The main telescopes have a 2-degree field of view and a 40-inch aperture. Because the system is 10,000 times more sensitive than the human eye in terms of the ability to "see" faint objects, it is operated only at night. Additionally, cloud cover or adverse weather conditions can influence the operation, due to its optical nature.

Background

Since the launch of Sputnik on October 4, 1957, deep space has become increasingly crowded. In fact, today there are over 10,000 known objects in orbit around the Earth.

The GEODSS (Figure 1–16) system is the successor to the Baker-Nunn camera, which was developed in the mid-1950s to provide surveillance data. The GEODSS concept was developed and researched by Massachusetts Institute of Technology Lincoln Laboratories at the Experimental Test Site located at Socorro, New Mexico. This Experimental Test Site is still in use by MIT for research supporting the next generation of optical sensors.

In January 1999, a new Optical Command, Control, and Communication Facility (OC3F) was installed at Edwards AFB in California. This became operational in February 2000 and can task the GEODSS telescopes via a dynamic scheduling system, increasing their accuracy by 75 percent.

Facts

Locations: Socorro, New Mexico; Maui, Hawaii; and Diego Garcia, British Indian Ocean Territories

Figure 1–16   GEODSS location. (*Source:* U.S. Air Force Space Command)

Range: 3,000–22,000 miles (approximately)
Number of Telescopes per Site: 3
Telescope Field of View: 2 degrees
Telescope Aperture: 40 inches
Sensitivity: 10,000 x human eye

Source: U.S. Air Force

Evolved Expendable Launch Vehicle (EELV)

The Evolved Expendable Launch Vehicle (EELV) is the space lift modernization program of the U.S. Air Force. The goal of the program is to "partner with industry to develop a national launch capability that satisfies both government and commercial payload requirements and reduces the cost of space launch by at least 25 percent." It is important to note that the EELV is a government-purchased service, not just government-purchased equipment.

The heritage launch systems of the U.S. Air Force include Delta, Atlas, and Titan, which date back to the 1960s and are still in service today. EELV will replace these systems. In comparison with these heritage systems, EELV is anticipated to save $6 billion in launch costs for the U.S. Air Force between 2002 and 2020 by partnership with commercial industry for launch processing as part of the service.

Features

The EELV program uses two national launch systems, Delta IV and Atlas V, from Boeing and Lockheed Martin, respectively. Part of the savings for the military comes from the partnership with these companies for operation and maintenance of the launch complexes. Boeing provides launch services on the East and West Coasts of the United States and Lockheed Martin on the East Coast.

The Delta IV launch vehicle from Boeing combines new and mature technology for launching medium or heavy payloads into space. There are five configurations of the launch vehicle, based around a common booster core (CBC). Delta IV uses a new Boeing RS-68 main engine that runs on liquid hydrogen and liquid oxygen and produces 650,000 pounds of thrust. The engine is environmentally friendly by providing only steam as a by-product of combustion.

The Atlas V launch vehicle from Lockheed Martin builds on its best practices from the Atlas and Titan programs. Atlas was originally developed as the first U.S. intercontinental ballistic missile and was also procured by NASA for space applications. The launch vehicle includes a structurally stable booster propellant tank, enhanced payload fairing options, and optional strap-on solid rocket boosters.

Some of the customers of the EELV program will include the DSCS, Defense Meteorological Satellite Program (DMSP), Milstar Satellite Communications System, Defense Support Program (DSP), Navstar GPS, plus satellites for the National Reconnaissance Office (NRO), Department of Defense experimental satellites, and NASA. The Air Force will also be transitioning to new space vehicles. The payloads are typically used for satellite imagery, weather forecasting and imagery, satellite communication, camouflage detection, and GPS-guided munitions, such as the JDAM weapons system and Tomahawk cruise missile.

Background

The program objectives for the EELV (Figure 1–17) are twofold: first, to increase the U.S. space launch industry's competitiveness in the international commercial launch services market and second, to implement acquisition reform initiatives resulting in reduced government resources necessary to manage system development, reduced development cycle time, and deployment of commercial launch services.

The EELV originated when Congress tasked the Department of Defense to conduct a study and develop a Space Launch Modernization Plan for fiscal year 1994. The EELV was one of four potential roadmaps arising as a result of the plan.

The first phase of the EELV program was a low-cost concept validation (LCCV), which was completed in November 1996. During this phase, there were four $30-million contracts awarded to Alliant Techsystems, the Boeing Defense and Space Group, Lockheed Martin Astronautics, and McDonnell Douglas Aerospace. The second phase was a $60-million contract awarded to Boeing and Lockheed Martin for preengineering and manufacturing development. Phase three, which includes the procurement of 28 government missions between 2002 and 2008, began in October 1998 with an Initial Launch Service contract of $3 billion awarded to Boeing and Lockheed Martin. The first three of these launches are listed in the facts section below. They included two commercial launches and one government launch of the DSCS payload.

The DSCS payload launch by a Boeing Delta IV completed the first mission for the U.S. Air Force EELV program on March 10, 2003 (Figure 1–17). The vehicle was launched from Cape Canaveral Air Force Station, Florida and deployed the satellite into orbit approximately 42 minutes after liftoff.

Facts

EELV Missions:
>> Lockheed Martin Atlas V Inaugural Flight, August 21, 2002
>> Boeing Delta IV (Med+ 4,2) Inaugural Flight, November 20, 2002
>> Boeing Delta IV (Medium) First Department of Defense payload (DSCS III A3), March 10, 2003

Source: EELV System Program Office, Los Angeles AFB

Figure 1–17   A Boeing Delta IV rocket successfully delivers to space the first satellite for the U.S. Air Force's EELV program on March 10, 2003. (*Source:* Boeing)

2

Ground Warfare

F rom external appearances, ground warfare may appear much the same as it has for several years, if not several decades. Tanks still look much the same from the outside, and soldiers' basic equipment has changed little in 50 years. Upon closer inspection, though, we find that the tanks and armored vehicles of the allied forces are well equipped for modern warfare and that our soldiers are starting to gain equipment that provides them with an increasingly better level of situational awareness and faster, more powerful, network-centric capabilities for command and control. In addition, these weapons platforms are continually increasing their lethality, survivability, and ability to operate from increased standoff distances from the enemy.

The M1A1 Abrams Main Battle Tank, for example, has protection against nuclear, biological, and chemical (NBC) contaminants via an overpressure system and has fire-on-the-move capability that allows it to engage enemy targets accurately while on the go. Its laser-guided main gun can also engage the enemy from up to four kilometers away in all types of conditions, day and night. Traveling at over 40 mph, it is also fast and agile, and can tackle 9-foot trenches and 60-degree slopes. The British Army's Challenger 2 has similar capabilities and features the secret Chobham armor, which can provide powerful protection against the latest in anti-tank missiles.

Along with this armored capability, today's soldier is also well equipped with a variety of protective and capability-enhancing equipment that provides an overmatch for most encounters. Night vision goggles provide a decided advantage over enemies whose military cannot afford the high cost of keeping up with this technology, especially the so-called third-generation image intensifiers, which work in extremely low light conditions. Suits such as the Joint Service Lightweight Integrated Suit Technology (JSLIST) enable the soldier to be protected against NBC contaminants. The suit features a removable inner lining consisting of micro-encapsulated carbon sphere technology, which replaces the charcoal lining of the earlier suits. The suits are lighter to wear and more flexible than their predecessors and can be laundered, which increases their practicality and useful life. Soldier equipment also includes the M40/42 chemical and biological protective masks for respiratory, eye, and face protection against a variety of contaminants. Although these masks have been in service a considerable time and are due to be replaced shortly, they provide a vital protective function for today's soldier.

Once the soldier is protected by heavy armor such as the Abrams and Bradley or the Challenger and Warrior of the British Army, and by protective equipment such as the JSLIST suits and chemical/biological masks, the next step is to ensure greater situational awareness and improved command and control. Recent technologies in use by the U.S. Army's 4th Infantry Division include the Tactical Internet and the Force XXI Battle Command Brigade and Below (FBCB2). Little has been disclosed by the military about the Tactical Internet and for good reasons. It provides a vital networking function, much like the public Internet, by helping connect soldiers—and their tanks and vehicles—with their commanders for network-centric warfare and critical communications.

The FBCB2 is the computer part of the system consisting of hardware and software that is used by soldiers in the field. It provides a visual display of the battlefield and maps out the positions of both friendly and enemy forces on a continuously updated graphical map. The FBCB2 also allows command and control instructions to be sent and received by using predefined standard message formats for information on enemy positions and calls for medical evacuation and fire and cease-fire commands. The Tactical Internet and the FBCB2 systems allow the modern warfighter to have greater situational awareness over the battlefield and gradually to replace paper maps and voice instructions with reliable, more comprehensive digital capabilities.

This chapter covers many of these existing and more recent capabilities and shows how the "heavy" forces are gaining increased digitization with systems such as the Tactical Internet and FBCB2. It also shows how our soldiers are gaining increased capabilities to take the battle to the enemy with improved situational awareness, lethality, and survivability.

M1A1 Abrams

The M1A1 Abrams is the main battle tank in use by the U.S. Army and the U.S. Marine Corps. The tank is a descendent of the M1 Main Battle Tank and has a 120-mm smoothbore main gun and a crew of four. Its advanced features include protection against NBC weapons via an NBC overpressure system, a 1,500-horsepower gas turbine engine, a cruising range of over 275 miles, top speed of 42 mph, and the ability to cross deep-water fords up to 4 feet in depth.

Features

The crew of four in the M1A1 consists of a tank commander, driver, loader, and gunner. The commander, loader, and gunner sit in the turret, and the driver sits in the front center part of the hull. The driver, who sits in a semi-reclined position, receives instructions from the commander as to where to drive the tank and can see via two or three periscopes that have a field of view of 120 degrees. The commander's station has six periscopes that provide a full 360-degree field of view. This includes an Independent Thermal Viewer (ITV) manufactured by

Texas Instruments, which provides day and night vision and automatic target cueing.

The 120-mm main gun is laser-guided and has rapid-fire capability. The gun is capable of engaging the enemy from ranges of up to 4,000 meters, as demonstrated during Operation Desert Storm. The main gun has day and night fire-on-the-move capability, which makes it highly agile and effective against enemy targets.

Despite the tank's weight of nearly 70 tons, it is able to climb scopes of up to 60 degrees. The tank's weight means that movement by air is next to impossible, and most tanks are moved via cargo ship. When the tanks are moved by air, they are usually carried by the C-5 Galaxy, the largest cargo plane of the U.S. Air Force, which can handle a single tank per flight.

Background

The M1 Abrams (Figure 2–1) was named after General Creighton W. Abrams, who was a former Army Chief of Staff and commander of the 37th Armored Battalion. The tank was originally produced in 1980 but its first test during real combat occurred in August 1990, during the Iraqi invasion of Kuwait. The fire-on-the-move capability of the tank, as well as its ability to target and engage the enemy at long range and during poor weather conditions, including dust and smoke, made it a resounding success on the battlefield. During the entire Gulf War, no crew members of Abrams tanks were lost, and only a small number of tanks were taken out of service due to damage on the battlefield.

Facts

Type: Main battle tank
Contractor: General Dynamics (Land Systems Division)
Powerplant: AGT-1500 turbine engine
Power Train: Hydrokinetic, fully automatic with four forward and two reverse gear ratios
Propulsion: 1,500-horsepower gas (multi-fuel) turbine engine
Length, Gun Forward: 385 inches (9.78 meters)
Width: 144 inches (3.66 meters)
Height: 114 inches w/o DWFK (2.89 meters)

Figure 2–1 Abrams M1A2 SEP during exercise evaluations with the 1st Cavalry Division at Fort Hood, Texas. (*Source:* U.S. Army, Photo by Nick Evans)

Weight Fully Armed: 67.7 tons (61.4 metric tons)
Caliber: 120 mm (M256 main gun)
Commander's Weapon: M2 .50-caliber machine gun
Loader's Weapon: 7.62-mm M240 machine gun
Coaxial Weapon: 7.62-mm M240 machine gun
Cruising Range: 289 miles (465.29 kilometers) without NBC system; 279 miles (449.19 kilometers) with NBC system
Sight Radius: 8 degrees at 8 power
Speed:
>> *Maximum*: 42 mph (67.72 kilometers per hour [kph]; governed)
>> *Cross-Country*: 30 mph (48.3 kph)
Ground Clearance: 19 inches (48.26 centimeters)
Obstacle Crossing:
>> *Vertical*: 42 inches (106.68 centimeters)
>> *Trench*: 9 feet wide (2.74 meters)
>> *Slope*: 60 degrees at 4.5 mph (7.24 kph)
Units: Two active duty battalions and two reserve battalions
Crew: 4-man crew comprised of a driver, loader, gunner, and tank commander
Warheads: M1A1 tank is capable of delivering both kinetic energy (sabot) and chemical energy (heat) rounds

Armament:

>> *Main*: 120-mm M256 main gun

>> *Secondary*: (1) .50-caliber M2 machine gun; (2) 7.62-mm M240 machine guns

Sensors: The 120-mm M256 main gun has a cant sensor, wind speed sensor, automatic lead, and ammunition temperature inputs to its ballistic fire control solution

Introduction Date: November 1990

Unit Replacement Cost: $4.3 million

Source: U.S. Marine Corps

M2A3 and M3A3 Bradley Fighting Vehicle System

The Bradley Fighting Vehicle System (BFVS) is an armored, tracked vehicle that provides protected transport for infantry squads or cavalry scouts on the battlefield. It consists of a crew of three, plus six infantry personnel or two scouts. In its infantry configuration it is designated as the M2 Infantry Fighting Vehicle (IFV), and in its scouting configuration it is designated as the M3 Calvary Fighting Vehicle. The vehicle can serve multiple functions, including transporting infantry to the battlefield, providing fire support once they are dismounted from the vehicle, and engaging enemy tanks and other vehicles as necessary. Fire support comes from the vehicle's M242 25-mm chain gun. This gun is capable of firing either armor-piercing or high-explosive ammunition at a standard fire rate of 200 rounds per minute.

Features

The Bradley is powered by a 600-horsepower turbo-diesel engine and can travel at up to 45 mph with a range of 300 miles. This enables it to keep up with the M1 Abrams main battle tank. In addition to its 25-mm chain gun, it can be equipped with a TOW (tube-launched, optically tracked, wire-guided) anti-tank missile that has a range of nearly 4,000 meters and can destroy any armored vehicle it chooses to engage. An M240C machine gun is mounted to the right of the chain gun and fires 7.62-mm rounds.

Background

The Bradley (Figure 2–2) replaces the M113 vehicles, which were armored personnel carriers. The Bradleys have greater power, acceleration, and suspension, and have been upgraded over the years to work in conjunction with the digital command and control facilities of the later versions of the M1 Abrams, such as the M1A2. Bradleys proved so successful in Operation Desert Storm that they destroyed more enemy armored vehicles than the M1 Abrams. Bradleys were also used to conduct armored patrols in Kirkuk during Operation Iraqi Freedom, along with M113 armored personnel carriers.

The Bradley family of vehicles was introduced in 1981 and included the Bradley Infantry Fighting Vehicle M2A3 and Bradley Cavalry Fighting Vehicle M3A3 mentioned here, as well as the Armored Medical Evacuation Vehicle (AMEV), Armored Medical Treatment Vehicle (AMTV), Bradley Fire Support Vehicle, Bradley M6 Linebacker, Bradley M2A2 ODS, Combat and Control Vehicle (C2V) M4, and Bradley Carrier M993.

Facts

Type: Armored, tracked vehicle
Prime Contractor: United Defense, Limited Partnership
Length: 21 feet, 2 inches
Width: 10 feet, 6 inches
Height: 9 feet, 9 inches
Weight: 50,000 pounds
Road Speed: 45 mph
Range: 300 miles
Engine: Cummins VTA-903T water-cooled 4-cycle diesel
Armament:
>> 25-mm cannon (chain gun)
>> 7.62-mm coaxially mounted machine gun
>> TOW missile launcher with twin tubes
Crew: 3
M2 IFV: 6 Infantry dismounts

Figure 2–2   Bradley M2A3 Infantry Fighting Vehicle during exercise evaluations with the 1st Cavalry Division at Fort Hood, Texas. (*Source*: U.S. Army, Photo by Nick Evans)

M3 CFV: 2 Cavalry scouts
Inventory: 1,602 systems
Total Program Cost: (TY$) $5.664 billion (total for all years)
Average Unit Cost: (TY$) $3.166 million
Full-Rate Production: FY00

Source: FAS

Challenger 2 Main Battle Tank

The Challenger 2 is the British Army's main battle tank. It is manufactured by Alvis Vickers, Limited and has been in service in Bosnia and Kosovo, as well as in Operation Iraqi Freedom. The tank is a descendent of the Challenger 1, which saw service during the Gulf War and featured the Chobham armor (named after the U.K. defense establishment in Surrey, England, Chobham is one of the most successful armors on the modern battlefield). The Challenger 2 replaced the Challenger 1 in 1994 and has over 150 improvements over its predecessor. The Perkins CV12 turbocharged diesel engine provides the tank with 1,200 horsepower and has a six-forward and two-reverse gearbox.

Features

The Challenger 2, which costs £5.6 million, features a 120-mm main gun—the L30—plus a 7.62-mm chain gun and 7.62-mm general-purpose machine gun (GPMG) for air defense. The tank's fire control system enables it to engage and destroy eight targets in 40 seconds using the L30 gun.

The turret can rotate 360 degrees. Smoke grenades round out the tank's artillery. The tank carries 4,000 rounds of 7.62-mm ammunition and can travel at a speed of 56 kph on road surfaces. The range is 450 kilometers by road and 250 kilometers by country. The crew of four includes the commander, operator/loader, gunner, and driver. Both the commander and gunner have access to the fire control system for locating enemy targets. Like the U.S. M1A1 Abrams, the tank features an NBC protective environment for the crew, and NBC protective suits are also provided. The crew compartment has air filtration and a heating and cooling system; it is separated from the ammunition for obvious safety reasons.

The Chobham armor, which first appeared on the Challenger 1, consists of a classified layered design to provide enhanced protection against the latest armor-piercing rounds. An interesting point is that this armor cannot be cast into shape during production of the tank. For this reason, it has altered the external shape of the Challenger to a more angular profile from that of its predecessors, such as the Chieftain.

Background

The British Army has the 386 Challenger 2 tanks (Figure 2–3), which first entered service in June 1988. In early 2003, there were reports that the Ministry of Defense had been considering retiring up to one fifth of these tanks as part of a move to more nimble forces with more logistically simple aircraft support, such as the Apache attack helicopter as opposed to the Challenger, which has a heavier logistics footprint, due to its weight. If this occurs, it will be a move toward an

Figure 2–3   Challenger 2 Main Battle Tank. (*Source:* Alvis Vickers, Ltd.)

agile force similar to the one Donald Rumsfeld has been advocating in the United States.

Historically, the tank has suffered from mechanical problems during desert operations where it can be troubled by sand but the latest development model, the 2E, has been enhanced to support these harsher environments.

During Operation Iraqi Freedom, many of the national newspapers in the United Kingdom reported the decisive outcome when 14 Challengers from the Royal Scots Dragoon Guards came up against 14 Iraqi Russian-built T-55 tanks in the southern city of Basra. The result was a resounding 14–0 victory for the British Army, which was hailed as one of the greatest tank victories since World War II.

Facts

Type: Main Battle Tank
Contractor: Alvis Vickers, Ltd.
Length Gun Forward: 11.55 meters
Hull Length: 8.3 meters
Height to Turret Roof: 2.49 meters
Width: 3.5 meters
Ground Clearance: 0.5 meters
Combat Weight: 62,500 kilograms

Main Armament: 1 x120 mm L30 CHARM (CHallenger main ARMament) gun
Ammunition Carried: Typically 50 rounds—APFSDS, HESH, Smoke
Secondary Armament: Coaxial 7.62-mm chain gun; 7.62-mm GPMG turret mounted for air defense
Ammunition Carried: 4,000 rounds 7.62 mm
Engine: Rolls-Royce CV12 with engine management system
Maximum Road Speed: 56 kph
Average Cross-Country Speed: 40 kph
Crew: 4

Source: British Army

Warrior Fighting Vehicle

The Warrior is the British Army's range of tracked fighting vehicles. The vehicles are NBC-proof and carry a full range of night vision equipment as standard. The Warrior family of vehicles includes a Milan carrier, a mechanized recovery vehicle, an engineer combat version, an artillery command vehicle, and an observation post vehicle. Warriors have been used extensively in the Liberation of Kuwait, during peacekeeping duties in Bosnia, and in the recent Operation Desert Storm, where over 500 vehicles were deployed to the region.

Features

As an armored combat vehicle, the Warrior is equipped with a 30-mm Rarden cannon and 7.62-mm Hughes chain gun. It can support a crew of three plus seven infantry soldiers. It is powered by a turbocharged Rolls Royce CV8 diesel engine producing 550–650 horsepower and giving it a maximum road speed of 75 kph. It has strong cross-country mobility and can tackle vertical obstacles of up to 0.8 meters and trench crossings of up to 2.5 meters.

The Warrior has a two-man turret that can be fitted with a 25-mm or 30-mm cannon (or up to a 120-mm stabilized cannon) or anti-tank missile launchers. The Warrior 2000 is the latest version and includes reduced radar, thermal, and acoustic signatures, and spaced aluminum armor that provides basic protection against 30-mm armor-piercing rounds.

Background

The Warrior (Figure 2–4) is manufactured by Alvis Vickers, Limited in the United Kingdom and is in service with the British armored infantry battalions, Royal Artillery, and Royal Electrical and Mechanical Engineers.

In June 2003, Alvis Vickers signed a contract with General Dynamics UK, Ltd., to supply a system called the Platform Battlefield Information System Application (PBISA) for the Challenger 2 Main Battle Tank worth £25 million. PBISA is part of the British Army's Digitization of the Battlespace (Land) Program and provides a battle-field management system for Warrior and Scimitar vehicles, as well as the Challenger 2. The system includes the integration of a Commander's Crew Station Display, Inertial Navigation System, Digitization Processing Computer (including Alvis Vickers' software), and Driver's Display Panel to provide enhanced network-centric warfare capabilities across the British Army vehicles.

Figure 2–4   Warrior 2000. (*Source:* Alvis Vickers, Ltd.)

Facts

Type: Armored, tracked vehicle
Contractor: Alvis Vickers, Ltd.
Weight Loaded: 24,500 kilograms
Length: 6.34 meters
Height to Turret Top: 2.78 meters
Width: 3.0 meters
Vertical Obstacle: 0.8 meters
Trench Crossing: 2.5 meters
Max Road Speed: 75 kph
Road Range: 500 kilometers
Engine: Rolls Royce CV8 turbocharged diesel, 550–650 horsepower
Crew: 3 (carries 7 infantry soldiers)
Armament: 30-mm Rarden cannon: Coaxial 7.62-mm Hughes chain gun

Source: British Army, Alvis Vickers, Ltd.

Night Vision Goggles (AN/PVS-7)

The AN/PVS-7 night vision goggles provide the Marine Corps with the current state of the art in night vision equipment. Night vision goggles can be vital in modern conflicts to provide the allies with the upper hand in night combat. In the case of desert warfare, at nighttime, the desert temperatures are lower, which helps both troops and equipment operate more effectively. Enemy soldiers are often not as well equipped with night vision equipment due to the relatively high unit costs involved and are, therefore, at an immediate disadvantage. For example, each American soldier was equipped and trained with night vision goggles for Operation Iraqi Freedom, something the Iraqi troops possessed in only limited quantities. In fact, there were many reports that the Iraqis were obtaining night vision equipment from Syria and Russia to make up for shortages in their own inventory.

Features

Night vision works by converting light energy (photons) into electrical energy (electrons), using an image intensifier tube. This image intensifier tube is the heart of the system and accelerates the electrons onto a phosphor screen, which causes the screen to glow and display the intensified image to the viewer. Third-generation image intensifiers are the latest generation of the technology and produce the best results in extremely low light by using a photocathode coated with gallium arsenide. In fact, all third-generation products require an export license from the U.S. State Department to be exported internationally.

The AN/PVS-7 night vision goggles are held in place by a helmet mounting or by using a face mask assembly secured by head straps, allowing soldiers to perform low-light-level or night tasks without having to hold the goggles. The goggles use a third-generation image intensifier and have a single tube leading to a binocular eyepiece assembly. Prisms and lenses are used to simulate binocular vision. The advantage of this system is that it is of lighter weight and can be worn on the head and more easily operated in a hands-free manner.

The goggles are provided with a shipping case, carrying case, eyepiece, and objective lens cap and filter, together with a demist shield to prevent fogging of the eyepiece. The AN/PVS-7D model also comes with an infrared light source that provides illumination. The two manufacturers for night vision goggles are ITT Industries and Litton. The goggles weigh just 680 grams and are operated by either two standard AA batteries or one standard military battery. The field of view provided is 40 degrees.

Background

As of December 1995, the U.S. Marine Corps inventory of AN/PVS-7B night vision goggles (Figure 2–5) was just 2,300. In May 2002, ITT Industries announced a U.S. Army contract that represented $450 million for third-generation night vision goggles over a five-year period for both aviators and ground forces. In addition to the equipment for ground troops, manufacturers such as ITT also make night vision equipment for aviators (AN/PVS-6 and AN/PVS-9) and night vision sights for rifles.

Figure 2–5   Night vision goggles.
(*Source:* U.S. Army)

Facts

Type: Image-intensifying, passive binoculars that allow the operator to perform tasks at night or under low-light-level conditions
Contractor: ITT, Litton
Length: 5.9 inches (14.99 centimeters)
Width: 6.1 inches (15.49 centimeters)
Height: 3.9 inches (9.91 centimeters)
Weight: 24 ounces (.68 kilograms)
Magnification: 1x
Range by Starlight:
>> *Man-Sized Target:* 100 meters
>> *Vehicle-Sized Target:* 500 meters
Range by Moonlight:
>> *Man-Sized Target:* 300 meters
Field of View: 40 degrees (circular)
Power Source: Mercury, nickel cadmium, or lithium battery (2.7V) (BA-5567 or AA cells)
Operation Time: 12 hours on one 2.7-volt battery
Unit Replacement Cost: $6,000

Source: U.S. Marine Corps

Joint Service Lightweight Integrated Suit Technology

With the increasing threat of NBC contaminants on the battlefield, the Joint Service Lightweight Integrated Suit Technology (JSLIST), represents the joint services program to provide protection against chemical and biological agents with the best suit available on the best economies of scale. The suit is designed to be of lighter weight and less bulky than previous chemical protective garments and reduces the heat stress involved in wearing it, compared with its predecessors. For desert climates, such as that experienced during Operation Iraqi Freedom, the reduced heat stress is critical because temperatures can range between 80 and 110 degrees in the spring and summer months.

Features

The JSLIST suit consists of a two-part overgarment of trousers and jacket plus multi-purpose rain/snow/chemical/biological overboots (MULO), which are worn over standard combat boots or other service-issued boots. The MULO has been designed to provide protection from chemical, biological, and environmental hazards while providing improved traction and resistance to petroleum, oils, and lubricants (POLs), as well as resistance to flame. The JSLIST suit is combined with protective gloves and masks to provide complete protection for what is known as Mission-Oriented Protective Posture (MOPP). It is provided in either four-color woodland or three-color desert camouflage colors, and most soldiers are equipped with two suits so that they have backups. The JSLIST features a removable inner lining consisting of micro-encapsulated carbon sphere technology, which replaces the charcoal lining of the earlier suits.

The JSLIST suit is provided in a vacuum-sealed pack. Once opened, the suits have a service life of 120 days. They can be worn for up to 45 days and laundered up to 6 times. After the 45 days of wear, 120 days after opening, or 6 times being laundered, they must be replaced. If the suits are contaminated, they need to be removed within 24 hours. Because the suits are designed to keep out chemical and biological agents they have very limited breathability and can be difficult to wear for extended periods of time. Depending on the tem-

Figure 2–6   JSLIST Suit.
(*Source*: U.S. Army)

perature and level of activity involved during wear, in some cases, this can be as little as 15–20 minutes.

Background

The JSLIST (Figure 2–6) program was created by a memorandum of agreement between the four services in 1993, with the U.S. Marine Corps as the lead service. Key requirements for the program included protection, lighter weight, greater flexibility, and the ability to be laundered. Laundering was an essential requirement because the previous suit, the Chemical Protective Overgarment (CPO), would disintegrate if laundered.

Production of the suits has been ramped up significantly in recent years, and recent General Accounting Office figures indicate that there are approximately 1.5 million JSLIST suits in service and a total of 4 million suits when the older suits are added to this figure.

Facts

Type: Provide service personnel with protection from NBC contaminants

Protection: Chemical agent vapors, aerosols, and droplets, and all known biological agents

Protection Period: 24 hours

Durability: 45 days of wear, 120 days of service life once opened, able to be laundered up to 6 times

Concentration Resistance: 10 mg/m^2

Dimensions:

>> *Length:* Size dependent

>> *Width:* Size dependent

>> *Height:* Size dependent

>> *Weight:* Size dependent

Storage Life: 10 years

Unit Replacement Cost: $253

Source: U.S. Marine Corps and U.S. Army

M40/42 Chemical Biological Protective Masks

The M40 and M42 series of chemical and biological masks provide respiratory, eye, and face protection against a variety of harmful substances, including chemical and biological agent vapors, aerosols, toxins, and radiological fallout particles. Used by the U.S. Army and Marine Corps, the M40/42 mask is fielded to active, reserve, and national guard forces, and is designed for either ground personnel or combat vehicle personnel.

Features

The M40/42 mask features a silicone rubber face piece with an in-turned face seal and binocular rigid lens system held in place with metal eye rings. A gas and aerosol filter is attached to the mask, using a cheek-mounted canister that can be fitted on either side of the mask. This can be beneficial in adapting for left- or right-handedness because the canister can be attached to the side of the face opposite that of the shoulder used to take aim with a rifle. The canister is also compatible with a variety of other NATO canisters, which helps to increase the functionality of the mask.

The M40/42 is provided in three sizes and can be obtained with corrective lens. It can be worn continuously for 8–12 hours and provides several enhancements beyond the basic protective function, such as the ability to drink while worn, and the use of microphone air adapters for combat vehicle and aircraft applications.

Background

The M40/42 (Figure 2–7) masks were brought into service to replace the M17, M25, and M9 masks. They have been in service for over a decade, and over 1 million have been produced. The latest versions of the M40/42 are the M40A1 and M42A1, which are more comfortable to wear due to a modified nosecup inside the mask. These newer models also feature a "quick-doff" hood and a second skin for additional protection.

The masks are scheduled to be replaced by the Joint Service General Purpose Mask (JSGPM), which is currently under development. The JSGPM will also replace the MCU-2A/P masks used by the Air Force and Navy.

Figure 2–7   M40 mask. (*Source:* U.S. Marine Corps)

Facts

Type: Provides respiratory, eye, and face protection against field concentrations of chemical and biological agents
Protection: Chemical and biological agent vapors, aerosols, toxins, and radiological fallout particles
Protection Probabilities:
>> 95 percent against 5,000 mg-min/m^3
>> 75 percent against 20,000 mg-min/m^3
>> 50 percent minimum probability of achieving no more than .002 percent penetration of *Bacillus globigii*
Breathing Resistance: Not greater than 55 mm of water at 85 liter/min
Unit Replacement Cost: $157

Source: U.S. Marine Corps

Marine Corps Combat Identification Program

The Marine Corps Combat Identification Program (MCBIP) is designed to provide "friend or foe" identification on the battlefield for U.S. Marine Corps armored units. This capability can help to reduce and prevent cases of friendly fire that have been a problem throughout the history of combat, due to misidentification and location problems. What typically occurs is that units are misidentified due to poor visibility or weather conditions, a fact often compounded by the increased range and accuracy of modern weapons systems. If a unit's location is not accurately known, it can be mistaken for enemy forces. In 1999 during the Gulf War, there were a total of 35 deaths and 72 casualties of U.S. troops due to friendly fire incidents. Although the numbers for Operation Iraqi Freedom were lower, the "friend or foe" identification challenge is a critical issue and one that is receiving increased attention.

Features

The Battlefield Combat Identification System (BCIS) employs an active millimeter wave communication system to interrogate, validate, and identify targets prior to engaging. The system consists of six major functional elements that include an interrogator antenna and a transponder antenna for question-and-answer types of dialog between the weapon system and the target. If a response is made, the target is a friend; if not, it is either a foe or a noncombatant. The interrogator antenna is mounted parallel to the sights on the main weapons system of long-range, direct-fire armored platforms. The transponder antenna is mounted on high-risk armored platforms deployed in the battle area.

The BCIS can operate in both ground-to-ground and air-to-ground scenarios. In the air-to-ground scenario, it can be attached to an AIM-9 Sidewinder missile on either rotary- or fixed-wing aircraft. The effective range of the system is between 150 and 5,500 meters for ground-to-ground identification and between 150 and 8,000 meters for air-to-ground identification. The way that BCIS works in operation is that it provides a visual or audible signal to gunners or commanders so that they can make shoot or don't-shoot decisions before engaging their targets. The identification process can be automatically triggered by the gunner's laser range finder, and the visual response can be provided directly in the sight so that eyes can remain on the target. Alternatively, an audible tone can be sounded on their intercom systems for the same purpose.

Background

The Battlefield Combat Identification System (Figure 2–8) program was developed after the Gulf War at the request of the Joint Chiefs of Staff in order to reduce the occurrence of direct-fire fratricide. Low-rate initial production was scheduled in 1999 and fielding to the 4th Infantry Division at Fort Hood, Texas began in 2001.

Facts

Type: To identify "friend or foe" for armor units in order to reduce/prevent fratricide
Contractor: TRW/Magnavox

Battlefield Combat Identification System (BCIS) Criteria

Probability of Correct Target ID: 90 percent (threshold) (under all battlefield conditions) 99 percent (objective)

Figure 2–8   Marine Corps Combat
Identification Program equipment.
(*Source*: U.S. Marine Corps)

Target Engagement Time: < 1 second
Multiple Interrogations/Reponses: ≥ 3 Simultaneous
Maximum Effective Range (Min–Max):
>> Ground-to-Ground 150–5,500 meters
>> Air-to-Ground 150–8,000 meters
Discrimination Between Targets: > ± 22.5 mils in azimuth or > 250
meters in range
Reliability: 1,242 hours (threshold); 2,760 hours (objective)
Unit Replacement Cost: Information N/A.

Source: U.S. Marine Corps

Force XXI Battle Command Brigade and Below

The Force XXI Battle Command Brigade and Below (FBCB2) is the
main digital command and control system for the U.S. Army at the
brigade level and below. It provides on-the-move, real-time and near-
real-time battle command information and is a key component of the
Army Battle Command System (ABCS). The ABCS is a collection of
systems that provides the capability of "network-centric warfare" to
the warfighter. ABCS provides a common operational picture from 10
different systems that include information on friend or foe, air
defense, airspace, weather, terrain, logistics, and fire support. FBCB2

plays a key role within these common operational pictures—particularly for the identification of friend or foe.

The FBCB2 system is comprised of hardware and software that is mounted in various Army platforms, such as the M1A1 Abrams Main Battle Tank and the M2A2 Bradley Fighting Vehicle. It provides a shared common picture of the battlefield that includes graphical color-coded displays of both friendly and enemy unit locations. The system helps to replace paper maps and voice radio communications for improved tactical decision-making on the battlefield from the brigade level down to the individual soldier.

Features

The FBCB2 hardware is comprised of a central processing unit (CPU), monitor, and keyboard similar in form to a laptop computer but ruggedized for the typically harsh environment that may include heavy vibration, temperature extremes, and exposure to dust and sand. It is mounted in Army platforms, including the M1A1 Abrams, M2A2 Bradley, M113A3 Armored Personnel Carrier, M981 Fire Support Team Vehicle (FIST-V), and the High-Mobility Multipurpose Wheeled Vehicle (HMMWV). The system includes position navigation and reporting capability, communications capability over terrestrial (ground-based) or satellite communications systems, and a combat identification capability using the BCIS.

All FBCB2 systems are connected to the Army's Tactical Internet so that they can exchange situational awareness data and conduct command and control across the brigade. Functionally, the end user of an FBCB2 system can adjust his or her view of the battlefield by selecting which overlays, graphics, and icons are shown on the display. Icons can also be grouped by unit type or echelon. The display looks much like a color map, showing blue icons for friendly forces and red icons for enemy forces overlaid on a terrain contour map. The map also displays reported battlefield obstacle locations.

In addition to the graphical display, the system helps to automate frequently used command and control messages by using standard message formats for requirements such as reporting on enemy locations, requesting medical evacuation, and calls to fire or cease firing. Once these commands are selected and dispatched in one platform, such as the Abrams tank, they can be sent rapidly to all other units to update their displays and send commands. The standard message formats are important because they help to optimize the bandwidth used on the Tactical Internet and allow the rapid transfer of information between systems, reducing the need for extensive user input. Standard message formats are also important because the ABCS system requires all data to be input by operators (with the exception of tracking friendly forces, which is done automatically by the system).

Background

Northrop Grumman Mission Systems is the prime contractor on the FBCB2 and is helping the U.S. Army transition from paper maps and voice radio communications toward greater use of digital communications. This gives the U.S. Army a technological edge for modern warfare by enabling quicker and better tactical decision making.

According to Northrop Grumman, in 2002, U.S. Army forces serving as NATO peacekeepers throughout Kosovo, Bosnia, and Italy were able to get a detailed picture of their surroundings by using a computer information network developed by its Mission Systems group that tracks vehicles and displays their locations on a digital map. FBCB2 (Figure 2–9) was named as one of the government's "Top Five Quality Software Projects" in 2002 by *The Journal of Defense Software Engineering*. The Northrop Grumman team also received the highest possible Level 5 maturity rating for the Software Engineering Institute's (SEI) Capability Maturity Model-Integrated (CMMI) for its work on the FBCB2 and the Tactical Internet Management System. The FBCB2 software is used by the U.S. Army's 4th Infantry Division at Fort Hood, Texas, and has received highly positive reviews during combat in Iraq.

Facts

Type: Main digital command and control system for the U.S. Army at the brigade level and below

Primary Contractor: TRW Data Technologies Division, Systems Integration Group (now Northrop Grumman Mission Systems)

Subcontractor: Raytheon Systems Company

Service: U.S. Army

Figure 2–9 Specialist William Goodman inside his HMMWV equipped with FBCB2 during exercise evaluations with the 1st Cavalry Division at Fort Hood, Texas. (*Source:* U.S. Army, Photo by Nick Evans)

Tactical Internet

The Tactical Internet provides the backbone for communications for the Army in much the same way that the conventional Internet provides for the rest of the world. It runs using standard Internet protocols and serves as the command, control, communications, and computer (C4) network, providing the backbone for information to be distributed from the ABCS and the FBCB2.

The transformational benefit of the Tactical Internet is that it increases the speed and power of command and control in war fighting. By acting as the underlying network for ABCS, it enhances the planning, monitoring, and control of combat operations and leads to improved lethality, survivability, and operational tempo.

Features

As the communications network supporting network-centric warfare, the Tactical Internet can operate in a range of stressful conditions, including harsh battle conditions, loss of key elements within the network, enemy interference, and hostile terrain. Its two main functions are to provide situational awareness (SA) and command and control between soldiers, platforms (such as tanks and fighting vehicles), and commanders. Like the public Internet, it is capable of passing both voice and data communications and performs various routing and network services to ensure successful delivery.

The applications that sit on top of the Tactical Internet include the ABCS applications that provide a common operational picture of the battlefield. The Tactical Internet links both local area networks (LANs) and wide area networks (WANs) up and down the military chain of command, including battalion and below, brigade, and division and higher. It links a variety of communications networks from satellite communication systems to tactical data radios. Some of these components include the Enhanced Position Location Reporting System (EPLRS) and Single-Channel Ground and Airborne Radio System (SINCGARS) for lower echelons; the Brigade Subscriber Node (BSN), which provides WAN connectivity for brigades; the Mobile Subscriber Equipment (MSE), which is the digital communications mode among brigade, division, and corps command posts; and the Near Term Data Radio (NTDR), which is the primary communication link between battalion and brigade. Like the public Internet, the Tactical Internet serves to connect all these various communication links, with their varying bandwidths, so that digital information can flow freely across any of these links to reach its intended recipients.

Due to the importance of the Tactical Internet to military operations and the sensitivity of the information on the network, it is operated at the Secret level, and direct connections to the public Internet are not permitted. The best way to protect networks such as the Tactical Internet is to isolate them physically from other networks so that there is no way that external attacks can be launched on the system.

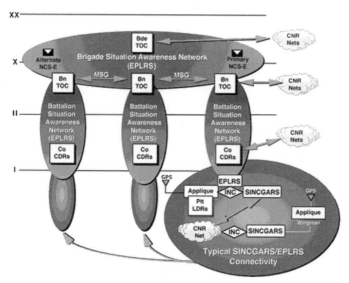

Figure 2–10   Tactical Internet. (*Source:* U.S. Army)

Background

The Tactical Internet (Figure 2–10) has been fielded both in testing and in combat service by the U.S. Army's 4th Infantry Division. Located at Fort Hood, Texas. The 4th Infantry Division is the Army's experimental unit known as Force XXI.

Facts

Type: Command, control, communications, and computer (C4) network providing the backbone for information to be distributed from the ABCS and the FBCB2

Applications: ABCS

Communications Systems: SINCGARS (1.7 kbps), EPLRS (6.7 kbps), NTDR (30 kbps), MSE (16 kbps), BSN (1,024 kbps), SMART-T (1,024 kbps)

Service: U.S. Army

Source: U.S. Army (Gunnery Department)

3

Munitions

M odern munitions include a wide variety of bombs and missiles that are used for air-to-surface, air-to-air, surface-to-air,
and plain on-the-ground warfare. In recent years, beginning
with the Gulf War, technology has enabled these munitions to
increase their range and accuracy while making them easier for coalition forces to "fire and forget." This fire-and-forget capability enables
them to launch their weapons and continue their other tasks as the
weapon is guided toward its intended target. The current trend is for
smarter, more accurate weapons that can be launched from increased
standoff distances from an increasing range of aircraft platforms to
protect our troops by keeping them out of range of enemy defenses.

In the Gulf War, one of the weapons of choice was the Tomahawk
cruise missile and various forms of laser-guided bombs (LGBs). The
LGBs were an improvement over conventional, or "dumb" bombs
that fall with gravity, because they could be guided to their targets
using laser designation. Despite the precision of LGBs, the problem

with this form of targeting was that aircraft pilots needed to remain in the vicinity of the target to designate the target with the laser until the actual bomb impact. This increased the danger to the air crew, and the laser designation meant that these bombs could be used effectively only in good weather conditions that permitted clear visibility of the target.

Subsequent to the Gulf War, there has been considerable progress in weapons technology that has exhibited increased standoff distances, improved all-weather capabilities, and autonomous guidance without the need for air crew or on-the-ground laser designation. The percentage of precision-guided munitions delivered has risen from about 8 percent during the first war in the Persian Gulf region to 80 percent during the second. There has also been an increase in the number of precision-guided munitions (PGMs) that have been capable of delivery during adverse weather. This number rose from 13 percent in the first Gulf War to 90 percent in Afghanistan.

One of the more recent technologies to enable these precision, adverse-weather capabilities has been the use of the Global Positioning System (GPS), coupled with inertially guided navigation. The best known weapons employing these techniques have been the Joint Direct Attack Munition (JDAM) and the Joint Standoff Weapon (JSOW). The JDAM is essentially a $21,000 strap-on kit that converts a dumb bomb into a GPS-guided smart bomb. The JSOW is a standoff glide weapon that can carry a variety of modular payloads. Both weapons saw action during Operation Iraqi Freedom and were responsible for hitting targets such as the Baathist Party Headquarters and the Iraqi Information Ministry.

In recent years, weapons have also been specially created, adapted, and hurried into service to meet specific mission requirements. The bunker buster was not even in the planning stages when Kuwait was invaded in 1990. This bomb, designed to penetrate hardened command centers deep underground, was rapidly developed and within months was in service during the Gulf War. Another weapon, the Massive Ordnance Air Blast (MOAB), was first seen by the public during tests at Eglin Air Force Base (AFB) in Florida. This weapon is currently the largest non-nuclear weapon in the U.S. military arsenal, and during tests its devastating effects were seen and heard up to 19 miles from the target site.

The Hellfire missile has also seen some innovative uses outside of its typical role on board Navy, Army, and Marine Corps helicopters. It gained prominence when it was used in November 2002 against six suspected al Qaeda terrorists in a vehicle in Yemen. It is also being adapted to carry a thermobaric warhead to enable its use against caves and bunkers.

There are also new weapons designed for non-lethal but equally decisive effects. The secretive "Blackout Bomb" is capable of shutting down the electrical power grid of an entire city. It releases hundreds of submunitions that fall to ground via parachute. These submunitions then release carbon fiber filaments that short-circuit power distribution equipment. The blackout bomb was used in Operation Allied Force against Serbia and possibly during Operation Iraqi Freedom.

Turning to missile defense, the Patriot Advanced Capability-3 (PAC-3) uses a new approach for destroying enemy ballistic missiles. Instead of exploding near its target with a fragmentation warhead, hoping to destroy or at least knock the target missile off course, it uses kinetic (or motion) energy to completely destroy its target with a head-on collision equivalent to a bullet hitting another bullet.

The Tomahawk cruise missile is gaining new capabilities, as well. The next generation, the Tactical Tomahawk, can be reprogrammed in flight to strike either any of 15 preprogrammed alternate targets or a new target designated via GPS coordinates. It can also loiter over a designated area and provide target information or battle damage assessment information back to its commanders using an onboard camera before being committed to use.

This chapter completes its coverage of present-day munitions with a look at some of the intercontinental ballistic missile (ICBM) and submarine-launched ballistic missile (SLBM) warheads that are a legacy of the Cold War and part of America's strategic nuclear deterrent—the Minuteman, Peacekeeper, and Trident Fleet Ballistic Missile.

GBU-28/GBU-37 "Bunker Buster"

The GBU-28 and GBU-37 are "bunker-buster" bombs that are used to penetrate hardened command centers deep underground and to destroy enemy weapons of mass destruction. The weapon was first introduced during the Gulf War and can penetrate over 20 feet of concrete or more than 100 feet of solid earth. It is typically launched from U.S. Air Force aircraft, including the F-15E Strike Eagle and the B-2 Spirit. The original weapon used during the Gulf War was designed and placed into combat operation in less than one month in February 1991 in order to attack Iraqi underground command centers.

Features

The GBU-28 is an LGB that carries a 4,400-pound penetrating warhead. It can be dropped by either the F-15E Strike Eagle or the B-2 Spirit. The GBU-37 is satellite-guided and is dropped from the B-2 Spirit at heights of 40,000 feet. The bomb measures approximately 19 feet in length and is 14.5 inches in diameter. The warhead, located inside a surplus 8-inch artillery gun tube, includes over 600 pounds of high explosives plus what is believed to be depleted uranium. Because this material is radioactive, it can be harmful if ingested. However, its alpha rays cannot pass though skin or clothing, so it is relatively safe in its solid form. Advanced fuzes inside the weapon mean that it can count the rooms it is passing through and can be set to detonate when it reaches a specific floor level. These fuzes can also be set to detonate when they encounter a designated air space or a specific altitude.

In addition to being used to penetrate hardened bunkers, the weapon can also be used to destroy weapons of mass destruction. It achieves this by carrying "agent defeat material" that can incinerate chemical and biological weapons with intense flash fires. This technique can help to prevent the spread of these agents into the air and into surrounding areas with flash fires that can burn at thousands of degrees Fahrenheit.

Background

When Kuwait was invaded in 1990, the GBU-28 (Figure 3–1) was not even in the planning stages. The U.S. Air Force rapidly put the bomb

Figure 3–1 The GBU-28/GBU-37 "Bunker Buster."(*Source:* U.S. Air Force)

together using a surplus 8-inch artillery gun tube for increased strength and weight. The first bomb was made on February 1, 1990. Flight and sled tests proved the bomb's ability to penetrate hardened targets and by February 27, the first two bombs had been delivered to the Gulf region. Both weapons were dropped from F-111s.

Two bunker-buster bombs were also used to destroy a national communications center that operated the Iraqi telephone system in Baghdad on March 27, 2003 during Operation Iraqi Freedom. They were dropped from a B-2 Spirit stealth bomber.

Facts

Targets: Fixed, hard targets, such as underground command centers and bunkers
Guidance: Laser-guided (GBU-28) and satellite-guided (GBU-37)
Length: 19 feet, 2 inches
Diameter: 14.5 inches
Penetration: Over 20 feet (concrete), over 100 feet (earth)
Warhead: 4,400 pounds with 630 pounds of high explosives and rest depleted uranium
Platform: F-15E Strike Eagle and B-2 Spirit
Service: U.S. Air Force
Date Deployed: 1991

BLU-114/B "Blackout Bomb"

The BLU-114/B "Blackout Bomb" is used to knock out the electrical power grid of an enemy by releasing hundreds of submunitions that fall to ground via a small parachute. These submunitions then release carbon fiber filaments that short-circuit electrical power distribution equipment and shut down the supply. The weapon is highly secretive, and very little is known or released about this high-tech yet simple device. What is known is that it was used in Operation Allied Force against Serbia and possibly again during Operation Iraqi Freedom.

Features

The BLU-114/B is dropped from a U.S. Air Force stealth fighter, such as the F-117A Nighthawk. It is believed that LGBs are used to deliver these submunitions accurately to their target area. Additionally, it is possible that a variant of the JSOW could be used to deliver the submunitions because it is designed to carry a variety of payloads within its modular design. The advantage of the JSOW would be that it is a "fire-and-forget" weapon that can be released from a long-standoff distance of up to 40 nautical miles and uses GPS for guidance. This would make the JSOW ideal for such a dangerous stealth mission to shut down an enemy electrical system.

Once released, the drink-can-sized submunitions, of which there could be several hundred within a single weapon, fall toward their target and are slowed by a small parachute. They then disperse a cloud of carbon fiber filaments just a few hundredths of an inch in thickness. These filaments float down until they strike their intended target, which is electrical power distribution equipment, such as transformers and switching stations. The filaments conduct electricity and cause an immediate short-circuit in the equipment, thus shutting down the power supply.

Background

During the Gulf War, the U.S. Navy used what was called a "Kit-2" dispenser inside a Tomahawk cruise missile in order to cause a blackout in parts of Iraq. This Kit-2 dispenser carried carbon fiber filaments for creating short-circuits on electrical equipment. The BLU-

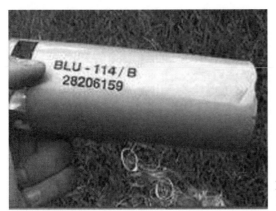

Figure 3–2   BLU-114/B.
(*Source*: FAS)

114/B (Figure 3–2) is believed to be descended from this initial use of the technology. It was first used as part of Operation Allied Force against Serbia on May 2 and May 9, 1999. The strike was successful in knocking out the power supply over 70 percent of the country, and canisters were later discovered with the BLU-114/B marking.

During Operation Iraqi Freedom, the blackout in Baghdad that occurred in early April 2003 as the allied forces captured the international airport was suspected to be due to the use of the BLU-114/B but was never confirmed by the military. In fact, this was denied by the military with statements that it did not want to target civilian infrastructure. The intent, if this was indeed the case, would have been to allow special operations forces to enter the city with greater cover of darkness and to provide allied troops with a greater advantage from night vision goggles.

Facts

Targets: Electrical power distribution equipment
Guidance: Laser-guided munitions or INS/GPS navigation based on carrier weapon system for the submunitions
Warhead: Carbon fiber filaments (submunitions)
Platform: F-117A Nighthawk
Service: U.S. Air Force
Date Deployed: 1999

Source: FAS and others

BLU-82/B "Daisy Cutter"

The BLU-82/B is a conventional 15,000-pound bomb that is one of the largest in the U.S. military inventory other than the more recent Massive Ordnance Air Blast (MOAB). The BLU-82/B, or "Daisy Cutter," has been used in Vietnam, in Iraq during the Gulf War, and in Afghanistan during Operation Enduring Freedom. Its primary purpose is for clearing minefields, clearing helicopter landing zones, and for psychological purposes against enemy troops.

Features

The BLU-82/B is known as a "Daisy Cutter" due to its massive blast just above ground level. The explosion is triggered by a 38-inch fuze, which sticks out from the nose of the bomb. This blast generates an air pressure of 1,000 pounds per square inch, which can clear and totally level an area of dense vegetation, including trees, approximately 260 feet in diameter. The weapons mine-clearing effects are reportedly up to 3 miles in diameter.

The bomb itself is a thin-walled, cylindrical metal tank filled with 12,600 pounds of an explosive slurry mixture called GSX. Due to the weight of the bomb, it can be dropped only from cargo planes such as the C-130 Hercules and variants such as the MC-130 Combat Talon. The bomb uses a cargo extraction parachute to pull it clear of the plane, then falls with a stabilization parachute following a ballistic (free-trajectory) path. Because the bomb is unguided, it needs to be released from the aircraft at a precise location in order to hit its intended target. The target has historically been mine clearance or clearance of dense jungle foliage to create helicopter landing zones.

Background

The BLU-82/B (Figure 3–3) was first used in Vietnam in March 1970 as a replacement for the 10,000-pound M121 bombs for blasting helicopter-landing zones in dense jungle areas. During Vietnam, the bomb was also used by the U.S. Air Force for tactical airlift operations called "Commando Vault," which is another name for this weapon. During the Gulf War, 11 BLU-82/Bs were used for mine clearing and for psychological effects. As part of the psychological

Figure 3–3   BLU-82/B. (*Source*: USAF Museum)

warfare, leaflets were also dropped that showed an image of the bomb together with the slogan "Flee and Live, or Stay and Die!" In Afghanistan during Operation Enduring Freedom, the weapons were used to target al Qaeda tunnels and caves.

Facts

Type: Air-to-surface conventional bomb
Contractor: Classified
Targets: Used for area clearance, including minefield and helicopter landing zones, as well as for psychological effects
Guidance: Ballistic
Length: 141.6 inches
Diameter: 54 inches
Weight: 15,000 pounds
Warhead: 12,600 pounds of GSX
Platform: MC-130 Combat Talon
Total Produced: 225
Service: U.S. Air Force
Date Deployed: 23 March 23, 1970

Source: FAS and others

Massive Ordnance Air Blast Bomb

The MOAB is currently the largest non-nuclear weapon in the U.S. military, giving it the nickname of the "Mother Of All Bombs." It first gained visibility when it was tested by the U.S. Air Force in Florida prior to the start of Operation Iraqi Freedom. Although it was shipped over to the Iraq region, it was not used during the conflict. It is thought to be used for psychological effect, due to its extensive mushroom cloud, in addition to use against above-ground, hardened targets and large troop formations. By detonating before impact, the bomb can maximize the horizontal target area affected.

Features

The MOAB is a 21,500-pound bomb that is dropped from the rear of a C-130 Hercules cargo plane. It is a successor to the 15,000 pound "Daisy Cutter" used in Vietnam and Afghanistan. A parachute is used to deploy the bomb, sitting on a sled, from the rear of the C-130. Once ejected from the aircraft, the bomb then glides toward its target, and when it nears the ground, it disperses a flammable mist and ignites it to create a large blast over a wide horizontal area.

MOAB uses satellite (GPS) and inertial guidance and has an aerodynamic body to help it find its target. The denotation typically occurs six feet above the ground. The MOAB is not the largest bomb ever to be created but is currently the largest within the U.S. military arsenal. Larger bombs have included the 22,000-pound Grand Slam dropped from Lancaster bombers during World War II and the 44,000-pound T-12 Cloudmaker carried by U.S. B-36 bombers in the 1950s.

Background

The MOAB (Figure 3–4) is an Air Force Research Laboratory technology project that began in fiscal year 2002 and is scheduled to be completed in late 2003. The first public images of the bomb were made available during the U.S. Air Force tests at Eglin AFB in Florida. During this test, on March 11, 2003, the explosion could be seen up to 19 miles away from the target site. Residents also heard the blast up to a similar distance. It is suspected that the bomb development and related tests were timed to coincide with the building political

Figure 3–4 Massive Ordnance Air Blast weapon is prepared for testing at the Eglin Air Force Armament Center. (*Source*: DefenseLink)

pressure mounting on Saddam Hussein prior to Operation Iraqi Freedom. The U.S. Air Force is believed to have another similar weapon in the works that is code-named "Big Blue" and is 30,000 pounds in size—50 percent larger than the current MOAB.

Facts

Type: Air-to-surface conventional bomb
Contractor: Dynetics
Targets: Used for area clearance, including large structures and troop formations, as well as for psychological effects
Guidance: Satellite and Inertial Navigation System (INS)
Length: 30 feet
Diameter: 40.5 inches
Weight: 21,500 pounds
Warhead: 18,000 pounds of explosives
Platform: C-130 Hercules cargo plane
Service: U.S. Air Force
Date Deployed: 2003 (Testing)

Source: DefenseLink

AGM-114B/K/M/N Hellfire

The Hellfire missile is a laser-guided, air-to-ground missile that is primarily fired from Navy, Army, and Marine Corps helicopters such as the Seahawk, Apache, and Super Cobra. It is used as an anti-tank weapon or for other point targets, such as ground vehicles, structures, and bunkers. It can also be used in air-to-air scenarios against other helicopters or slow-moving fixed-wing aircraft. The weapon gained prominence with the public when it was used in November 2002 against suspected al Qaeda terrorists in a vehicle in Yemen.

Features

The Hellfire is manufactured by Boeing and Lockheed Martin and features a solid-propellant rocket for power. The missile travels at subsonic speeds and features a laser seeker for guidance. Laser designation of the target can be made either within the aircraft or from a ground-based position.

The Hellfire warhead varies, according to the missile designation. The warhead is typically a shaped charge or blast fragmentation warhead but more recently, the AGM-114N has been used as a thermobaric Hellfire. The thermobaric warhead produces increased heat and pressure when it explodes and can be used against caves and bunkers more effectively than the conventional warheads.

Background

The name *Hellfire* (Figure 3–5) is short for Helicopter-launched fire-and-forget missile. It was first funded in 1972; later in the same year, the Hellfire Project Office was established. The program was a result of the Army's requirement to "develop a helicopter-launched, direct/ indirect fire-and-forget, laser semi-active guided, terminal homing, anti-tank, hard-point weapon system." After a series of tests, it was approved for full-scale production in March 1982. In March 1988, the 1st Attack Helicopter Battalion, 6th CAV, III Corps was the first operational unit to fire Hellfire missiles.

Figure 3–5   AGM-114 Hellfire. (*Source*: Boeing)

The first combat use of the Hellfire missile was on December 20, 1989, when AH-64 Apache helicopters fired seven Hellfire missiles during Operation Just Cause in Panama.

In August 1990, Hellfire equipment was deployed to support Operation Desert Shield and later Operation Desert Storm. The first shots of Operation Desert Storm occurred when eight Apache helicopters used Hellfire missiles and Hydra-70 rockets to target and destroy two Iraqi early warning radar sites in January 1991.

On March 22, 2003, the first kill by an armed unmanned aerial vehicle occurred in Iraq when a Predator UAV destroyed a radar-guided anti-aircraft artillery piece using a Hellfire II missile outside the Iraqi town of Al Amarah. During Operation Iraqi Freedom, the U.S. fired over 500 Hellfire missiles from a total of approximately 20,000 guided munitions, according to the April 30, 2003, "By the Numbers" report from the U.S. Air Force Assessment and Analysis Division.

Facts

Type: Point target/anti-armor weapon, semi-active laser seeker
Four Variants: AGM-114B/K/M/N
Contractor: Boeing, Lockheed Martin
Powerplant: Solid-propellant rocket
Length: 5.33 feet (1.6246 meters)
Launch Weight: 98–107 pounds (44.45–48.54 kilograms)
Diameter: 7 inches (17.78 centimeters)
Wingspan: 28 inches (0.71 meter)
Speed: Subsonic
Warhead: Shaped charge, blast fragmentation, thermobaric
Aircraft Platforms:
>> *Navy:* SH-60B/HH-60H Seahawk
>> *Army:* AH-64 Apache
>> *Marine:* AH-1W Super Cobra

Source: U.S. Navy

AIM-9 Sidewinder

The AIM-9 Sidewinder is a supersonic, heat-seeking, air-to-air missile used by the U.S. Air Force and U.S. Navy on fighter aircraft such as the F-15 and Sea Harrier. The Sidewinder has been produced for 27 other nations and is one of the most successful weapons in the U.S. inventory, due to its longevity, low cost, and the high number of missiles produced.

Features

The AIM-9 is included here not because it is particularly new but because of its successful track record and the continual evolution of the missile over time since its inception in the 1950s. Over time, this missile has increased its speed, range, maneuverability, and warhead capabilities, in addition to its reliability, maintainability, and shelf-life.

The AIM-9 features a high-explosive blast fragmentation warhead, an infrared guidance system, and a rocket motor for propulsion. The infrared guidance system allows it to home in on the exhaust heat signature of target aircraft. This enables both day and night operation and avoids problems with electronic countermeasures. Over time, with subsequent upgrades, the missile has increased its ability to engage with targets from increased launch angles and distances such that the pilot does not have to be positioned directly behind and close to the target aircraft. In fact, the control surfaces behind the nose of the missile enable it to pull many tens of Gs when pursuing its target so that it can take sharp turns and accelerate during engagement.

Background

The AIM-9 (Figure 3–6) is a weapon for symmetric warfare, when one fighter takes on another fighter in aerial combat. Given the currently asymmetrical nature of today's battlefield, the weapon has not seen much combat action in recent years because many enemy aircraft fail to get off the runway to engage.

The AIM-9A was first fired in September 1953. The AIM-9B entered operational use in 1956 with the U.S. Air Force. Successive generations included the E, J, L, M, and P variants, the 9X being a future variant that is currently under development. Improvements in the early models included the greater maneuverability, speed, and range of the J model in 1977; the ability to attack from all angles with the L model in 1976; and the improved defense against infrared countermeasures, enhanced background discrimination capability, and reduced-smoke rocket motor of the M model in 1983. The AIM-9M is the current operational model.

Facts

Type: Air-to-air missile
Contractor: Raytheon and Loral Martin
Powerplant: Hercules and Bermite Mk-36 Mod 11 single-stage, solid-propellant rocket motor
Length: 9 feet 5 inches (2.87 meters)
Diameter: 5 inches (0.13 meters)
Finspan: 2 feet 3/4 inches (0.63 meters)
Speed: Supersonic (Mach 2.5+)

Figure 3–6   AIM-9X Sidewinder. (*Source*: Raytheon)

Warhead: Blast fragmentation (conventional) weighing 20.8 pounds
Launch Weight: 190 pounds (85.5 kilograms)
Range: 10+ miles (8.7 nautical miles, 16 kilometers)
Guidance System: Solid-state infrared homing system
Introduction Date: 1956
Unit Cost: $41,300 (U.S. Navy), $84,000 (U.S. Air Force)

Source: U.S. Air Force and U.S. Navy

Joint Direct Attack Munition

The JDAM is a low-cost guidance tail kit manufactured by Boeing Corporation and used by the U.S. Navy and Air Force, with the Air Force as the lead service. The JDAM kit converts existing free-fall bombs into guided "smart" bombs by using INS and GPS as part of the tail kit. The JDAM greatly improves the accuracy of general-purpose bombs, works in any weather conditions, including clouds, rain, and snow, and can be launched from up to 15 miles from the target. JDAM accuracy is within 13 meters or less of "circular error probable" (CEP). CEP is an indicator of the accuracy of a missile or projectile and is used as a factor in determining probable damage to a target. It is the radius of a circle within which half of the missiles or projectiles are expected to fall.

Features

The JDAM kits attach to a variety of general-purpose warheads, including the 2,000-pound BLU-109/MK 84 and the 1,000-pound BLU-110/MK 83. One of the technical features of the JDAM is that it can operate with or without GPS guidance. As mentioned, with GPS guidance, it can achieve an accuracy of within 13 meters or less. Without GPS guidance, it can rely on the INS on board the tail kit to obtain an accuracy of 30 meter CEP for flight times of less than 100 seconds. This means that the weapon can be effective even in conditions where GPS data is unavailable, such as due to GPS jamming technologies in effect from the enemy.

The JDAM kit is comprised of the tail kit itself plus strakes, or fins, which are attached to the main body of the bomb to facilitate guided flight. The target coordinates are transferred from the carrying aircraft to the weapon either before takeoff or during flight prior to deployment. The weapon can be carried by a number of Air Force and Navy fighters and bombers, including the B-1, B-2, B-52, F-15E, F-16, F-22, F-117, and F/A-18. More than one JDAM can be launched on a single pass and can be directed at single or multiple targets on the ground.

Background

Operation Desert Storm highlighted the need for adverse weather precision-guided munitions. At the time, most bombs used were unguided weapons with limited accuracy, due to mid- to high-attitude deployments. Additionally, poor weather limited the ability to use precision-guided munitions, such as LGBs. Research and development began in 1992 to look into "adverse weather precision-guided munitions" to solve these problems, and the first JDAMs (Figure 3–7) were certified as operational-capable on the B-2 in July 1997. JDAMs were used in combat for the first time during Operation Allied Force in Kosovo in 1999 and later during Operation Iraqi Freedom by both British and American aircraft in April 2003. During Iraqi Freedom, successful targets for the JDAMs included the Baathist Party headquarters and the Iraqi Information Ministry. JDAMs have also been

Figure 3–7   Joint Direct Attack Munition. (*Source*: U.S. Air Force)

involved in friendly fire accidents, such as an incident that killed three U.S. soldiers in Kandahar, Afghanistan in December 2001.

Facts

Type: Guided air-to-surface weapon
Contractor: Boeing
Length (JDAM and warhead):
>> GBU-31 (v) 1/B: 152.7 inches (387.9 centimeters)
>> GBU-31 (v) 3/B: 148.6 inches (377.4 centimeters)
>> GBU-32 (v) 1/B: 119.5 inches (303.5 centimeters)
Weight (JDAM and warhead):
>> GBU-31 (v) 1/B: 2,036 pounds (925.4 kilograms)
>> GBU-31 (v) 3/B: 2,115 pounds (961.4 kilograms)
>> GBU-32 (v) 1/B: 1,013 pounds (460.5 kilograms)
Wingspan:
>> GBU-31: 25 inches (63.5 centimeters)
>> GBU-32: 19.6 inches (49.8 centimeters)
Range: Up to 15 miles (24 kilometers)
Ceiling: 45,000+ feet (13,677 meters)

Guidance System: GPS-aided INS
Unit Cost: Approximately $21,000

Source: U.S. Navy

AGM-154 Joint Standoff Weapon

The JSOW is a low-cost, precision-guided, air-to-ground weapon system used by U.S. Navy and Air Force strike aircraft. It can be deployed at increased standoff distances from enemy targets out of range of most enemy fire, such as medium-range surface-to-air missiles (SAMs). This standoff distance, which ranges from 12 to 40 nautical miles, based on whether the weapon is launched at low or high altitude, enables greater aircraft survivability. The JSOW uses INS and GPS information for midcourse guidance as in the JDAM. One of its three variants also incorporates infrared imaging terminal guidance for increased accuracy.

Features

Because the JSOW is designed specifically as a standoff glide weapon with an aerodynamically efficient airframe, it has further standoff distance than the JDAM. The unpowered JSOW can be launched at standoff distances of 12–40 nautical miles. A powered version of the JSOW is even more effective and can reach standoff distances of up to 120 nautical miles. The JDAM, in contrast, has less efficient aerodynamic capabilities because it is essentially an add-on tail kit to general-purpose, free-fall bombs.

The JSOW is especially useful for initial attacks on land and sea targets, such as air defense sites, parked aircraft, and other facilities where enemy defenses have not been softened and where there is an increased threat of attack from the ground. Like the JDAM, the JSOW can be launched from a variety of altitudes and in a variety of weather conditions, such as clouds, rain, and snow during day or night. Its GPS and INS help it to stay on course toward predetermined targets without any pilot intervention.

The JSOW measures about 13 feet in length and weighs between 1,000 and 1,500 pounds, based on its payload. It has a modular design that allows for various payloads to be carried, including lethal and non-lethal items. In fact, the modular design can allow anything from warheads to pamphlets to be carried as a payload. The three current variants of the JSOW include the AGM-154A, which carries 145 BLU-97/B submunitions; the AGM-154B, which carries 6 BLU-108/B submunitions; and the AGM-154C, which carries the BLU-111/B variant of the Mk-82, 500-pound general-purpose bomb.

The JSOW is carried by a number of U.S. Navy and Air Force aircraft, including the F/A-18, F-16, B-52, and B-2 aircraft, and will soon be flying on the B-1 and F-15E.

Background

Engineering and manufacturing development of the JSOW (Figure 3–8) was begun by Texas Instruments in 1992. In 1997, the Texas Instruments division working on the JSOW, the Defense Systems & Electronics division, was acquired by Raytheon Corporation.

The JSOW AGM-154A variant was first used in combat during air strikes against anti-aircraft defense sites in Iraq. Three JSOWs were launched by Navy F/A-18C Hornet strike fighters against the Iraqi targets on January 25, 1999. In 2003, during Operation Iraqi Freedom, F/A-18 Hornets launched from the USS *Kitty Hawk* used JSOW weapons to target various sites in Baghdad during severe sand-storms. The GPS guidance of the weapons allowed them to perform accurately even when visibility was greatly reduced.

In terms of procurement, the Navy awarded an $80 million contract to Raytheon on March 19, 2003 for the production of 337 JSOW-As, allocating 313 for the Navy and 24 for the Air Force. This contract is expected to be completed by February 2005. In total, the Pentagon plans to spend over $4 billion to purchase 14,000 JSOWs through the year 2007. The JSOW will be employed on the following aircraft: F/A-18A/B, C/D, and E/F; AV-8B; F-14A/B and /D; F-16C/D; F-15E; F-117; B-1B; and B-52.

Facts

Type: Air-to-surface standoff weapon for use against a variety of targets, depending on payload
Contractor: Raytheon

Guidance: GPS/INS

Length: 160 inches (4.1 meters)

Diameter: Box-shaped 13 inches on a side

Weight: From 1,065 pounds (483 kilograms) to 1,500 pounds (681 kilograms), depending on payload, sensor, and propulsion combination

Wingspan: 106 inches

Aircraft Compatibility: F/A-18, F-16, AV-8B, P-3

Range:

>> Low-altitude launch 12 nautical miles

>> High-altitude launch 40 nautical miles

Warhead:

>> BLU-97 Combined-effects bomblets

>> BLU-108 Sensor-fuzed weapon

>> BLU-111 500-pound general-purpose warhead

Date Deployed: January 1999

Unit Cost: $150,000

Source: U.S. Navy

Figure 3–8   Joint Standoff Weapon. (*Source:* U.S. Navy)

Patriot Advanced Capability-3

The PAC-3 is a land-based, guided SAM defense system that can protect against tactical ballistic missiles, cruise missiles, and hostile fixed-wing aircraft and helicopters using a "hit-to-kill" approach. Instead of using fragmentation warheads that explode near the target, as in the prior Patriot missiles, the PAC-3 system uses the kinetic (motion) energy of the missile to completely destroy its targets in a head-on collision. In terms of the accuracy required to achieve this capability, this is like a bullet hitting another bullet. With the proliferation of ballistic missiles and even the increased terrorist threats against commercial airliners, such as the recent failed attempts in Kenya, the PAC-3 forms an essential part of the U.S. Army's defense and will be in service at least until 2008.

Features

With its "hit-to-kill" approach, the PAC-3 system represents a far more effective method for countering enemy missile threats. The fragmentation warhead exploded in close proximity to the target typically only damages or redirects the threat because there is no direct impact. Conversely, the "hit-to-kill" approach can totally destroy the threat and its contents, which may include biological or chemical agents. When compared with the earlier versions of Patriot, the PAC-3 is also smaller and more accurate. Accuracy is improved by way of the Ka-band millimeter Wave (mmW) seeker, which is an onboard active radar seeker that provides terminal guidance to the target.

The entire Patriot system (or "fire unit," as it is called) is comprised of a radar, launcher, and engagement control station (ECS). The radar is a 5,000-element phased-array radar with no moving parts that can perform target search, detection, and tracking plus target identification, target illumination, missile guidance, and countermeasures protection. The launcher is trailer-mounted and can hold 16 PAC-3 missiles per launcher. This is another improvement over the PAC-2 configuration, which supported only four missiles per launcher. The launcher can be operated up to 1 kilometer away via a remote VHF or fiberoptic data link. The launcher is not required to be aimed prior to launch of the missiles. The engagement control station is used for battle management, command, control, and communications. A human operator can view a display screen showing sector coverage and any incoming targets. Operation can either be "man-in-the-loop" or completely automated.

When the PAC-3 missile is launched, it is initially guided by the ground radar portion of the fire unit until the onboard active seeker acquires and engages the target. In-flight corrective maneuvers can then be applied in order to hit the target.

Background

The original Patriot was proven in combat during Operation Desert Storm, when it was used to intercept Iraqi SCUD missiles. Production for the Patriot began in 1980, and it is currently deployed by the United States, Germany, Saudi Arabia, Kuwait, The Netherlands, Japan, Israel, Taiwan, and Greece. The PAC-2 (Figure 3–9) version of the system was fielded in January 1991.

Research Development Test and Evaluation (RDT&E) and procurement responsibility for the PAC-3 are due to transfer to the U.S. Army in 2003. The Missile Defense Agency (MDA) is also integrating the PAC-3 system in its layered Ballistic Missile Defense System (BMDS) that combines several programs into a complete system that can engage enemy targets in all phases of flight path, from the boost phase through the midcourse phase and into the terminal phase.

Facts

Type: Air defense system against tactical ballistic missiles, cruise missiles, and aircraft
Contractor: Lockheed Martin
Guidance: Inertial plus active onboard radar seeker (Ka-band mmW seeker)
Length: 17 feet 1 inch
Diameter: 10 inches
Weight: 312 kilogram
Number per launcher: 16
Maximum Speed: Mach 5
Maximum Range: 15 kilometers
Maximum Altitude: 15 kilometers

Figure 3–9   Patriot launch. (*Source*: Raytheon)

Warhead: "Hit-to-kill" using simple kinetic energy (motion) plus 73-kilogram HE blast/fragmentation with proximity fuze
Date Deployed: 1980
Cost: Over $3 billion in past 10 years (over 9,000 missiles and 170 fire units)

Source: FAS, Raytheon, and others

Tomahawk Cruise Missile

The Tomahawk Cruise Missile is the U.S. Navy's surface- and submarine-launched, precision-strike standoff weapon. It is used as a weapon of choice for critical, long-range, precision-strike missions against high-value, heavily defended enemy targets. Over 1,000 missiles have been used in military operations, including Operation Desert Storm, Iraq, Bosnia, Operation Desert Fox, and Operation Allied Force. The latest generation Tomahawk, the Tactical Tomahawk, had its first test with a live warhead in May 2003 and flew over 700 nautical miles on a sea test range.

Features

The Tomahawk missile is approximately 18 feet in length and 20 inches in diameter. It is powered by a solid propellant after launch until it reaches its cruising speed of approximately 550 mph, at which time a turbofan engine takes over for the cruise portion of its flight. The missile flies at subsonic speeds and low altitudes, and is able to navigate to its target by using a combination of guidance systems. In the Block II configuration, these guidance systems include INS, Terrain Contour Marching (TERCOM), and Digital Scene Matching Area Correlation (DSMAC). In Block III, introduced in 1994, the navigation capabilities are enhanced with the addition of GPS navigation, which can be used instead of or in addition to the Block II navigation capabilities. The benefit of GPS, of course, is that it frees the missile from having to rely on terrain matching to find its target. Time of Arrival (TOA) control means that these missiles can be timed to hit their targets in conjunction with anticipated events or with the arrival of other missiles.

The missile is difficult to detect on radar, due to its small cross-section and low-altitude flight. In addition, it has a low thermal profile because the turbofan engine makes it difficult to locate via infrared detection. In terms of the warhead configurations, the Tomahawk can carry either a 1,000-pound blast/fragmentary unitary warhead or a general-purpose submunition dispenser with combined-effects bomblets.

Tomahawk missiles are deployed worldwide on numerous U.S. Navy surface ships and submarines, including Aegis-class cruisers, guided-missile destroyers, and Seawolf- and Los Angeles-class submarines.

The Tactical Tomahawk represents the next-generation Tomahawk and has many advanced capabilities. First, the missile can be reprogrammed in flight to strike either any of 15 preprogrammed alternate targets or a new target designated via GPS coordinates. The missile has the capability to loiter over a designated area and can provide target information or battle damage assessment information back to its commanders, using an onboard camera. This gives them the ability to verify the target area and assess potential existing damages prior to committing this expensive weapon to its target destination.

Background

First introduced in 1986, the Tomahawk (Figure 3–10) has been fielded successfully in many campaigns, including Operation Desert Storm in 1991, Iraq in 1993, Bosnia in 1995, Iraq in 1996, Operation Desert Fox in 1998, and Operation Allied Force in 1999. It has been highly praised for its long range, lethality, and accuracy.

During Operation Iraqi Freedom, the Los Angeles-class attack submarine USS *Cheyenne* (SSN 773) was one of the U.S. Navy's first ships to launch a Tomahawk cruise missile on March 18, 2003. This number grew to four ships and two submarines launching Tomahawks on March 19, and by March 21, a total of 30 U.S. Navy and coalition warships had launched Tomahawk missiles.

The first flight of the Tactical Tomahawk occurred in August 2002 at the Naval Air Systems Command's Western Test Range, Pt. Mugu, California. Johns Hopkins University Applied Physics Laboratory (APL) served as the strike controller during the test and exchanged messages with the missile via satellite during its 550-mile flight.

The first launch of the Tactical Tomahawk from an operational surface ship occurred in April 2003 from USS *Stethem* (DDG 63) off southern California. In May 2003, Raytheon and the U.S. Navy fired the first test of Tactical Tomahawk, again from USS *Stethem*, with a live warhead as part of their technical evaluation flights. The Tactical Tomahawk is scheduled for introduction into the fleet in 2004 and will cost less than half the cost of a newly built Block III missile.

Facts

Type: Long-range subsonic cruise missile for striking high-value or heavily defended land targets

Contractor: Raytheon

Powerplant: Williams International F107-WR-402 cruise turbofan engine; CSD/ARC solid-fuel booster

Length: 18 feet 3 inches (5.56 meters); with booster: 20 feet 6 inches (6.25 meters)

Weight: 2,900 pounds (1,315.44 kilograms); 3,500 pounds (1,587.6 kilograms) with booster

Figure 3–10   Tactical Tomahawk. (*Source*: Raytheon)

Diameter: 20.4 inches (51.81 centimeters)
Wingspan: 8 feet 9 inches (2.67 meters)
Range: 870 nautical miles (1,000 statute miles; 1,609 kilometers)
Speed: Subsonic about 550 mph (880 kph)
Guidance System: TERCOM, DSMAC, and GPS (Block III only)
Warheads: 1,000 pounds or conventional submunitions dispenser
with combined-effect bomblets
Date Deployed: 1986—IOC; 1994—Block III; 2004—Tactical
Tomahawk
Unit Cost: approximately $600,000 (from last production contract)

Source: U.S. Navy

LGM-30 Minuteman III

The LGM-30 Minuteman III is a solid-fuel ICBM that is a key part of
the U.S. strategic nuclear deterrent. It represents the major land portion of the strategic nuclear "triad," which is comprised of the ability
to launch nuclear weapons from land, sea, and air. Ballistic missiles

are defined as those that assume a free-falling ballistic trajectory after an initial self-powered ascent. The ballistic trajectory is acted upon only by gravity and the aerodynamic drag of the missile.

There are currently 500 Minuteman IIIs located at three U.S. air force bases in the U.S. Midwest. The Boeing-manufactured missiles are capable of traveling at approximately 15,000 mph with a range of over 6,000 miles and a maximum altitude of over 700 miles. The Minuteman weapon system has been in operation since the early 1960s and has gradually been scaled back in terms of the number of missiles and the number of nuclear warheads after the START I and START II arms control treaties between the United States and the Soviet Union.

Features

Minuteman III missiles can be launched within minutes from underground silos in the Midwest. The hardened launch silos protect them from attack and are connected to a Launch Control Center (LCC) approximately 50 feet under the ground. Two officers man these launch control centers in round-the-clock alert status. The President and Secretary of Defense are able to have reliable, direct communications with each launch crew by way of a variety of secure communications systems. If this connectivity is lost for any reason between the land-based launch control center and the missile launch facilities, the Air Force has specially configured E-6B aircraft that can assume command and control of the missiles from the skies.

The Minuteman III missiles are nearly 60 feet in length and have a diameter of 5.5 feet. Their payload consists of one or more nuclear warheads per missile. Initially, the Minuteman III carried three warheads in what is known as a multiple independently targeted reentry vehicle (MIRV). This enables warheads to target different areas within the overall target area of the missile and reduces the enemy's chances of destroying the missiles before impact.

Background

Minuteman I came into existence due to the need for the United States to keep up with the Soviet Union in terms of ICBM development in the 1950s. The first generation of ICBMs within the United

States, the Atlas and Titan I, were propelled by liquid fuel. This meant that they required several hours on the launch pad in preparation for firing. Instead of liquid fuel, the Minuteman I was a solid-fuel ICBM that could be launched within minutes from underground silos, thus minimizing the chances of a preemptive strike prior to launch. This capability greatly improved the U.S. nuclear deterrent, and the first Minuteman I was deployed in 1962 after planning began in 1957. By 1965, there were 800 Minuteman Is deployed at five bases across the United States.

Minuteman II was produced in 1964 and provided greater range and accuracy than its predecessor. Strategic Air Command started deploying Minuteman IIs in 1966, and by 1969 there were a total of 500 Is and 500 IIs in service.

Minuteman III (Figure 3–11), the latest version of the Minuteman, was first deployed by the U.S. Air Force's Strategic Air Command in June 1970. In 1975, there were 550 Minuteman IIIs deployed with a total of 1,650 nuclear warheads, plus 450 Minuteman IIs. The START I and START II arms control treaties negotiated by the United States and Russia have reduced the current inventory to 500 missiles with one warhead per missile.

The current Minuteman missiles reside at three locations within the U.S. Midwest: F.E. Warren AFB, Wyoming; Malmstrom AFB, Montana; and Minot AFB, North Dakota. Current plans call for the Minuteman IIIs to remain in active service until 2020.

Facts

Type: Intercontinental ballistic missile
Contractor: Boeing
Powerplant: 3 solid-propellant rocket motors
>> First stage—Thiokol
>> Second stage—Aerojet-General
>> Third stage—United Technologies Chemical Systems Division
Length: 59.9 feet (18 meters)
Weight: 79,432 pounds (32,158 kilograms)
Diameter: 5.5 feet (1.67 meters)
Range: 6,000+ miles (5,218 nautical miles)

Figure 3–11 Minuteman III ICBM.
(*Source*: Boeing)

Speed: Approximately 15,000 mph (Mach 23 or 24,000 kph) at burnout
Ceiling: 700 miles (1,120 kilometers)
Thrust: First stage 202,600 pounds
Load: Reentry vehicle: Lockheed Martin Missiles and Space Mk-12 or Mk-12A
Guidance systems:
>> *Inertial system:* Boeing North American
>> *Ground electronic/security system:* Sylvania Electronics and Boeing
Date Deployed: June 1970; production cessation, December 1978
Inventory: Active force, 500; Reserve, 0; ANG, 0
Unit cost: $7 million

Source: U.S. Air Force

LG-118A Peacekeeper

The LG-118A Peacekeeper is the newest ICBM in the U.S. inventory and the most accurate. Manufactured by Boeing, it was placed into service in December 1986. The four-stage rocket ICBM is capable of delivering 10 independently targeted warheads that are housed in the reentry system at the top section of the missile. The current active force of Peacekeeper missiles is 50, located at F.E. Warren AFB in Wyoming. The United States is revising its policies toward nuclear weapons, and the Peacekeepers are scheduled to be deactivated in the near future, leaving just the 500 Minuteman IIIs for the land-based nuclear deterrent.

Features

The Peacekeeper has a length of 71 feet and a diameter of 7 feet 8 inches. Like the Minuteman III, it has a range of over 6,000 miles (a range of over 5,500 kilometers classifies a missile as an ICBM) and travels at up to 15,000 mph during its trajectory toward its target.

The three major sections of the missile include the boost system, the post-boost vehicle system, and the reentry system. Like other ICBMs, the Peacekeeper is launched under power during the boost phase of its flight, glides in a ballistic trajectory during the midcourse phase of flight, then reenters the Earth's atmosphere during the terminal phase. During the boost phase, three stages of the rocket use a solid propellant to accelerate the rocket into space. Once these three stages have burned out and have been separated, the fourth stage, which uses a storable liquid propellant, maneuvers the rocket in space so it is ready to deploy the reentry vehicles. The reentry vehicles consist of 10 cone-shaped Avco Mk-21 payloads, each carrying a nuclear warhead. These are separated from the remaining reentry system by a small explosive cartridge, then follow a ballistic trajectory to the ground.

Background

The Peacekeeper's (Figure 3–12) first test flight was on June 17, 1983 from Vandenburg AFB in California. During this test, the missile trav-

Figure 3–12   LG-118A Peacekeeper.
(*Source:* U.S. Air Force)

eled 4,190 miles and dropped six unarmed test reentry vehicles onto a missile test range in the Pacific Ocean.

The initial operating capability was achieved with 10 Peacekeepers deployed at F.E. Warren AFB in December 1986. Full operational capability was achieved two years later in December 1988 with a squadron of 50 missiles.

Facts

Type: Strategic deterrence
Contractor: Boeing
Powerplant:
>> *First Three Stages:* Solid propellant
>> *Fourth Stage:* Storable liquid (by Thiokol, Aerojet, Hercules, and Rocketdyne)
Warheads: 10
Load: Avco Mk-21 reentry vehicles
Guidance System:
>> Inertial: integration by Boeing North American
>> IMU: Northrop and Boeing North American

Thrust: First stage, 500,000 pounds
Length: 71 feet (21.8 meters)
Weight: 195,000 pounds (87,750 kilograms), including reentry vehicles
Diameter: 7 feet, 8 inches (2.3 meters)
Range: Greater than 6,000 miles (5,217 nautical miles)
Speed: Approximately 15,000 mph at burnout (Mach 20 at sea level)
Date Deployed: December 1986
Inventory: Active force, 50; ANG, 0; Reserve, 0
Unit Cost: $70 million

Source: U.S. Air Force

Trident Fleet Ballistic Missile

Trident is an SLBM that has been in service with the U.S. Navy since 1979 when Trident I (C4) was first deployed. The primary function of the Trident missiles is strategic nuclear deterrence. The missiles can travel over 4,000 nautical miles and are deployed in Ohio-class (Trident) submarines.

Features

Trident missiles represent 50 percent of the total number of U.S. strategic warheads that are part of the triad of the strategic deterrent—on land, sea, and air. Each Ohio-class ballistic missile submarine, of which there are 18, carries 24 Trident missiles. The three-stage, solid-propellant missiles are launched by pressurized gas from their launch tubes. Then, once the missile is clear of the submarine, the first motor of the three stages kicks in to propel the missile toward its target. By the time the third stage motor kicks in after about two minutes of flight, the missile is traveling at greater than 20,000 feet per second.

The missiles are 44 feet in length and 83 inches in diameter, weigh 130,000 pounds, and have an inertial guidance system for navigation. While on deterrent missions aboard Ohio-class submarines, the missiles have no preprogrammed target coordinates, but these coordinates can be rapidly loaded into the system using sea-based communications links.

Background

The Trident missile (Figure 3–13) is the U.S. Navy's latest fleet ballistic missile and supercedes the earlier Polaris (A1), Polaris (A2), Polaris (A3), and Poseidon (C3) SLBMs, which date back to 1956 with the Polaris (A1) program. As mentioned, Trident I (C4) was first deployed in 1979 and Trident II (D5) in 1990.

The Trident II (D5) is also carried aboard four Vanguard Class nuclear-powered submarines belonging to the British Royal Navy. These have replaced Polaris as the United Kingdom's nuclear strategic deterrent. The Vanguard Class submarine has 16 missile tubes and carries a total of 48 warheads, 3 per missile. Tridents entered service in the United Kingdom in December 1994 and were purchased under the terms of the 1963 Polaris Sales Agreement.

With over 10 years since initial deployment, the Trident II has set a record of over 87 consecutive and successful test launches. Also during this time, the U.S. Navy conducted over 200 deterrent patrols, with the first patrol being the USS *Tennessee* in March 1990, sailing from Submarine Base, Kings Bay, Georgia.

Facts

Trident I (C4)

Type: Strategic nuclear deterrence
Contractor: Lockheed Martin Missiles & Space
Propulsion: 3-stage solid-propellant rocket
Length: 34 feet (10.2 meters)
Weight: 73,000 pounds (33,142 kilograms)
Diameter: 74 inches (1.8 meters)
Range: 4,000 nautical miles (4,600 statute miles or 7,360 kilometers)
Guidance System: Inertial
Warhead: Nuclear MIRV
Date Deployed: 1979

Trident II (D5)

Type: Strategic nuclear deterrence
Contractor: Lockheed Martin Missiles & Space

Figure 3–13   Trident fleet ballistic missile. (*Source:* Lockheed Martin Missiles & Space)

Powerplant: 3-stage solid-propellant rocket
Length: 44 feet (13.41 meters)
Weight: 130,000 pounds (58,500 kilograms)
Diameter: 83 inches (2.11 meters)
Range: Greater than 4,000 nautical miles (4,600 statute miles, or 7,360 kilometers)
Guidance System: Inertial
Warheads: Nuclear MIRV
Date Deployed: 1990
Unit Cost: $30.9 million

Source: U.S. Navy

4

Naval Warfare

T oday's naval fleet comprises the most modern and sophisticated aircraft carriers, weapons systems, cruisers, destroyers, and submarines in the world. Together, the naval fleet is able to "control the sea and project power, defense, and influence beyond the sea."

As the needs of the modern Navy move from the deep ocean toward the littorals (the shallow regions between land and sea), the fleet's capabilities are being adjusted accordingly to help the Navy transform itself to meet its new mission. Modifications to existing ships and submarines are providing incredible capabilities for projecting power forward from the sea and on shore to aid our joint force commanders.

The Nimitz-class carriers are the equivalent of small cities and carry over 80 combat aircraft and 6,000 sailors. They have expected service lives of up to 50 years and can go for 20 years without refueling their two nuclear reactors. With a displacement of approximately

97,000 tons and a length of over 1,000 feet, these aircraft carriers are the ultimate symbol of military strength and deterrence.

The Ticonderoga-class cruisers and Arleigh Burke-class destroyers of the surface combatant fleet are equipped with the world's most sophisticated naval defense system. The Aegis Weapons System can search, track, and defend against aircraft, missiles, surface ships, submarines, and torpedoes. Its multi-function, phased-array radar, the AN/SPY-1, can simultaneously track over 100 targets at all angles from directly overhead to the horizon. The Aegis Weapons System and its flagship Ticonderoga-class cruisers are also helping with a new mission. The Aegis Ballistic Missile Defense (Aegis BMD) program is moving the power of Aegis toward defending against ballistic missile threats in support of the Missile Defense Agency.

Today's submarines include attack submarines, ballistic-missile submarines, and guided-missile submarines. As the needs of Cold War deterrence are yielding to the newer demands of fighting in the littorals, several of the fleet ballistic-missile submarines are being repurposed to become guided-missile submarines. These guided-missile submarines, or SSGNs, provide a transformational force for the U.S. Navy by combining elements of stealth, precision strike, Special Operations Forces, and mission agility with the potential to develop and test new capabilities for future missions, such as unmanned undersea vehicles and remote mine-hunting systems.

The SSGN can carry up to 154 Tomahawk missiles plus up to 66 Special Operations Forces. In addition, it is capable of a variety of intelligence, surveillance, and reconnaissance (ISR) missions and can deploy Special Forces while submerged by using SEAL delivery vehicles (SDVs) or the Advanced SEAL Delivery System (ASDS) mini-submarines. These mini-subs can travel over 125 nautical miles to reach land and make the SSGN a highly effective platform for covert operations.

This chapter takes a look at these and other exciting vessels, such as the stealthy *Sea Shadow*, and uncovers some of the latest Navy aircraft carriers, ships, and submarines in current service around the world.

Nimitz-Class Aircraft Carrier

The Nimitz-class carriers are the largest warships in the world. Their mission is to respond to global crises ranging from peacetime presence to full-scale war. During peacetime, their mission is to provide a credible, sustainable, independent forward presence and a highly visible deterrence to potential aggressors. During times of crisis, the mission is to serve as the cornerstone of joint and allied operations, and in the event of war, the mission is to launch air attacks on enemies and to protect friendly forces as directed by the President. The latest of the Nimitz-class carriers, the USS *Ronald Reagan* (CVN 76), was commissioned on July 12, 2003, at the Norfolk Naval Station in Norfolk, Virginia.

Features

The Nimitz-class carriers are the most modern and sophisticated aircraft carriers in the world. They are powered by two nuclear reactors, which can operate for 20 years without refueling, with four shafts leading to their propellers. In terms of size and speed, they have a displacement of approximately 97,000 tons, a length of over 1,000 feet, a flight deck width of over 250 feet, and a top speed in excess of 30 knots. Each carrier is home to over 80 combat aircraft and 6,000 sailors, and has an expected service life of 50 years.

The steam-powered catapults on board the USS *Ronald Reagan* can thrust a 60,000-pound aircraft from zero to 165 mph in 2 seconds within a distance of 300 feet. The arresting cables, which are used to catch the aircraft and decelerate them upon landing, can bring the aircraft from 150 mph to a full stop in a distance of about 320 feet. Weapons systems on board the USS *Ronald Reagan* include NATO Sea Sparrow missiles, Rolling Airframe Missiles (RAMs), guns, and electronic warfare capabilities. The RAMs replace the Phalanx Close-In Weapons System (CIWS) used on other carriers. They consist of the infrared seeker of the Stinger missile coupled with the warhead, rocket motor, and fuse from the Sidewinder missile, as opposed to the rapid-fire 20-mm gun system of the CIWS.

Some of the systems innovations onboard the USS *Ronald Reagan* include an Integrated Communication Advanced Network (ICAN) installed throughout the ship, plus digital communications run on a laser fiber backbone. Digital flat panels are installed on the bridge, and the ship's console uses a touch-screen format.

The carriers are in essence small cities, with their own supply departments, post offices, dental departments, medical departments, and chaplains. The supply departments provide 20,000 meals a day and can stock a 90-day supply of refrigerated and dry storage goods. Onboard distillation plants provide 400,000 gallons of fresh water daily, which is enough to supply 2,000 homes.

The USS *Ronald Reagan* is also the first carrier since the USS *Nimitz* (CVN 68) to have major carrier design changes. The changes include a redesigned island, a bulbous bow, and various flight deck modifications. The new island design provides a 270-degree view of all aircraft on deck and within the carrier airspace. This expanded view over the previous carriers provides better visibility and control over the flight deck. The flight deck angle has been increased slightly from 9.05 degrees to 9.15 degrees from the centerline to allow for unobstructed simultaneous launching and recovery of aircraft. This seemingly small adjustment means that the carrier has improved sortie rates so that it can operate at increased tempo during times of conflict. Finally, the bulbous bow provides the carrier with increased list, stability, and speed.

Background

The Nimitz-class carriers are the latest in a line of aircraft carriers that includes the Kitty Hawk, John F. Kennedy, and Enterprise classes. Ten Nimitz-class carriers are scheduled to be built with the completion of the final carrier, *George H.W. Bush* (CVN 77), currently under construction. The *Bush* will serve as the first ship in the transition to a new class of carriers known as CVN 21.

The shipbuilder for the Nimitz-class is Newport News Shipbuilding Company, now a part of Northrop Grumman. Northrop Grumman is now the sole supplier of U.S. Navy aircraft carriers and exclusive provider of their refueling services. The company is also one of only two companies capable of designing and building nuclear-powered submarines.

Figure 4–1 USS *Ronald Reagan* (CVN 76). (*Source:* U.S. Navy, Photo by Photographer's Mate 2nd Class James Thierry)

Construction and commission of an aircraft carrier can take several years from the time of initial contract award to final delivery to the Navy and commissioning. The name of the USS *Ronald Reagan* (Figure 4–1) was announced in February 1995 after initial contact award in December 1994. The keel was laid in February 1998 and the island house lifted aboard in November 2000. The ship was christened by Mrs. Nancy Reagan on March 4, 2001 and underwent sea trials in May 2003. It was delivered to the Navy on June 20, 2003 and commissioned on July 12, 2003.

Facts

General Characteristics, Nimitz Class

Builder: Newport News Shipbuilding
Powerplant: 2 nuclear reactors, 4 shafts
Length, overall: 1,092 feet (332.85 meters)
Flight Deck Width: 252 feet (76.8 meters)
Beam: 134 feet (40.84 meters)
Displacement: Approx. 97,000 tons (87,996.9 metric tons) full load
Speed: 30+ knots (34.5+ mph)
Aircraft: 85

Ships:
>> USS *Nimitz* (CVN 68), San Diego, Calif.
>> USS *Dwight D. Eisenhower* (CVN 69), Newport News, Va.
>> USS *Carl Vinson* (CVN 70), Bremerton, Wash.
>> USS *Theodore Roosevelt* (CVN 71), Norfolk, Va.
>> USS *Abraham Lincoln* (CVN 72), Everett, Wash.
>> USS *George Washington* (CVN 73), Norfolk, Va.
>> USS *John C. Stennis* (CVN 74), San Diego, Calif.
>> USS *Harry S. Truman* (CVN 75), Norfolk, Va.
>> USS *Ronald Reagan* (CVN 76), Norfolk, Va.
>> *George H.W. Bush* (CVN 77) (under construction)
Crew: Ship's Company: 3,200; Air Wing: 2,480
Armament: 2 or 3 (depending on modification) NATO Sea Sparrow launchers, 20-mm Phalanx CIWS mounts (3 on *Nimitz* and *Dwight D. Eisenhower* and 4 on *Vinson* and later ships of the class)
Date Deployed: May 3, 1975 (USS *Nimitz*)
Cost: about $4.5 billion each

Source: U.S. Navy

Aegis Weapons System

Aegis is the U.S. Navy's total weapon system designed to protect naval battle groups against multiple, incoming threats from air, surface, or subsurface. It consists of a radar, computer-based command and decision element, and missile systems that enable it to search, track, and defend against aircraft, missiles, surface ships, submarines, and torpedoes. It is the world's premier naval defense system on board U.S. Navy cruisers and destroyers and is also in use with the Spanish, Norwegian, Japanese, and Korean fleets overseas.

Features

One of the main components of the Aegis system is the automatic, detect-and-track, multi-function phased-array radar, the AN/SPY-1. This radar has four fixed-array structures instead of conventional rotating radar antennas and can send out radar beams in all directions at once. This gives it the capability simultaneously to track over

100 targets at all angles from directly overhead to the horizon. Another key feature is the command and decision system and the weapons control system. These systems provide simultaneous response to incoming threats from initial detection to kill. The Aegis system is equipped on Ticonderoga-class cruisers (CG 47) and Arleigh Burke-class destroyers (DDG 51); a version of the AN/SPY-1 radar, the SPY-1F, has been built for smaller vessels, such as the frigates of the Spanish navy.

In terms of surface-to-air missile capability, the Aegis system is integrated with what is termed the *Standard Missile* (SM). This medium- to long-range missile provides air defense for the fleet area, as well as for ship self-defense. It can be launched from the Mk-41 Vertical Launcher System (VLS) or Mk-26 Guided-Missile Launcher System and has a range of up to 200 nautical miles. In flight, the missile can be given midcourse commands from the Aegis Weapons System and is guided by inertial navigation and semiactive radar or an infrared sensor for terminal homing. The SM-2 variant of the Standard Missile has had over a thousand firings over the last two decades and has successfully engaged a variety of surface ships, helicopters, manned aircraft, and cruise missiles.

A recent focus for the Aegis program has been to enhance support for ballistic missile defense. The latest variants of the Standard Missile, such as the SM-3, are being tested for their ability to engage incoming ballistic missile targets during their ascent and midcourse phases of flight. The program, managed jointly by the U.S. Navy and Missile Defense Agency (MDA), is the Aegis BMD program.

Background

The Aegis system (Figure 4–2) was developed in response to the threat of incoming enemy aircraft and anti-ship missiles on naval battle groups in the late 1960s. During this time in the Cold War, the threat was of a coordinated attack by the Russians with multiple incoming weapons aimed at the fleet in order to overcome its shipboard defenses.

The Aegis system started out as the Advanced Surface Missile System (ASMS) and was later renamed to AEGIS in December 1969. A series of upgrades have kept the weapons system up to date with the latest technologies, and today the system is in its seventh generation

Figure 4–2   Aegis Weapons System. (*Source:* U.S. Navy)

and has been sold to other allied navies around the world. The first Engineering Development Model of the Aegis system was installed in the test ship, USS *Norton Sound*, in 1973.

Lockheed Martin is the prime contractor for the Aegis system, including the AN/SPY-1 radar, and these systems are used on board Ticonderoga-class cruisers (CG 47) and Arleigh Burke-class destroyers (DDG 51).

The Aegis BMD program is currently using an Aegis-class cruiser, USS *Lake Erie*, as the test ship for a series of tests to demonstrate the systems capability against stressful ballistic missile targets in the Pacific Missile Range Facility in Hawaii. In 2002, the program achieved two successful ballistic missile intercepts, which demonstrated less stressful target scenarios.

Facts

Type: Naval defense system against air, surface, and subsurface threats

Contractor: Lockheed Martin Naval Electronics & Surveillance Systems

Platforms: Ticonderoga-class cruisers (CG 47) and Arleigh Burke-class destroyers (DDG 51)

Weapons: Standard Missile (SM)

Service: U.S. Navy

Source: U.S. Navy, Lockheed Martin

Ticonderoga-Class Cruisers

The Ticonderoga-class cruisers are large combat vessels that have multi-mission roles in support of carrier battle groups, surface action groups, amphibious assault groups, and as an integral part of inter-diction forces. As Battle Force-Capable (BFC) units, these cruisers can defeat hostile ships, submarines, and aircraft while simultaneously delivering long-range land attacks.

Features

The Ticonderoga-class cruisers have a length of 567 feet, a beam of 55 feet, and a full load displacement of 9,600 tons. They are capable of traveling at speeds in excess of 30 knots. Their power plant consists of four General Electric gas turbine engines that produce 80,000 shaft horsepower in total.

The primary weapons system on board the Ticonderoga-class cruisers is the Aegis Weapons System for unrivaled defense of the entire battlespace, including anti-air, anti-surface, and anti-submarine warfare. The weapons on board include surface-to-air SMs, Harpoon anti-ship missiles, Tomahawk cruise missiles, anti-submarine rockets, torpedoes, the Phalanx CIWS, and five-inch, rapid-fire deck guns.

Electronic warfare countermeasures include decoys and passive detection systems. For anti-submarine warfare at a distance of up to 100 miles, the Ticonderoga class has a hull-mounted sonar, an acoustic array sonar towed behind the ship, and the SH-60B LAMPS Mk-3 Helicopter.

Figure 4–3 Ticonderoga-class guided-missile cruiser USS *Chosin* (CG 65). (*Source:* U.S. Navy photo by Photographer's Mate 3rd Class Yesenia Rosas)

Background

The Ticonderoga-class cruisers (Figure 4–3), which use the Spruance-class hull form, were initially designated as Guided Missile Destroyers DDG but were later designated as Guided Missile Cruisers CG on January 1, 1980. These ships were the first to be equipped with the Aegis Weapons System. Today, they are considered the "flagships" of Aegis and are the principal sea-based ABM missile launch platforms as the Aegis Weapons System is used for ballistic missile defense in addition to its long-standing role of naval defense in support of the fleet.

The Ticonderoga-class cruiser, USS *Lake Erie* (CG 70), currently serves as the test ship for the Aegis BMD program. The USS *Lake Erie* was commissioned on July 24, 1993 and is homeported at Pearl Harbor, Hawaii.

Facts

General Characteristics, Ticonderoga Class

Builders:
>> *Ingalls Shipbuilding*: CG 47–50, CG 52–57, 59, 62, 65–66, 68–69, 71–73

>> *Bath Iron Works*: CG 51, 58, 60–61, 63–64, 67, 70
Power Plant: 4 General Electric LM 2500 gas turbine engines; 2 shafts, 80,000 shaft horsepower total
SPY-1 Radar and Combat System Integrator: Lockheed Martin
Length: 567 feet
Beam: 55 feet
Displacement: 9,600 tons (9,754.06 metric tons) full load
Speed: 30+ knots
Aircraft: 2 SH-2 Seasprite (LAMPS) in CG 47–48; 2 SH-60 Sea Hawk (LAMPS III)
Cost: About $1 billion each
Ships:
>> USS *Ticonderoga* (CG 47), Pascagoula, Miss.
>> USS *Yorktown* (CG 48), Pascagoula, Miss.
>> USS *Vincennes* (CG 49), Yokosuka, Japan
>> USS *Valley Forge* (CG 50), San Diego, Calif.
>> USS *Thomas S. Gates* (CG 51), Pascagoula, Miss.
>> USS *Bunker Hill* (CG 52), San Diego, Calif.
>> USS *Mobile Bay* (CG 53), San Diego, Calif.
>> USS *Antietam* (CG 54), San Diego, Calif.
>> USS *Leyte Gulf* (CG 55), Norfolk, Va.
>> USS *San Jacinto* (CG 56), Norfolk, Va.
>> USS *Lake Champlain* (CG 57), San Diego, Calif.
>> USS *Philippine Sea* (CG 58), Mayport, Fla.
>> USS *Princeton* (CG 59), San Diego, Calif.
>> USS *Normandy* (CG 60), Norfolk, Va.
>> USS *Monterey* (CG 61), Norfolk, Va.
>> USS *Chancellorsville* (CG 62), Yokosuka, Japan
>> USS *Cowpens* (CG 63), Yokosuka, Japan
>> USS *Gettysburg* (CG 64), Mayport, Fla.
>> USS *Chosin* (CG 65), Pearl Harbor, Hawaii
>> USS *Hue City* (CG 66), Mayport, Fla.
>> USS *Shiloh* (CG 67), San Diego, Calif.
>> USS *Anzio* (CG 68), Norfolk, Va.
>> USS *Vicksburg* (CG 69), Mayport, Fla.
>> USS *Lake Erie* (CG 70), Pearl Harbor, Hawaii
>> USS *Cape St. George* (CG 71), Norfolk, Va.
>> USS *Vella Gulf* (CG 72), Norfolk, Va.
>> USS *Port Royal* (CG 73), Pearl Harbor, Hawaii

Crew: 24 officers, 340 enlisted

Armament: Mk-26 missile launcher (CG 47–51) medium-range SM or Mk-41 VLS (CG 52–73) medium-range SM; Vertical Launch ASROC (VLA) missile; Tomahawk cruise missile; 6 Mk-46 torpedoes (from 2 triple mounts); 2 Mk-45 5-inch/54-caliber lightweight guns; 2 Phalanx CIWS

Date Deployed: January 22, 1983 (USS *Ticonderoga*)

Source: U.S. Navy

Arleigh Burke-Class Destroyers

The Arleigh Burke-class destroyers are the latest, most capable and survivable surface combatants in the U.S. Navy fleet. They incorporate the Aegis weapons system for air defense and can operate as part of carrier battle groups or on other offensive or defensive missions.

Features

Typically, destroyers perform anti-submarine warfare missions, whereas guided-missile destroyers can perform multiple roles, including anti-submarine warfare, anti-air warfare, and anti-surface warfare. The Arleigh Burke-class destroyers are over 500 feet in length, with a beam of nearly 60 feet and a displacement of over 8,000 tons. Powered by four General Electric gas turbines, they are capable of speeds in excess of 30 knots.

As a guided-missile destroyer, the Arleigh Burke (DDG 51)-class destroyers are equipped with a full spectrum of armaments, including the SM, Harpoon missiles, Vertical Launch ASROC (VLA) missiles, and Tomahawk missiles, together with Mk-46 torpedoes, an Mk-45 gun, and two 20-mm Phalanx CIWS. The SM provides medium- to long-range surface-to-air coverage; the Harpoon provides anti-ship coverage; the VLA missiles provide anti-submarine coverage; and the Tomahawk cruise missiles provide capability for land attack warfare. The Phalanx system provides last resort close-in defense against anti-ship missiles with a 20-mm rapid-fire gun capable of operating at 4,500 rounds per minute.

The Aegis weapons system is the centerpiece of the Arleigh Burke defense capability and comprises a complete system, including the AN/SPY-1 multi-function phased-array radar, computer-based command and decision elements, and integrated missile systems. The Aegis weapons system is also equipped on Ticonderoga-class cruisers (CG 47), as well as the Arleigh Burke-class. As the world's premier naval defense system, it can provide defense against all incoming threats, whether airborne, surface, or subsurface.

The Arleigh Burke-class destroyers are also strengthened for survivability. They include protection against underwater shock; nuclear air blasts; radar detection; electronic countermeasures; and chemical, biological, or nuclear agents. The stealth capability to minimize radar detection is accomplished by the ship's angular construction. Other stealth features include minimized acoustic and infrared signatures. The ship's complement includes 30 officers and 302 enlisted personnel.

Background

The Arleigh Burke class (Figure 4–4) was originally designed to defend the fleet against Soviet aircraft, cruise missiles, and nuclear attack submarines.

The first in the class, the *Arleigh Burke* was commissioned on July 4, 1991, and was named after the famous destroyer squadron combat commander and three-time Chief of Naval Operations (CNO). The 45th ship of the 62 ships currently authorized by Congress, the *James E. Williams* was christened on June 28, 2003, in Pascagoula, Mississippi.

On June 11, 2003, the USS *Arleigh Burke* (DDG 51) returned to her homeport of Norfolk, Virginia after a five-month deployment in support of Operation Enduring Freedom and Operation Iraqi Freedom. As part of the Theodore Roosevelt Carrier Strike Group, *Arleigh Burke* had fired 26 Tomahawk cruise missiles at targets in Iraq.

Facts

General Characteristics, Arleigh Burke Class

Builders: Bath Iron Works, Ingalls Shipbuilding

Figure 4–4   USS *Arleigh Burke*. (*Source:* U.S. Navy, Photo by Master Chief Journalist Kevin Copeland)

Powerplant: 4 General Electric LM 2500-30 gas turbines; 2 shafts, 100,000 total shaft horsepower.
SPY-1 Radar and Combat System Integrator: Lockheed Martin
Length:
>> *Flights I and II (DDG 51–78):* 505 feet (153.92 meters)
>> *Flight IIA (DDG 79–98):* 509.5 feet (155.29 meters)
Beam: 59 feet (18 meters)
Displacement:
>> *Hulls 51–71:* 8,315 tons (8,448.04 metric tons) full load
>> *Hulls 72–78:* 8,400 tons (8,534.4 metric tons) full load
>> *Hulls 79 and on:* 9,200 tons (9,347.2 metric tons) full load
Speed: Excess of 30 knots
Aircraft: None. LAMPS III electronics installed on landing deck for coordinated DDG 51/helo ASW operations
Ships:
>> USS *Arleigh Burke* (DDG 51), Norfolk, Va.
>> USS *Barry* (DDG 52), Norfolk, Va.
>> USS *John Paul Jones* (DDG 53), San Diego, Calif.
>> USS *Curtis Wilbur* (DDG 54), Yokosuka, Japan

>> USS *Stout* (DDG 55), Norfolk, Va.
>> USS *John S. McCain* (DDG 56), Yokosuka, Japan
>> USS *Mitscher* (DDG 57), Norfolk, Va.
>> USS *Laboon* (DDG 58), Norfolk, Va.
>> USS *Russell* (DDG 59), Pearl Harbor, Hawaii
>> USS *Paul Hamilton* (DDG 60), Pearl Harbor, Hawaii
>> USS *Ramage* (DDG 61), Norfolk, Va.
>> USS *Fitzgerald* (DDG 62), San Diego, Calif.
>> USS *Stethem* (DDG 63), San Diego, Calif.
>> USS *Carney* (DDG 64), Mayport, Fla.
>> USS *Benfold* (DDG 65), San Diego, Calif.
>> USS *Gonzalez* (DDG 66), Norfolk, Va.
>> USS *Cole* (DDG 67), Norfolk, Va.
>> USS *The Sullivans* (DDG 68), Mayport, Fla.
>> USS *Milius* (DDG 69), San Diego, Calif.
>> USS *Hopper* (DDG 70), Pearl Harbor, Hawaii
>> USS *Ross* (DDG 71), Norfolk, Va.
>> USS *Mahan* (DDG 72), Norfolk, Va.
>> USS *Decatur* (DDG 73), San Diego, Calif.
>> USS *McFaul* (DDG 74), Norfolk, Va.
>> USS *Donald Cook* (DDG 75), Norfolk, Va.
>> USS *Higgins* (DDG 76), San Diego, Calif.
>> USS *O'Kane* (DDG 77), Pearl Harbor, Hawaii
>> USS *Porter* (DDG 78), Norfolk, Va.
>> USS *Oscar Austin* (DDG 79), Norfolk, Va.
>> USS *Roosevelt* (DDG 80), Mayport, Fla.
>> USS *Winston S. Churchill* (DDG 81), Norfolk, Va.
>> USS *Lassen* (DDG 82), San Diego, Calif.
>> USS *Howard* (DDG 83), San Diego, Calif.
>> USS *Bulkeley* (DDG 84), Norfolk, Va.
>> USS *McCampbell* (DDG 85), San Diego, Calif.
>> USS *Shoup* (DDG 86), Everett, Wash.
>> USS *Mason* (DDG 87), Norfolk, Va.
>> USS *Preble* (DDG 88), San Diego, Calif.
>> USS *Mustin* (DDG 89), San Diego, Calif.
>> *Chafee* (DDG 90), under construction
>> *Pinckney* (DDG 91), under construction
>> *Momsen* (DDG 92)
>> *Chung-Hoon* (DDG 93)

>> *Nitze* (DDG 94)
>> *James E. Williams* (DDG 95)
>> *Bainbridge* (DDG 96)
>> *Halsey* (DDG 97)
>> *Forrest Sherman* (DDG 98)
>> *Farragut* (DDG 99)
Crew: 23 officers, 300 enlisted
Armament: SM; Harpoon; VLA missiles; Tomahawk; 6 Mk-46 torpedoes (from 2 triple tube mounts); 5-inch/54-caliber Mk-45 (lightweight gun); 2 20-mm Phalanx CIWS
Date Deployed: July 4, 1991 (USS *Arleigh Burke*)

Source: U.S. Navy

Attack Submarines (SSN)

Attack submarines are the U.S. Navy's nuclear-powered submarines, comprised of the Los Angeles, Seawolf, and Virginia classes, designed to combat enemy submarines and surface ships and to take on a variety of other broad-spectrum missions. They represent a multi-mission platform that can perform peacetime engagements, ISR, Special Operations, precision strikes, sea denial, and deterrence, using their characteristics of stealth, endurance, firepower, and mobility. Their nuclear reactor powerplant means that they have virtually unlimited propulsion power and can remain at sea for weeks or even months at a time.

Features

The main submarine of the attack fleet is the Los Angeles (SSN 688) class. These fast, heavily-armed submarines can carry 25 torpedo-tube-launched weapons, including the Mk-48 torpedo and the Tomahawk cruise missile. The Mk-48 is a self-propelled guided missile that operates underwater at a speed of greater than 28 knots. It detonates on contact or in close proximity to its target and has a warhead of 650 pounds of high explosives. The Mk-48 is one of the three main torpedoes in the U.S. Navy inventory and is carried by all Navy submarines. The Los Angeles class has four torpedo tubes, and some later submarines have VLS tubes that increase their firepower.

The Los Angeles-class submarines carry a crew of approximately 130 men. They have a length of 360 feet and can travel at a speed in excess of 20 knots. The latest 23 submarines in the Los Angeles class are called the "Improved 688s" (I688s). Their enhancements include quieter operation, an advanced combat system, improved under-ice operations, and twelve vertical launch tubes for Tomahawk cruise missiles. Improved under-ice operations include diving planes moved from the sail to the bow and a strengthened sail for breaking through ice.

The next class in the SSN class is the Seawolf. This submarine builds on the capabilities of the Los Angeles class with improved stealth, mobility, and firepower. It is quieter than the Los Angeles class, can travel greater than 25 knots, and has eight torpedo tubes instead of four. The Seawolf's robust design supports missions such as surveillance, intelligence collection, special warfare, covert cruise-missile strike, mine warfare, and anti-submarine and anti-surface ship warfare.

In recent years, the focus of submarine warfare has shifted toward the littoral regions in addition to the "blue-water" traditional domain of the submarine. Because of this change in requirements and due to the large costs involved in operating the submarine fleet, in 1991, Admiral Kelso, CNO, ordered the design of an "affordable" submarine as a follow-on to the Seawolf class. This heralded the beginning of the New SSN (NSSN), the Virginia-class SSN. The Virginia class is designed to operate in the coastal region while maintaining its open-ocean capability. It will include Tomahawk cruise-missile capability and will add support for advanced sonar systems for anti-submarine and mine warfare; a reconfigurable torpedo room for special missions; ASDS and nine-man lockout trunk to launch unmanned underwater or aerial vehicles for mine reconnaissance, intelligence gathering, and other missions; enhanced stealth; and enhanced electronic support measures (ESM).

Background

The first submarine of the Los Angeles class, USS *Los Angeles* (SSN 688), was deployed in November 1976. In 1991, the USS *Louisville* (SSN 724) gained the recognition of being the first submarine to fire a Tomahawk cruise missile in a combat situation during Operation Desert Storm. Today, there is a fleet of over 50 submarines in this class with the most recent being the USS *Cheyenne* (SSN 773), which was commissioned in September 1996. The USS *Cheyenne* is the newest submarine in the Pacific submarine force and is the 62nd Los Angeles-class submarine. With the last of this class having been deployed, the numbers of Los Angeles-class submarines will decrease yearly as they reach the end of their service lives of approximately 25–30 years.

The first submarine in the Seawolf class, USS *Seawolf* (SSN 21), completed its sea trials in July 1996. The class was originally intended to grow to a total of 29 submarines in support of Cold War efforts. The end of the Cold War meant that budgets and needs were reevaluated, and today the class has been restructured to just three submarines: the USS *Seawolf* (Figure 4–5), the USS *Connecticut*, and the *Jimmy Carter*, which is under construction at the time of this writing.

In September 1999, the USS *Virginia* (SSN 774) keel-laying ceremony took place at Quonset Point, Rhode Island. Initial construction began at General Dynamics Electric Boat, Connecticut and Newport News, Virginia. The USS *Virginia* is expected to be complete in 2004. The Virginia-class submarines are the latest generation of attack submarines and will be covered in detail later in Chapter 8.

Figure 4–5   USS *Seawolf* (SSN 21) completing sea trials in July 1996. (*Source:* U.S. Navy)

Facts

General Characteristics, Seawolf Class

Builders: General Dynamics Electric Boat
Powerplant: 1 nuclear reactor, 1 shaft
Length: 353 feet (107.6 meters)
Draft: 35 feet (10.67 meters)
Beam: 40 feet (12.2 meters)
Displacement: 8,060 tons (8,189.35 metric tons) surfaced; 9,150 tons (9,296.84 metric tons) submerged
Speed: 25+ knots (28+ mph, 46.3+ kph)
Cost: About $2.1 billion each
Ships:
>> USS *Seawolf* (SSN 21), Groton, Conn.
>> USS *Connecticut* (SSN 22), Groton, Conn.
>> *Jimmy Carter* (SSN 23), (under construction)
Crew: 13 officers; 121 enlisted
Armament: Tomahawk missiles, Mk-48 torpedoes, 8 torpedo tubes

General Characteristics, Los Angeles Class

Builders: Newport News Shipbuilding; General Dynamics Electric Boat
Powerplant: 1 nuclear reactor, 1 shaft
Length: 360 feet (109.73 meters)
Beam: 33 feet (10.06 meters)
Displacement: Approximately 6,900 tons (7010.73 metric tons) submerged
Speed: 20+ knots (23+ mph, 36.8+ kph)
Ships:
>> USS *Los Angeles* (SSN 688), Pearl Harbor, Hawaii
>> USS *Philadelphia* (SSN 690), Groton, Conn.
>> USS *Memphis* (SSN 691), Groton, Conn.
>> USS *Bremerton* (SSN 698), San Diego, Calif.
>> USS *Jacksonville* (SSN 699), Norfolk, Va.
>> USS *Dallas* (SSN 700), Groton, Conn.
>> USS *La Jolla* (SSN 701), Pearl Harbor, Hawaii
>> USS *City of Corpus Christi* (SSN 705), Guam
>> USS *Albuquerque* (SSN 706), Portsmouth, N.H.
>> USS *Portsmouth* (SSN 707), San Diego, Calif.

>> USS *Minneapolis-St. Paul* (SSN 708), Norfolk, Va.
>> USS *Hyman G. Rickover* (SSN 709), Norfolk, Va.
>> USS *Augusta* (SSN 710), Groton, Conn.
>> USS *San Francisco* (SSN 711), Guam
>> USS *Houston* (SSN 713), San Diego, Calif.
>> USS *Norfolk* (SSN 714), Norfolk, Va.
>> USS *Buffalo* (SSN 715), Pearl Harbor, Hawaii
>> USS *Salt Lake City* (SSN 716), San Diego, Calif.
>> USS *Olympia* (SSN 717), Pearl Harbor, Hawaii
>> USS *Honolulu* (SSN 718), Pearl Harbor, Hawaii
>> USS *Providence* (SSN 719), Groton, Conn.
>> USS *Pittsburgh* (SSN 720), Groton, Conn.
>> USS *Chicago* (SSN 721), Pearl Harbor, Hawaii
>> USS *Key West* (SSN 722), Pearl Harbor, Hawaii
>> USS *Oklahoma City* (SSN 723), Norfolk, Va.
>> USS *Louisville* (SSN 724), Pearl Harbor, Hawaii
>> USS *Helena* (SSN 725), San Diego, Calif.
>> USS *Newport News* (SSN 750), Norfolk, Va.
>> USS *San Juan* (SSN 751), Groton, Conn.
>> USS *Pasadena* (SSN 752), Pearl Harbor, Hawaii
>> USS *Albany* (SSN 753), Norfolk, Va.
>> USS *Topeka* (SSN 754), Pearl Harbor, Hawaii
>> USS *Miami* (SSN 755), Groton, Conn.
>> USS *Scranton* (SSN 756), Norfolk, Va.
>> USS *Alexandria* (SSN 757), Groton, Conn.
>> USS *Asheville* (SSN 758), San Diego, Calif.
>> USS *Jefferson City* (SSN 759), Bangor, Wash.
>> USS *Annapolis* (SSN 760), Groton, Conn.
>> USS *Springfield* (SSN 761), Groton, Conn.
>> USS *Columbus* (SSN 762), Pearl Harbor, Hawaii
>> USS *Santa Fe* (SSN 763), Pearl Harbor, Hawaii
>> USS *Boise* (SSN 764), Norfolk, Va.
>> USS *Montpelier* (SSN 765), Norfolk, Va.
>> USS *Charlotte* (SSN 766), Pearl Harbor, Hawaii
>> USS *Hampton* (SSN 767), Norfolk, Va.
>> USS *Hartford* (SSN 768), Groton, Conn.
>> USS *Toledo* (SSN 769), Groton, Conn.
>> USS *Tucson* (SSN 770), Pearl Harbor, Hawaii
>> USS *Columbia* (SSN 771), Pearl Harbor, Hawaii

>> USS *Greeneville* (SSN 772), Pearl Harbor, Hawaii
>> USS *Cheyenne* (SSN 773), Pearl Harbor, Hawaii
Crew: 13 officers, 121 enlisted
Armament: Tomahawk missiles, VLS tubes (SSN 719 and later), Mk-48 torpedoes, 4 torpedo tubes (Seawolf has 8)
Date Deployed: November 13, 1976 (USS *Los Angeles*)

Source: U.S. Navy

Fleet Ballistic Missile Submarines (SSBN)

The fleet ballistic missile submarines (SSBN) are nuclear-powered submarines within the U.S. Navy that have the sole mission of strategic deterrence. The current generation of SSBNs is the Ohio class, which was first commissioned in 1981, replacing the earlier submarines built during the 1960s. Each Ohio-class submarine carries 24 Trident submarine-launched intercontinental ballistic missiles (SLBMs). The fleet of 18 submarines assigned to the Atlantic and Pacific Oceans represents the sea-based "leg" of the U.S. strategic triad and accounts for over 50 percent of the total U.S. strategic warheads. The submarines also provide the most survivable and enduring nuclear strike capability, compared with the land-based missile systems and manned bombers within the triad. The deterrent capability of these submarines is due to the fact that historically during the Cold War, any attack by the Soviets could be immediately countered in a retaliatory strike using the SSBN fleet, which can be neither detected nor destroyed. This capability continues to this day, although the Clinton Administration's Nuclear Posture Review and the START II arms control treaty is reducing the size of the fleet from 18 to 14 in active service.

Features

The Ohio-class submarines are among the quietest, fastest, largest, and most powerful submarines in the world. Their normal operating schedule is to be at sea for 77 days and back at port for a 35-day maintenance period. Two complete crews are assigned to each SSBN. Each crew has 15 officers and 140 enlisted personnel, called the

"Blue" and "Gold" crews. To make port calls more efficient, the submarines have three large logistics hatches that can help speed resupply and repair. The modular nature of the design means that major overhauls are required only every 15 plus years.

The submarines are powered by a nuclear reactor with a single shaft drive and have a length of 560 feet and a beam of 42 feet. They can travel at up to 20 plus knots and to depths of 800 plus feet.

Background

The first submerged launch of a ballistic missile was conducted in 1963 aboard the USS *George Washington* (SSBN 598). The Ohio-class submarine (Figure 4–6), commissioned in 1981, replaced the older Ethan Allen, Lafayette, and Benjamin Franklin classes. Of the 18 Ohio-class submarines produced, the first eight carried the Trident I C-4 ballistic missile, and the later ten carried the improved Trident II D-5. Currently, four of the submarines equipped with the Trident I are being retrofitted to Trident II, and the other four are being converted to guided-missile submarines (SSGN) over the next few years.

Currently, half the fleet is stationed at Bangor, Washington and the other half at Kings Bay, Georgia. The last Ohio-class submarine to be manufactured, the USS *Louisiana* (SSBN 743), was commissioned in September 1997 at the Naval Submarine Base, Kings Bay.

Figure 4–6   Ohio-class ballistic missile submarine. (*Source:* General Dynamics)

Plate 1
The B-2 Spirit is a multi-role, long-range bomber operated by the U.S. Air Force that can deliver conventional or nuclear weapons and penetrate deep into enemy defenses using its advanced stealth technology. (*Source:* Northrop Grumman)

Plate 2
Developed for the Air Force, the F-117A Stealth Fighter is the first operational aircraft to exploit low-observable stealth technology. It is designed to penetrate dense threat environments at night and attack high-value targets with pinpoint accuracy. (*Source:* Lockheed Martin)

Plate 3
The Merlin Helicopter for the British Royal Navy is a new multi-mission helicopter designed primarily for anti-surface-ship and anti-submarine warfare. (*Source:* Lockheed Martin)

Plate 4
The RQ-4A Global Hawk is a high-altitude, long-endurance, unmanned aerial vehicle (UAV) that provides the U.S. Air Force with near-real-time, high-resolution images from intelligence, surveillance, and reconnaissance missions. (*Source:* Northrop Grumman)

Plate 5
The U.S. Air Force's Navstar Global Positioning System (GPS) is designed to instantaneously provide precise, three-dimensional navigation information to properly equipped military and civilian users under all weather conditions around the world. (*Source:* Boeing)

Plate 6
The Challenger 2 is the British Army's main battle tank. It is manufactured by Alvis Vickers Limited and has been in service in Bosnia and Kosovo as well as during Operation Iraqi Freedom. (*Source:* Alvis Vickers Ltd.)

Plate 7
The AN/PVS-7 night vision goggles provide the Marine Corps with the current state-of-the-art in night vision equipment. Night vision goggles can be vital in modern conflicts in order to provide allies with the upper hand in night combat. (*Source:* Northrop Grumman)

Plate 8
The Force XXI Battle Command Brigade and Below (FBCB2) is the main digital command-and-control system for the U.S. Army at the Brigade and below level. It provides on-the-move, real-time, and near-real-time battle command information and is a key component of the Army Battle Command System (ABCS). (*Source:* Northrop Grumman)

Plate 9
The Massive Ordnance Air Blast, or MOAB, is currently the largest non-nuclear weapon in the U.S. military giving it the nickname "Mother Of All Bombs." It first gained visibility when it was tested by the U.S. Air Force in Florida prior to the start of Operation Iraqi Freedom. (*Source:* Department of Defense)

Plate 10
The Patriot Advanced Capability-3 is a land-based, guided surface-to-air missile defense system that can protect against tactical ballistic missiles, cruise missiles, and hostile fixed-wing aircraft and helicopters using a "hit-to-kill" approach. The figure shows a direct impact during a real-life test. (*Source:* Lockheed Martin)

Plate 11
Joint Standoff Weapon (JSOW) represents a new generation of advanced missiles developed by Raytheon Systems Company—and now in production for the U.S. Navy and U.S. Air Force. (*Source:* Raytheon)

Plate 12
The Joint Direct Attack Munition (JDAM) is a guidance kit that converts existing unguided free-fall bombs into precision-guided "smart" munitions. The JDAM dramatically improves the accuracy of precision strike munitions in adverse weather and can be dropped by an aircraft from up to 15 miles from the target. (*Source:* Boeing)

Plate 13
Upon completion of acceptance sea trials, the Nimitz-class aircraft carrier *Ronald Reagan* (CVN 76) returns to Norfolk Naval Station in Norfolk, VA, where it was commissioned July 12, 2003. (*Source:* Northrop Grumman)

Plate 14
Technicians and Navy personnel at the AEGIS air combat system test and crew training facility in Moorestown, NJ. (*Source:* Lockheed Martin)

Plate 15
Northrop Grumman's Advanced SEAL Delivery System (ASDS) leaves Pearl Harbor aboard the Los Angeles–class submarine USS *Greeneville* (SSN 772) to begin launch and recovery testing. (*Source:* Northrop Grumman)

Plate 16
The *Sea Shadow* began life in the mid-80s in secrecy and was not revealed to the public until 1993. It is pictured here at its debut in the ocean near San Francisco Bay. (*Source:* Lockheed Martin)

Plate 17
The Joint Strike Fighter is the next-generation multi-role combat aircraft to replace the F-16, A-10, F-18C/D, British Harrier, and other aircraft. Designated F-35, the supersonic Joint Strike Fighter has three variants: Conventional Take Off and Landing for the U.S. Air Force, Carrier Variant for the U.S. Navy, and the STOVL variant for the U.S. Marines. (*Source:* Lockheed Martin)

Plate 18
The RAH-66 Comanche is the U.S. Army's next-generation armed reconnaissance helicopter. The helicopter's primary role will be to perform armed reconnaissance in support of AH-64 Apache attack helicopters. It will also have projected missions of light attack, air combat and special operations. (*Source:* Boeing)

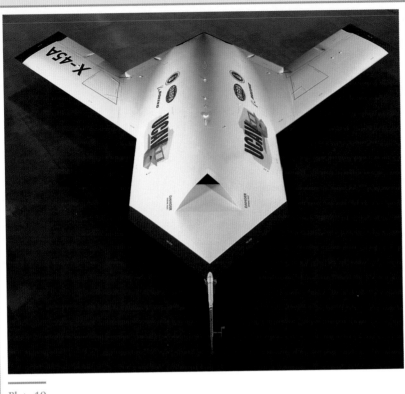

Plate 19
An artist concept of an operational U.S. Air Force Unmanned Combat Air Vehicle. (*Source:* Boeing)

Plate 20
The Hornet Micro Air Vehicle (MAV) set a record on March 21, 2003, when it completed the first fuel cell powered flight of an unmanned aerial vehicle. During the day, the Hornet was flown three times for a total endurance of 15 minutes. (*Source:* DARPA)

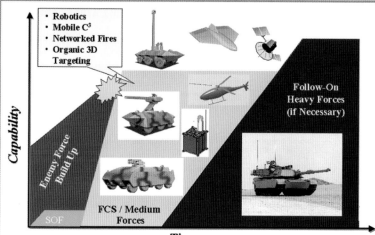

Plate 21
The Future Combat Systems (FCS) program has the goal of designing and developing a networked system-of-systems comprised of eighteen manned and unmanned ground and aerial vehicles and sensors connected via an advanced communications network. (*Source:* DARPA)

Plate 22
The Unmanned Ground Combat Vehicle (UGCV) is part of the U.S. Army's Future Combat Systems (FCS) program and is focused on developing unmanned vehicle prototypes that can carry reconnaissance, surveillance and targeting, or weapons payloads in support of network-centric warfare. (*Source:* DARPA)

Plate 23

Objective Force Warrior program is aimed at enhancing the soldier's lethality, survivability, communications, and responsiveness. It includes a head-to-toe protective system, lightweight weapons systems, networked communications, advanced power systems, and warfighter physiological status monitoring. (*Source:* Natick Soldier Center)

Plate 24

The Future Warrior is a soldier uniform concept demonstration program that aims to show how the future soldier may be equipped in the 2025 timeframe. (*Source:* Natick Soldier Center)

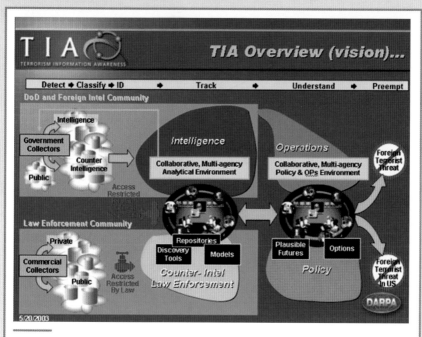

Plate 25

Terrorism Information Awareness (TIA) aims to develop a prototype system and network for the detection, classification, and identification of potential foreign terrorists so that the United States can take pre-emptive action before events of terrorism occur. (*Source:* DARPA)

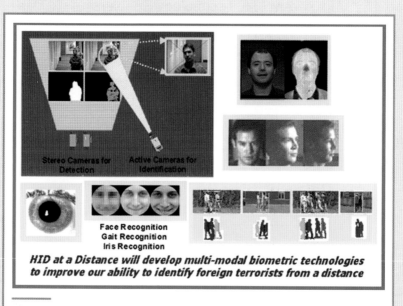

Plate 26

Human Identification at a Distance (HumanID) aims to develop automated biometric identification technologies to detect, recognize, and identify humans at great distances. (*Source:* DARPA)

Plate 27
The VoxTec Phraselator is a one-way translation device that was used in
Afghanistan by U.S. military forces in support of Operation Enduring Freedom
and also during Operation Iraqi Freedom by coalition forces. (*Source:*
www.phraselator.com)

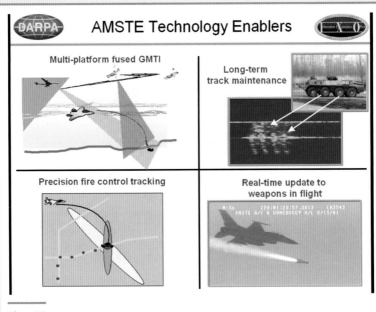

Plate 28
Affordable Moving Surface Target Engagement (AMSTE) has a goal to
develop and demonstrate the ability to target moving surface threats
from long range, to rapidly engage them with precision stand-off
weapons, and to do so economically. (*Source:* DARPA)

Plate 29
An artist's concept of the Airborne Laser. (*Source:* Boeing; Artwork by Mike Casad)

Plate 30
The CVN 21 Future Carrier is the Navy's next-generation aircraft carrier, which is scheduled to begin construction in 2007 with delivery planned for 2014. (*Source:* Northrop Grumman)

Plate 31
The Littoral Combat Ship (LCS) is part of the family of ships within the future Surface Combatant Navy. It is a small, fast, and highly maneuverable focused mission ship that is designed for warfighting in the littorals. (*Source:* Raytheon)

Plate 32
The Virginia-class submarine is the U.S. Navy's newest attack submarine, optimized for operation in the littorals, the shallow coastal regions of the ocean near the shore, and features advanced technologies in the areas of firepower, maneuverability, and stealth. (*Source:* U.S. Navy)

Facts

Builders: General Dynamics Electric Boat
Powerplant: 1 nuclear reactor, 1 shaft
Length: 560 feet (170.69 meters)
Beam: 42 feet (12.8 meters)
Displacement: 16,764 tons (17,033.03 metric tons) surfaced; 18,750 tons (19,000.1 metric tons) submerged
Speed: 20+ knots (23+ mph, 36.8+ kph)
Ships:
Homeported at the Naval Submarine Base, Bangor, Washington:
>> USS *Michigan* (SSBN 727)—conversion to SSGN scheduled for October 2003
>> USS *Georgia* (SSBN 729)—conversion to SSGN scheduled for 2004
>> USS *Henry M. Jackson* (SSBN 730)
>> USS *Alabama* (SSBN 731)
>> USS *Alaska* (SSBN 732)
>> USS *Nevada* (SSBN 733)
>> USS *Pennsylvania* (SSBN 735)
>> USS *Kentucky* (SSBN 737)

Homeported at the Naval Submarine Base, Kings Bay, Georgia:
>> USS *Tennessee* (SSBN 734)
>> USS *West Virginia* (SSBN 736)
>> USS *Maryland* (SSBN 738)
>> USS *Nebraska* (SSBN 739)
>> USS *Rhode Island* (SSBN 740)
>> USS *Maine* (SSBN 741)
>> USS *Wyoming* (SSBN 742)
>> USS *Louisiana* (SSBN 743)

Ships Undergoing Conversion to SSGN:
>> USS *Ohio* (SSBN 726)—out of service October 29, 2002, for conversion to SSGN, Puget Sound Naval Shipyard
>> USS *Florida* (SSBN 728)—conversion to SSGN scheduled for October 2003, Norfolk, Va.
Crew: 15 officers, 140 enlisted
Armament: 24 tubes for Trident I and II, Mk-48 torpedoes, 4 torpedo tubes
Date Deployed: November 11, 1981 (USS *Ohio*)

Source: U.S. Navy

Guided-Missile Submarines (SSGN)

The SSGN is a guided-missile submarine that is a converted fleet bal-listic missile submarine (SSBN) using Tomahawk or Tactical Toma-hawk missiles instead of the Trident missiles of the SSBN. The mission of the SSGN fleet is to support combat land attack operations with tactical missiles and to provide the ability to transport and sup-port up to 66 Special Operations personnel for months at a time. The submarines provide a transformational force for the U.S. Navy by combining these elements of stealth, precision strike, Special Opera-tions Forces, and mission agility with the potential to develop and test new capabilities, such as unmanned undersea vehicles and remote mine-hunting systems for future missions.

Features

The SSGN can carry up to 154 Tomahawk missiles plus up to 66 Spe-cial Operations Forces. Like the SSBN, it has a length of 560 feet and a beam of 42 feet. Its speed is 20+ knots, and its crew consists of 15 officers and 140 enlisted personnel. In addition to land attack via Tomahawk missiles and the insertion of Special Operations Forces, the submarines can also perform ISR, battlespace preparation, and sea control.

Special Forces can be deployed while the submarine is submerged by using SDVs or ASDS mini-submarines. These mini-subs can travel over 125 nautical miles to reach land and make the SSGN a highly effective platform for covert operations. Special Operations Forces can be supported for up to 90 days on the SSGN, compared with 15 days on a fast attack submarine (SSN).

Background

The four submarines being converted to SSGN (Figure 4–7) from the SSBN fleet include the USS *Ohio*, USS *Michigan*, USS *Florida*, and USS *Georgia*. The USS *Ohio* entered the conversion yard in Novem-ber 2002. Conversions are scheduled to continue to be initiated in the 2003 and 2004 timeframe and to be complete by 2008.

Figure 4–7   Guided-missile submarine (SSGN). (*Source:* U.S. Navy)

The four submarines are expected to be deployed two per coast so that they can balance the support provided to EUCOM, CENTCOM, and PACOM. Additionally, every other crew turnover will be performed at a forward-deployed location, which may include Guam, La Maddalena, Italy, or Diego Garcia, according to the U.S. Navy.

Facts

Builders: General Dynamics Electric Boat
Powerplant: 1 nuclear reactor, 1 shaft
Length: 560 feet (170.69 meters)
Beam: 42 feet (12.8 meters)
Displacement: 16,764 tons (17,033.03 metric tons) surfaced; 18,750 tons (19,000.1 metric tons) submerged
Speed: 20+ knots (23+ mph, 36.8+ kph)
Ships:
>> USS *Ohio* (SSBN 726)—out of service October 29, 2002 for conversion to SSGN
>> USS *Michigan* (SSBN 727)—conversion to SSGN scheduled for October 2003
>> USS *Florida* (SSBN 728)—conversion to SSGN scheduled for October 2003

>> USS *Georgia* (SSBN 729)—conversion to SSGN scheduled for 2004

Crew: 15 officers, 140 enlisted

Armament: Up to 154 Tomahawk missiles each (140 on SOF-config-ured SSGNs)

Source: U.S. Navy

Sea Shadow (IX 529)

The *Sea Shadow* is a test craft that was originally developed by the Defense Advanced Research Projects Agency (DARPA), the U.S. Navy, and Lockheed Martin. The program was begun in the mid-1980s to research various technologies that could be applied to future surface ships. These technologies and techniques included automated ship control, advanced structures, reduced manning, sea-keeping, and signature control (stealth). After being in lay-up status since 1994, the *Sea Shadow* was reactivated for technology testing of future surface ships on March 18, 1999 and is in active service today.

Features

The *Sea Shadow* has a highly unique and immediately recognizable shape with its dual hull design and characteristic stealth contours reminiscent of the F-117A fighter. Spy fans may remember the James Bond movie, *Tomorrow Never Dies*, which featured a similar-looking craft. In this case, truth is indeed stranger than fiction.

The *Sea Shadow* is powered by a diesel electric power plant with two propellers and has a steel hull and steel superstructure, and an overall length of 164 feet. Stealth technologies are important for sur-face craft due to the threat of anti-surface ship weapons. Stealth tech-niques can help to minimize the overall signature of the ship and enhance survivability by making it harder for these weapons to acquire and home in on their targets. Because a surface ship's signa-ture can include not just radar reflection but also infrared profile, electronic and acoustic emissions, wake, magnetic field, and optical signature, the *Sea Shadow* was designed to investigate the limits of controlling these numerous signatures. For example, the twin hull design, called a SWATH hull design, helps to minimize wake in addition to providing greater stability in difficult, rough sea states.

The *Sea Shadow* requires a crew of just 10 or less (some accounts report a crew of just 8) and can travel at a speed of 10 knots. As an advanced technology demonstrator, the *Sea Shadow* is used to host a variety of projects that require integration into shipboard systems, including high-performance distributed computing, artificial intelligence for combat systems, ship control, and advanced communication.

Background

The *Sea Shadow* (Figure 4–8) began life in the mid-1980s in secrecy as an unacknowledged program. It was assembled inside the Hughes Mining Barge (HMB-1) in Redwood City, California. The HMB-1 is a fully enclosed, submersible dock. The craft was not revealed to the public until the 1993–1994 time frame, when it underwent daylight testing. It was inactivated in 1994 and kept in lay-up status until March 18, 1999, when the Navy Wire Service announced its reacti-

Figure 4–8 *Sea Shadow. (Source:* U.S. Navy)

vation for technology testing of future surface ships, such as the DD-21 (now the DD(X)). It is currently homeported at Naval Station San Diego. *Sea Shadow* has influenced several ship designs, including the Navy's Arleigh Burke-class destroyers and the T-AGOS-class ships.

Facts

Type: Stealth ship
Contractor: Lockheed Martin Missiles & Space
Powerplant: Diesel electric
Length: 164 feet (49.99 meters)
Beam: 68 feet (20.73 meters)
Draft: 14.5 feet (4.42 meters)
Displacement: 560 tons (568.99 metric tons) full load
Hull Material: Steel hull, steel superstructure
Number of Propellers: 2
Crew: 10
Delivery Date: March 1, 1985

Source: U.S. Navy, Naval Vessel Register

II

Tomorrow's Battlefield

"Thus it is that in war the victorious strategist only seeks battle after the victory has been won, whereas he who is destined to defeat first fights and afterwards looks for victory."

–Sun Tzu, *The Art of War*

O ver the last several decades, we have witnessed the transformation of the military from its legacy capability of heavy armor and deterrent against a known Cold War threat toward a new capability that combines both strength and agility. This new capability combines the heavy armor of traditional military aircraft, helicopters, ships, submarines, aircraft carriers, tanks, munitions, and forces together with the addition of lighter, faster equipment, improved stealth technologies, computer-networked command and control, improved situational awareness, greater use of autonomous vehicles and precision-guided munitions, increased standoff capability, ability to fight in the littorals, and various other force multipliers. The end result is a military that is more strategically responsive, deployable, agile, versatile, lethal, survivable, and sustainable to meet the current and future demands of both traditional and asymmetric warfare.

This combination of strength and agility is the new formula for today's battlefield and for the battlefield of tomorrow. Today we face ever-increasing asymmetric threats from adversaries who aim for our vulnerabilities. In a way, the new threat is not that much different than the old threat. Asymmetric techniques were used by the Germans during the Blitzkrieg, and the element of surprise was used at Pearl Harbor with well-known consequence. Today's asymmetries, however, operate across a wider array of dimensions, including time, place, target, and technique. The asymmetry is no longer just technology or a novel technique against a known target. The new threat is less predictable, less well known, and can take many forms, including the escalating threat of terrorism. It can strike at any time and any place, directed against almost any conceivable target at home or abroad—whether political, economic, civilian, or military—using a spectrum of methods of varying degrees of sophistication.

While transforming itself for both traditional and asymmetric warfare, military doctrine aims to reduce casualties on both sides. Instead of the historical use of general-purpose munitions, cluster bombs, and even atomic weapons, which as an understatement can devastate vast areas and inflict heavy loss of life, the philosophy of modern warfare is to engage the enemy from a distance, to use autonomous vehicles for surveillance and reconnaissance, and to use precision-guided munitions for precise strikes. The approach is to apply just the right amount of force in the right place at the right time in order to achieve the mission objectives. Although the human element is still very much in control and a necessary presence on the ground, the automation and networking of military equipment means that initial reconnaissance and surveillance—and even entire battles—can be fought with increased standoff distances. By the time ground forces advance to within harm's way, the battle is often already won. As we have unfortunately experienced in Iraq, modern peacekeeping and rebuilding efforts can often be more hazardous than modern warfare.

As we look into the future, these trends of automation and networking are becoming ever more apparent. We'll see increased autonomy, increased digitization, and increased reliance on technology. The armed services are transitioning themselves to embrace the system-of-systems concept as embodied in programs such as the U.S. Army's Future Combat Systems (FCS) initiative. This program is now in its $15 billion system development and demonstration (SDD) phase and aims to replace traditional "heavy" ground platforms, such as the Abrams tank and the Bradley Fighting Vehicle, with a new breed of

18 manned and unmanned ground and aerial vehicles and sensors. These components of the FCS program will be networked together in a system of systems that can support the warfighter by providing the ability "to see first, understand first, act first, and finish decisively as the means to tactical success." It will also bring the Army closer to its vision of the Objective Force by the end of this decade.

To explore where these trends are taking the modern battlefield, we need to look across a number of areas. We need to look across the spectrum of science and technology organizations within the military itself to the myriads of defense contractors and services companies, and even out to the academic world and sciences, such as biology, chemistry, geophysics, information technology, materials science, mathematics, nanotechnology, oceanography, physics, and telecommunications.

In addition to looking within the armed services themselves, one of the most important places to look for these trends and for current innovation is within the "technological engine" for transforming the Department of Defense—the Defense Advanced Research Projects Agency (DARPA). Interestingly, if you consider the airplane, tank, radar, jet engine, helicopter, electronic computer, stealth technologies, and even the Internet, it is surprising that none of these technologies, which have transformed warfare in both the 20th and 21st centuries, owed their initial development to a doctrinal requirement or request of the military.[*] In fact, these capabilities were all accelerated into military service by DARPA.

This is exactly DARPA's goal: to accelerate the adoption of emerging technologies from fundamental research and discovery into technologies and systems that are ready for internal exploitation by the services. Figure P2–1 shows the timeline and investment focus for DARPA, taken from its fiscal year 2003 strategic plan.

DARPA's role is to find people and ideas on the so-called far side and to accelerate those ideas to the near side as quickly as possible. Once these technologies approach the near side, it will have been proven sufficiently that they can be adopted by the armed services. DARPA's mission is as follows:

---

[*] John Chambers, ed., *The Oxford Companion to American Military History* (New York: Oxford University Press, 1999), p. 791.

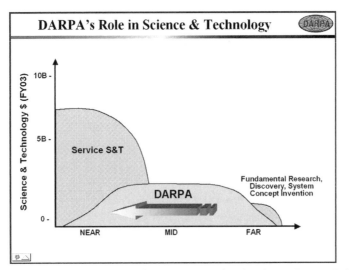

Figure P2–1   DARPA's role in science and technology. (*Source:* DARPA)

DARPA's mission is to maintain the technological superiority of the U.S. military and prevent technological surprise from harming our national security by sponsoring revolutionary, high-payoff research that bridges the gap between fundamental discoveries and their military use.

The comment about technological surprise in DARPA's mission statement is significant. Any technological surprise has the potential to put the recipient of that surprise at high risk. It alters the playing field and can create asymmetry in terms of which player has superiority over the adversary. An incumbent such as the United States could be quickly put on the defensive. When Sputnik was launched in 1957, the United States was essentially taken by surprise. DARPA was founded in the following year with the intent that such technological surprise would never happen again.

Many of the technologies that we have covered in Part I were accelerated into service by DARPA. This includes the Ground Surveillance Radar, Stealth Fighter, Joint STARS, *Sea Shadow,* Global Positioning System, Predator, and Global Hawk, as shown in Figure P2–2.

Some of the newer technologies that DARPA is focused on include its current eight strategic thrusts: counter-terrorism; assured use of space; networked manned and unmanned systems; robust self-forming networks; detection, identification, tracking, and destruction of elusive surface targets; characterization of underground structures; biorevolution; and cognitive computing. Additionally, DARPA maintains what it calls "enduring foundations of research" in areas such as materials, microsystems, and information technology.

In Part II, we'll explore examples of several of these DARPA research areas, together with other technologies and systems under investigation and initial development by the armed services. As in Part I, the chapters will be divided into those related to air warfare, ground warfare, munitions, and naval warfare. However, the transformation of the battlefield is making these distinctions in terms of the services or the type of warfare increasingly less significant. For example, autonomous vehicles are being applied across all lines of service and are emerging as unmanned aerial vehicles (UAVs), unmanned ground vehicles (UGVs), and unmanned underwater vehicles (UUVs). Network-centric warfare is linking all these technologies and making them usable across the services as part of the integrated battlefield comprised of a networked "system of systems."

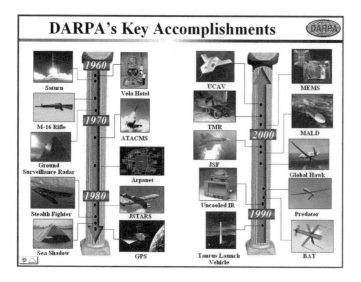

Figure P2–2   A summary of key DARPA accomplishments spanning more than four decades. (*Source:* DARPA)

As another example, the Joint Strike Fighter is being developed using a single airframe to support the U.S. Air Force, Navy, and Marine Corps, together with the British Royal Navy. Clearly, modern warfare is practiced with close cooperation across the U.S. armed services and often with strong allied involvement, both on the drawing board and on the battlefield.

In light of this, chapters covering ground warfare, such as Chapter 6, include coverage of information technologies that have relevance to all services. As the mass of data captured by the military from intelligence reports, warfighters, sensors, and other sources is converted into meaningful and actionable information, it can be rapidly disseminated across any service that has a need for the information. An example is the Terrorism Information Awareness (TIA) program that combines data from multiple sources and applies a variety of data mining and analysis techniques to track and predict terrorist behavior more accurately before it occurs. Additionally, input sources of data may come from a variety of services and be combined for real-time missions, such as integrated surveillance and precision strike against elusive, moving targets. An example is the Affordable Moving Surface Target Engagement (AMSTE) program that is covered in Chapter 7 on munitions.

The battlefield of tomorrow clearly leverages both manned and unmanned systems tied together using the latest information technologies to create a more agile, lethal, survivable, and affordable force. This section of the book aims to illustrate some of these programs that are helping transform the military through advanced technology.

5

Air Warfare

T he Air Force vision for the 21st century is called *global engagement*. The vision is grounded in the Joint Vision 2010 and Joint Vision 2020 of the Chairman of the Joint Chiefs of Staff and aims to "provide America with the air and space capabilities required to deter, fight, and win."

In its document, "Global Engagement: A Vision for the 21st Century Air Force," the U.S. Air Force noted that the service was transitioning from "an *air* force into an *air and space* force on an evolutionary path to a *space and air* force." With many military functions—such as intelligence, surveillance, and reconnaissance—migrating to space, it is increasingly important for the Air Force to ensure continued unrestricted access to space in addition to dominance in the air. Therefore, the focus of the Air Force is on air and space superiority as a core competency, in addition to rapid global mobility, precision engagement, global attack, information superiority, and agile combat support.

This chapter looks at some of the many programs within the U.S. Air Force that are designed to realize this vision by increasing our capabilities in both air and space. Manned aircraft such as the F-35 Joint Strike Fighter (JSF) and the F-22 Raptor are increasing the capabilities of modern aircraft in areas such as stealth and speed, as well as advanced lethality, survivability, and supportability. As capabilities such as stealth and speed are being pushed to the limits, the Air Force is also ensuring that these new aircraft are highly affordable and well leveraged across the services. The JSF is a prime example, with the same basic airframe being used to develop three variants of the aircraft for the U.S. Air Force, U.S. Navy, U.S. Marine Corps, and British Royal Navy. The F-22 Raptor, the world's most capable, technologically advanced air dominance fighter, brings unique combinations of stealth, supercruise speed (lengthy cruise durations at supersonic speed), and advanced integrated avionics to the future battlefield. Another first is the RAH-66 Comanche, the world's first stealth helicopter, which has projected missions of light attack, air combat, and special operations. To illustrate just how far the envelope is being pushed in terms of advanced stealth, this helicopter will have a radar cross-section from the front less than 360 times that of the Apache. In addition, its heat signature is so low that heat-seeking missiles are unable to lock onto it, due to its highly efficient mixing of exhaust gases with cooler air prior to emission.

While the innovations within manned fighters and helicopters are bringing world-class capabilities to the U.S. Air Force in terms of stealth, agility, and survivability, some of the other action is happening on the unmanned side of the fence. Upcoming unmanned aerial vehicles (UAVs) include an impressive array ranging from the unmanned combat air vehicle (UCAV) to the tiny Wasp and Hornet micro-air vehicles (MAVs) in development at the Defense Advanced Research Projects Agency (DARPA). In between these two extremes are a variety of UAVs with an equally broad variety of missions. The Organic Air Vehicle (OAV) has a mission of short-range airborne reconnaissance and surveillance for the individual soldier and small units. As part of the U.S. Army's Future Combat System (FCS), it will provide the capability for the warfighter to increase his or her situational awareness by looking "around the corner" and "over the hill." The Wasp and Hornet MAVs provide backpackable capabilities for the warfighter for reconnaissance and surveillance in difficult-to-access or hostile areas, such as underground caves, heavily forested areas, confined areas, and even inside buildings. Beyond the basic research into flight at such small scales, these DARPA programs around MAVs are exploring how various materials can be leveraged to provide multiple functions, such as wing structure and battery power all from a single material.

One of the most futuristic programs in the lineup is the X-43 experimental hypersonic flight research program being conducted by the NASA Dryden Flight Research Center, Edwards, California, and the NASA Langley Research Center, Hampton, Virginia. It is a multi-year NASA and industry program that aims to demonstrate hypersonic flight using air-breathing engines instead of rocket engines. The benefit of hypersonic flight with these air-breathing engines is that it allows increased payload capacity over conventional rocket engines and the potential for improved affordability and safety. Instead of carrying rocket fuel, these hypersonic vehicles, traveling at over five times the speed of sound, can use the outside air and pass it through a scramjet engine to provide their thrust. Although initial tests have had some setbacks, these programs are truly at the forefront of aviation and typify the high-risk, high-reward payoffs that organizations such as NASA and DARPA are pursuing on a daily basis.

F-35 Joint Strike Fighter

The JSF is a next-generation, multi-role strike fighter aircraft that is designed to affordably support the needs of the U.S. Air Force, Marine Corps, Navy, and allies with advanced lethality, survivability, and supportability. It is anticipated to move into service in 2008 in order to bring enhanced fighter capabilities to the U.S. and allied forces and to replace their aging inventories of aircraft such as the U.S. Air Force F-16 and A-10, the U.S. Navy F/A-18A/C/D, the U.S. Marine Corps AV-8B, and the British Royal Air Force Harrier and Royal Navy Sea Harrier. The JSF program aims to achieve a 70–90 percent commonality of costs across three variants of the aircraft for each of the services in order to greatly reduce initial production costs and ongoing support, training, and maintenance costs. The JSF program is an international cooperative program currently in the system development and demonstration (SDD) phase, worth $18.9 billion and led by Lockheed Martin teamed with Northrop Grumman and BAE SYSTEMS.

Features

The main concept behind the JSF is to leverage a common design and the same basic airframe to support the unique needs of each of the individual services. In this way, the U.S. military and its allied partners, including the United Kingdom, aim to affordably meet the requirements for the advanced tactical fighter aircraft of tomorrow.

The three main variants of the JSF required by the services include a conventional takeoff and landing (CTOL) variant for the U.S. Air Force, a short takeoff and vertical landing (STOVL) variant for the U.S. Marine Corps, and a carrier variant (CV) for the U.S. Navy. These three variants have been designated X-35A, B, and C, respectively. The U.S. Air Force variant is the simplest in design of the three and will be produced in the greatest numbers. The U.S. Marine Corps variant requires the Harrier-like ability for STOVL. This is accomplished in the JSF via a shaft-driven, lift-fan system attached to a Pratt & Whitney engine. The U.S. Navy variant requires strengthening for catapult launches and arrested landings on board modern carriers. It also features larger wing and tail control surfaces for low-speed approaches needed for carrier landings.

In terms of its mission, the JSF is a supersonic, stealth aircraft that can be used in air-to-ground roles with 24-hour, adverse weather, precision engagement of heavily defended enemy targets. In this role, it can complement the mission of the F-22 and fighters such as the F/A-18E/F. Weapons capability includes an internal laser designator, internal gun or missionized external gun, and support for a variety of munitions, including Joint Direct Attack Munitions (JDAMs), laser-guided bombs (LGBs), and air-to-air missiles, such as the Advanced Short-Range Air-to-Air Missile (ASRAAM) and Advanced Medium-Range Air-to-Air Missile (AMRAAM).

For propulsion, the JSF uses a Pratt & Whitney engine that will compete in production with an interchangeable engine manufactured by General Electric and Rolls Royce. All three variants of the JSF will be able to use either engine interchangeably in terms of functionality and physical specification in order to reduce risks.

The JSF features many military and technical firsts, including the Navy's first stealth fighter, the first time a shaft-driven lift-fan has been used for STOVL, and a new technology for reducing airflow into the engine to subsonic speeds during supersonic flight. Traditionally, this airflow reduction has required movable parts, such as the moving baffles within the engines on the Concorde, but on the JSF this is achieved with no moving parts.

Background

The Concept Demonstration Phase (CDP) of the JSF project (Figure 5–1) was started in November 1996, with Lockheed Martin and Boeing selected to design and build initial concept aircraft. This phase lasted 51 months at a cost of $2.2 billion, with the goal of demonstrating aircraft commonality and modularity, STOVL, hover and transition, and low-speed carrier approach-handling qualities.

In October 2001, the Defense Department announced the selection of Lockheed Martin as the winner of the next phase of the project. This was the SDD phase, which was formerly known as the Engineering and Manufacturing Development (EMD) phase. The SDD phase comprised an $18.9 billion award for the team of Lockheed Martin, Northrop Grumman, and BAE SYSTEMS, plus a $4 billion award to Pratt & Whitney Military Engines for the production of the F135 propulsion system.

A total of 3,002 aircraft are scheduled to be produced for the United States and United Kingdom, including 2,000 for the U.S. Air Force, 642 for the U.S. Marine Corps, 300 for the U.S. Navy, and 60 for the British Royal Navy.

Facts

Type: Next-generation, multi-role strike fighter aircraft
Contractor: Lockheed Martin teamed with Northrop Grumman and BAE SYSTEMS
Length: 45 feet
Wingspan: 30–36 feet
Height: N/A
Weight: 22,500–24,000 pounds (empty)

Figure 5–1   Joint Strike Fighter. (*Source*: Lockheed Martin)

Maximum Takeoff Weight: Approximately 50,000 pounds
Ceiling: N/A
Engine: Pratt & Whitney (baseline), General Electric/Rolls Royce
(alternate)
Speed: Supersonic
Combat Radius: Over 600 nautical miles
Armament: JDAMs, PGMs, AMRAAM, ASRAAM
Crew: 1
Planned Inventory: 3,002 (2000 USAF, 642 USMC, 300 USN,
60 UK RN)
First Flight: 1999
Delivery: 2008
Unit Cost: $28–$38 million (FY 2004 dollars)

Source: FAS and others

F-22 Raptor

The F-22 Raptor is a fast, agile, and stealthy air superiority fighter
being developed by the U.S. Air Force that provides first-look, first-

shot, first-kill capability for the modern battlefield. The Raptor is being developed by a team that includes Boeing, Lockheed Martin, and Pratt & Whitney, and is scheduled for introduction within the Air Combat Command starting in 2005. Due to its combination of stealth, supercruise speed, and advanced integrated avionics, it is being hailed as one of the world's most capable, technologically advanced combat aircraft.

Features

The purpose of the F-22 program is to create an air dominance fighter that can be used for the next three decades to guarantee freedom of mobility for ground, air, and naval forces. The combination of stealth, supersonic speed, and information exploitation enables it to have considerable overmatch capability against other aircraft and to rapidly evade enemy air defenses. The balanced design of the aircraft also includes practical and economic aspects, such as reliability, maintainability, supportability, and affordability, into the overall requirements. As an example, the aircraft's engine is designed to support supercruise speed without requiring the use of afterburners, which consume heavy amounts of fuel. A first among production aircraft, the engine therefore achieves the performance requirements of supercruise with the advantages of a low-fuel-consumption engine without afterburners. The Raptor uses two Pratt & Whitney F119-PW-100 engines that are rated in the 35,000-pound thrust category. The stealth properties on the F-22 are also easier to maintain than earlier aircraft coatings and give the F-22 the radar signature of a small bird or even a bee.

The avionics onboard the F-22 include a common integrated processor (CIP) that has the equivalent computing throughput of two Cray supercomputers, expert systems, advanced data fusion cockpit displays, integrated electronic warfare system (INEWS) technology, integrated communications, navigation and identification (CNI) avionics technology, and fiberoptic data transmission.

In terms of armament, the F-22 can be outfitted in a couple of different configurations, depending on its use in an air-to-air or air-to-ground role. In the air-to-air role, it can carry six AIM-120C AMRAAMs and two AIM-9 Sidewinder missiles. In the air-to-ground role, it carries two 1,000-pound JDAMs, two AIM-120Cs, and two

Figure 5–2 F-22 Raptor. (*Source*: Boeing)

AIM-9s. The aircraft has three internal bays on its underside that can be used for weapons storage to provide an improved combat configuration with reduced radar signature.

Background

The F-22 (Figure 5–2) is slated to replace the aging U.S. fleet of F-15 Eagle fighters and was originally conceived as a counter to the agile Soviet aircraft in the 1980s. In 1985, the Air Force requested proposals for what was then named the Advanced Tactical Fighter (ATF) program. The prototype F-22, the YF-22, flew for the first time on September 29, 1990. At the end of the 54-month demonstration and validation phase in April 1991, the Air Force announced the winning team of Boeing, Lockheed Martin, and General Dynamics. In August 1991, the Lockheed Martin and Boeing team was awarded a $9.55 billion contract for EMD of the F-22.

The first flight of the F-22 aircraft occurred on September 7, 1997. The Air Force plans to procure 339 F-22s, and production is scheduled to run through 2013.

Facts

Type: Fighter, air-dominance
Contractor: Boeing and Lockheed Martin
Major Subcontractors (partial list): Northrop Grumman, Texas Instruments, Kidde-Graviner, Allied-Signal Aerospace, Hughes Radar Systems, Harris, Fairchild Defense, GEC Avionics, Lockheed Sanders, Kaiser Electronics, Digital Equipment, Rosemount Aerospace, Curtiss-Wright Flight Systems, Dowty Decoto, EDO, Lear Astronics, Parker-Hannifin, Simmonds Precision, Sterer Engineering, TRW, XAR, Motorola, Hamilton Standard, Sanders/GE Joint Venture, Menasco Aerospace
Wingspan: 44 feet, 6 inches
Length: 62 feet, 1 inch
Height: 16 feet, 5 inches
Powerplant: 2 Pratt & Whitney F119-PW-100 engines capable of supercruise and thrust vectoring
Speed: Mach 1.8 (supercruise: Mach 1.5)
Ceiling and Weight: Classified
Armament: 2 AIM-9 Sidewinders; 6 AIM-120C AMRAAMs; 20-mm Gatling gun; 2 1,000-pound JDAMs
Crew: 1
Personnel (approximate): USAF Program Office, 350; Lockheed Martin Aeronautical Systems, 1,000; Boeing, 1,500; Lockheed Martin Tactical Aircraft Systems, 1,200; Pratt & Whitney, 1,700.
First Flight: September 7, 1997
Flight Test Aircraft: 9
Initial Operational Capability: Late 2005
Planned Production: 339

Source: U.S. Air Force, Lockheed Martin

RAH-66 Comanche

The RAH-66 Comanche is the U.S. Army's next-generation armed reconnaissance helicopter. The helicopter's primary role will be to perform armed reconnaissance in support of AH-64 Apache attack helicopters. It will also have projected missions of light attack, air combat, and special operations. Designed for the digital battlefield, the Comanche is the centerpiece of the Army's aviation modernization plan, bringing unique capabilities in stealth and flexibility. First deliveries of the aircraft are expected in 2006.

Features

The Comanche is the world's most advanced rotorcraft with a number of advanced technology features that will enable it to support the Army's transition to an Objective Force that is responsive, deployable, agile, versatile, lethal, survivable, and sustainable. The advanced features on the Comanche include a low-observable airframe, high speed and aerobatic maneuverability, a sophisticated mission equipment package, and a design for easy field maintenance and repair.

The Comanche is a twin-turbine, two-seat helicopter with highly advanced stealth properties. Its radar cross-section from the front is 360 times smaller than the AH-64 Apache and 250 times less than the OH-58D Kiowa Warrior helicopter. The Comanche achieves this effect via a highly angular design plus internal weapons carriage and fully retractable landing gear. In addition to radar, the Comanche also has low observability of acoustic and infrared emissions that give it a two- to six-times lower sound signature, both to humans and to acoustic sensors, and a two- to four-times lower infrared signature than other helicopters. The five-bladed rotor design, which helps with noise suppression, allows the helicopter to approach 40 percent closer to its targets than the Apache without being detected acoustically. The low-infrared signature is achieved by mixing the exhaust gases from the engine with cool air prior to discarding the mixture from slots in the Comanche's tail. This low heat signature is reportedly so low that a heat-seeking missile is unable to find and lock onto the aircraft.

The Comanche's mission equipment package includes a digital avionics suite, an integrated helmet-mounted heads-up display, a night vision pilotage system and electro-optical target acquisition and detection system, high-resolution sensors, self-healing digital mission electronics, and triply redundant onboard system diagnostics. Survivability is enhanced through the use of onboard countermeasures; a ballistically tolerant composite airframe, flight controls, fuel system and rotors; and the ability to operate in nuclear, biological, and chemical (NBC) contaminated environments.

For weaponry, the Comanche uses a three-barrel turreted 20-mm gun with 500 rounds, internal and external missile stations, advanced technology-aided target detection and classification, and compatibility with most U.S. and NATO missiles and rockets. It can be rearmed and refueled in under 15 minutes and can self-deploy to Europe, Africa, Asia, the Caribbean, and Central and South America, meaning that it can be rapidly put into service without the wait of loading and unloading via Air Force transport aircraft. When transport via cargo aircraft is required, the Comanche is designed for rapid loading and unloading, and requires fewer personnel and support equipment than other helicopters.

Background

The first flight of the Boeing-Sikorsky RAH-66 Comanche (Figure 5–3) prototype was made on January 4, 1996. The program entered its $3.1 billion EMD phase in mid-2000. The final flight of the first prototype occurred in January 2002, and during that time the aircraft logged more than 380 flight hours and 300 flight missions mostly aimed at evaluating its flight control software and handling qualities.

For fiscal year 2004, the Comanche program represented the second highest program in the Army's top 10 research, development, and acquisition programs. It came in second after the FCS program with an investment of $1,079 million, compared with the FCS investment of $1,815 million. It is anticipated that the Comanche program will reach full production in about 2010 and that 1,213 Comanche helicopters will be built for service in the U.S. Army.

Facts

Type: Armed reconnaissance helicopter
Contractor: Boeing Helicopter and Sikorsky Aircraft
Length: 46.78 feet
Width: 39.04 feet
Weight: 9,300 pounds (empty); 12,339 pounds (primary mission)
Powerplant: 2 T800-LHTEC-801 turboshaft engines
Dash Speed: 175 knots

Figure 5–3   RAH-66 Comanche. (*Source*: Boeing)

Cruise Speed: 160 knots

Vertical Rate of Climb: 895 feet per minute

Maximum Range: 1,200 nautical miles

Armament: Air-to-air Stinger, Hellfire, 20-mm 3-barrel turreted gun, Hydra-70 rockets

Crew: 2

First Flight: January 4, 1996

Source: Boeing, FAS

V-22 Osprey

The V-22 Osprey is a tiltrotor VSTOL multi-mission aircraft designed to meet the requirements of the U.S. Marine Corps, U.S. Navy, and U.S. Special Operations Forces. It is designed to support Marine Corps requirements for transporting assault troops and cargo, and U.S. Navy requirements for combat search and rescue, plus fleet logistics support and special warfare support.

Features

The main feature of the V-22 Osprey is that it is capable of taking off vertically like a helicopter, then rotating its engine nacelles to fly like a conventional turboprop aircraft. This duel functionality gives the Osprey the ability to fly faster and at higher altitudes than conventional helicopters. Its maximum speed of 275 knots is about twice the speed of other helicopters.

The aircraft can carry up to 24 combat troops or 20,000 pounds of cargo and uses two large proprotors with a diameter of 38 feet each and three blades per rotor. The two proprotors are connected to one another via a single interconnect shaft so that both can be powered by a single engine in the event of engine failure in either one of the two engines.

The airframe of the V-22 is made up of a graphite-reinforced epoxy composite material that provides good strength-to-weight ratio, compared with metal construction. An electronic warfare package includes radar warning, missile warning, and countermeasures support.

Background

The Osprey (Figure 5–4) was designed to replace the Marine Corps CH-46E and CH-53D helicopters and the Air Force MH-53J and MH-60G. It will also augment the MC-130 for Special Operations missions. The first prototype flew on March 19, 1989. Due to several accidents involving loss of life, as well as cost concerns, the V-22 Osprey program has been proceeding at a very careful pace. During its history, it has been cancelled by the Bush administration in 1989, restarted by the Clinton administration, and grounded temporarily until safety concerns could be resolved.

It returned to flight on May 29, 2002, and is now involved in continued flight testing, which is expected to last for a couple of years. The current focus is on high rates of descent, low-speed maneuvering, and shipboard landings. The current plan calls for production of 11 Ospreys per year until a second operational evaluation, due to be conducted in 2005. Production may then increase up to 39 aircraft per year by 2009. Another goal of the program office is to reduce the flyaway cost of the Osprey by 21 percent by the year 2010.

Facts

Type: Tiltrotor VSTOL multi-mission aircraft
Contractor: Boeing, Bell Helicopter Textron, Allison Engine
Length: 57.33 feet
Width: 83.33 feet
Height: 21.76 feet (nacelles fully vertical)
Blade Diameter: 38.00 feet
Blade Construction: Graphite/Fiberglass
Blades per Hub: 3
Weight: 33,140 pounds (empty)
Powerplant: 2 Allison T406-AD-400 engines
Maximum Speed: 275 knots
Vertical Rate of Climb: 1,090 feet per minute
Maximum Rate of Climb: 2,320 feet per minute
Range: 515 nautical miles (amphibious assault), 2,100 nautical miles (self-deployment)
Service Ceiling: 26,000 feet
Crew: Cockpit 2, cabin 24
First Flight: March 19, 1989

Source: Boeing, FAS

Figure 5–4   V-22 Osprey. (*Source*: Boeing)

X-45A Unmanned Combat Air Vehicle

The UCAV program is a joint program of DARPA, the U.S. Air Force, and Boeing. The aim of the program is to demonstrate the technical feasibility, military utility, and operational value of a UCAV system for suppression of enemy air defenses (SEAD) and strike missions.

Features

With the success of UAVs such as Predator and Global Hawk used primarily for intelligence, surveillance, and reconnaissance missions, the next evolutionary step is to consider UAVs for actual combat operations. For suppression of enemy air defenses, this can take human pilots out of harm's way. For strike missions, this can greatly reduce the time between target identification and engagement with precision munitions. In both cases, a UAV can also greatly reduce costs, compared with manned aircraft. In fact, DARPA estimates that UAVs will cost 65 percent less to produce than future manned fighters and 75 percent less to operate and maintain than current systems.

The UCAV program aims to demonstrate several concepts in a spiral development process so that changes can be accommodated to meet changing warfighter needs. The X-45A UCAV designed by Boeing was created to demonstrate the technical feasibility of the concept and included an aircraft, mission control system, and storage container as part of the overall system. The aircraft can conduct fully autonomous missions with preplanned objectives and targeting information or can be updated while in flight with new instructions from battle planners on the ground. The mission control system has satellite relay and direct line-of-sight communications capability with the aircraft, and one person can control up to four aircraft at a time. To meet the rapid response requirements to deal with conflicts around the world, the UCAV can be shipped via container and assembled within one hour. These storage containers can also store the aircraft for up to 10 years.

Boeing produced two X-45A demonstrators that successfully showcased their capabilities to support the program objectives for technical feasibility, including taxi testing, initial flight, multi-vehicle control capability by a single operator, and various hardware and software tests. The X-45B demonstrator is a larger and more capable version of the X-45A. The X-45C demonstrator adds capabilities to support the Air Force's needs for greater range and loiter capability, plus the Navy's needs for a UCAV-N demonstrator. The UCAV-N is the Navy's version of the UCAV with additional capabilities to support aircraft carrier operations, including precision landings. The X-45C also adds support for two 2,000-pound JDAMs.

Background

The UCAV program started in 1998 with the initial awards for Phase I. The award for production of the two X-45A demonstrator aircraft was made on April 12, 1999, to Boeing's "Phantom Works" advanced R&D unit. The first flight of the X-45A was made on May 22, 2002, at the NASA Dryden Flight Research Center at Edwards Air Force Base in California. The flight of the second of the two aircraft was made on November 21, 2002 (Figure 5–5).

The Block I series of demonstrations were completed on February 28, 2003, and included 16 flights and nearly 13 flight hours with the two Boeing aircraft. Demonstrations included wing attachment, autonomous taxi, concept of operations simulations, distributed control, loss of communication response, and four-dimensional navigation. Distributed control demonstrated the ability for control of the UCAV to be seamlessly passed between a mission control shelter and a mission control van and back again. The loss of communication response demonstration proved the ability of the UCAV to return to base and land safely upon loss of communications with the mission control system, as per its contingency plan. Finally, the four-dimensional navigation demonstrated the ability to coordinate time of arrival at a waypoint, as well as position, so that multiple UCAVs can make coordinated attacks.

In August 2002, a contract award of $460 million was made for the X-45B. This included a $60 million award for completing the X-45A effort. The award included two X-45B aircraft, with the first to be completed in the summer of 2004 and the second to be completed in early 2005.

In April 2003, DARPA kicked off a Joint UCAV (J-UCAV) program so that the UCAV program of the Air Force and the UCAV-N

Figure 5–5 The second Boeing X-45A Unmanned Combat Air Vehicle completes a successful first flight at NASA's Dryden Flight Research Center at Edwards Air Force Base in California on Thursday, November 21, 2002. (*Source*: Boeing)

program of the Navy could be combined to focus on a common set of service objectives. Both Northrop Grumman and Boeing have been selected as contractors for this program. Boeing is planning the first flight of the X-45C for 2006. Initial operational capability for the UCAV is anticipated by 2008.

Facts

Program: X-45A UCAV
Type: Suppression of enemy air defenses (SEAD) and strike missions
Contractor: Boeing
System: Aircraft, mission control system, storage container
Length: 27 feet
Wingspan: 34 feet
Weight: 8,000 pounds
Payload: Precision-strike munitions
Altitude: 35,000 feet
Speed: 0.75 Mach
First Flight: May 22, 2002

Unmanned Combat Armed Rotorcraft

The Unmanned Combat Armed Rotorcraft (UCAR) is a joint DARPA and U.S. Army program that aims to demonstrate the technical feasibility, military utility, and operational value for a UCAR system to perform armed reconnaissance and attack missions within the Army Objective Force system-of-systems architecture.

Features

The UCAR program is not as mature as the UCAV program but aims to provide for the U.S. Army many of the same benefits that the UCAV provides for the U.S. Air Force. Some of the key features include reducing the risk to manned platforms by operating ahead of them and allowing for autonomous collaboration with both manned and unmanned air and ground systems. The UCAR is designed to be operated from existing platforms, such as the Comanche helicopter, the Army Airborne Command and Control System, or ground-based command and control systems. Like the UCAV, the UCAR is capable of identifying and engaging ground targets using its own sensors and firepower. The UCAR is planned to carry both lethal and non-lethal weapons, including missiles, rockets, and guns. Its system concept includes the ability for dynamic retasking so that plan changes can be made while in flight; autonomous operation so that entire missions can be flown without the need for human intervention; and collaborative mission execution so that it can be operated in close collaboration with many other manned and unmanned systems as part of the Army's Objective Force system-of-systems architecture.

As part of its role within the Objective Force, the UCAR will be tasked with identifying and prosecuting targets that are employing camouflage, concealment, and deception (CC&D) to hide or evade allied forces. The UCAR flies at low altitudes and has a variety of multi-spectral sensors that can operate at day and night and during adverse weather conditions. Another goal is to have the UCAR operate at increased distances from its targets to improve survivability. In terms of affordability, the goal is 20–40 percent that of the Comanche cost.

Background

The UCAR program (Figure 5–6) is still in its early stages, and no demonstrators are yet flying. The phases of the UCAR program include a concept development Armed phase, preliminary design phase, system development and testing phase, and finally a system maturation and demonstration phase. These phases are scheduled to last from mid-2002 until the end of 2009.

During Phase I, between mid-2002 and mid-2003, four contractors were chosen for concept development and system trades. These contractors were Boeing, Lockheed Martin, Northrop Grumman, and Sikorsky Aircraft, with each receiving $3 million in funding.

Future phases for the UCAR program include the development of two demonstration systems (X-vehicles) during Phase III and a third demonstration system during Phase IV. The final phase ends with a transition to the U.S. Army at the end of 2009 and anticipated fielding of the UCAR in the 2010–2012 timeframe.

Figure 5–6   Unmanned Combat Armed Rotorcraft. (*Source*: Boeing)

Facts

Program: UCAR
Type: Armed reconnaissance and attack missions within the Army Objective Force system-of-systems architecture
Contractors: Boeing, Lockheed Martin, Northrop Grumman, Sikorsky Aircraft
Service: DARPA, Tactical Technology Office (TTO)/U.S. Army
Started: FY 2002

Organic Air Vehicle

The OAV is a joint DARPA and U.S. Army program that aims to develop a small VTOL UAV for short-range airborne reconnaissance and surveillance for the individual soldier and small units. The OAV is specifically intended for use at the "organic" level, which means down to the smallest operational unit. The program is a component of the U.S. Army's FCS initiative.

Features

The OAV consists of a ducted fan concept that gives it the ability for both VTOL and cruise flight. The device can weigh between 20 and 75 pounds, depending on mission and platform characteristics, with duct diameters ranging from 6 to 36 inches. The requirements call for an endurance of 15–25 minutes and a range of 1–2 kilometers. The OAV is powered by a diesel fuel engine and has a ceiling of 8,000 feet. For stealth reasons, the requirements also call for a low acoustic signature so that the vehicle is less easily heard by enemy forces, who would most likely attempt to shoot it down.

The size of the vehicle is designed so that it can be carried in a soldier's backpack and easily deployed to help soldiers increase their situational awareness of the battlefield. The vehicle can fly autonomously, requiring no piloting, and simply needs soldiers to instruct it where to fly and land via a remote computer control and display interface. By supporting a variety of payloads, the OAV can be used for a variety of missions, including imaging in confined urban areas, biological and chemical agent detection, tagging and targeting,

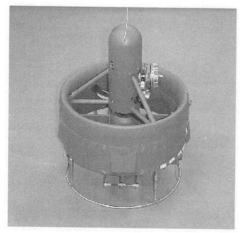

Figure 5–7 Organic Air Vehicle.
(*Source*: DARPA)

and battle damage assessment. As a relocatable sensor, it is able to help solders "look around corners" and "look over hills" without putting themselves in danger. The vehicle is designed to perform in all weather conditions and to require little operator intervention.

Background

In April 2001, DARPA awarded two $3 million agreements for the OAV program (Figure 5–7) to Micro Craft Inc. and Honeywell. Over the past several years, the program has determined requirements for OAVs to be used as sensor platforms, developed OAVs capable of operating in adverse weather, selected platforms and payloads for design and prototyping efforts, and continued prototyping development and testing.

Facts

Program: OAV.
Type: Small VTOL UAV for use by the individual soldier or small unit for surveillance and reconnaissance. Enables soldiers to enhance their situational awareness by having over-the-hill and around-the-corner surveillance
Contractors: Micro Craft Inc. and Honeywell
Service: DARPA, TTO/U.S. Army
Started: FY 2001

PLATFORM CHARACTERISTICS SET A
Soldier-Level Asset:

>> Soldier Transportable
>> Gross Weight: 20 pounds
>> Endurance: 15 minutes
>> Range: 1 kilometer
>> Payload: 1 pound
>> Ceiling: 8,000 feet MSL
>> Low Acoustic Signature: 75 dB at 20 feet
>> VTOL or STOL
>> Diesel Fuel Engine
>> Payload Type: EO/IR

Performance characteristics based on Army Standard Day (4,000 feet, 95 degrees F).
Performance values noted above are approximate.

PLATFORM CHARACTERISTICS SET B
Platoon-Level Asset:

>> Carrier Transportable (Hummer size)
>> Gross Weight: 75 pounds
>> Endurance: 25 minutes
>> Speed: Vmax > 40 kts
>> Range: 2 kilometer
>> Payload: 7 pounds
>> Ceiling: 8,000 feet MSL
>> Low Acoustic Signature: 75 dB at 100 feet
>> Day/Night Operations
>> VTOL
>> Diesel Fuel Engine
>> Tethered Options Will Be Considered
>> Primary Payload Type: EO/IR
>> Alternate Modular Payloads: Acoustic, mine detection, comm-relay, SIGINT

Performance characteristics based on Army Standard Day (4,000 feet, 95 degrees F).
Performance values noted above are approximate.

Source: Boeing

Hummingbird Warrior

The Hummingbird Warrior is a joint DARPA and U.S. Army program that aims to develop a VTOL UAV for airborne surveillance and targeting against ground targets. The program is a component of the U.S. Army's FCS initiative. It differs from the OAV in that it has greater endurance and range, flies at higher altitudes with a wider field of view, and performs a wider range of missions than the "perch-and-stare" sensor missions of the OAV.

Features

The Hummingbird Warrior is helicopter-shaped with a hingeless, three-blade rotor that can vary its speed for controlling VTOL and low-power loiter over a specific area of interest. The hingeless rotor concept has the potential to significantly increase the endurance of the UAV and its range, when compared with traditional designs. Endurance is targeted for 24–48 hours and range for over 2,000 nautical miles.

Under the Army's FCS program, the Hummingbird Warrior is called the A160. The A160 vehicle will be evaluated for a number of functions, including surveillance and targeting, serving as a communications and data link, deploying other unmanned sensors and vehicles, resupplying forces in the field, and lethal and non-lethal weapons delivery.

As a data link, the Hummingbird Warrior would provide airborne communications between ground sensors and vehicles, command nodes, and satellite communications. As a deployment platform, it may deploy ground sensors, unmanned ground vehicles, and MAVs.

Background

Some of the current plans for the Hummingbird Warrior A160 program (Figure 5–8) include studies into satellite communications, survivability, and resupply. Other tests include the evaluation of de-icing systems plus sand, dust, and salt protection systems, so that the Hummingbird can operate in harsh environments.

Figure 5–8   Hummingbird Warrior. (*Source*: Frontier Systems)

The flight portion of the program plans to evaluate the hingeless rotor concept. Continued ground and flight testing will help to provide information on the performance, reliability, and maintainability of this type of design.

Facts

Program: Hummingbird Warrior
Type: VTOL UAV for airborne surveillance and targeting against ground targets
Contractors: Frontier Systems
Service: DARPA, TTO/U.S. Army

Micro Air Vehicle

The MAV program is a DARPA program that aims to demonstrate a backpackable, affordable, easy-to-operate, and responsive reconnaissance and surveillance system. Like the OAV, this vehicle is designed to be used by small units and individual soldiers in order to obtain real-time battlefield information in a variety of environments. It differs from the OAV in that the DARPA MAV program and other related programs have historically focused on the technologies necessary for small-scale flight and on the concept of multifunctional materials that combine the function of structure, such as a small wing, with that of another system function, such as power, repair, or ballistic protection. Two of the best known MAV vehicles are the Wasp and Hornet, manufactured by AeroVironment, and it is these vehicles that will be the focus of discussion.

Features

Although the MAV is not a part of the FCS program, it is a critical technology that has already been demonstrated in flight and that can provide considerable benefits for the warfighter in the years to come. One of the main areas of application for the MAV is to provide reconnaissance and surveillance in difficult-to-access or hostile areas, such as underground caves, heavily forested areas, confined areas, and even inside buildings as a digital "fly on the wall."

An example of the current MAV aircraft is the Wasp. This aircraft has a wingspan of 13 inches and combines its battery pack along its wing structure to provide a multi-functional system that has a weight of only 6 ounces. A lithium-ion battery is used to provide power due to its high-energy density. This battery provides 143 watts per kilogram and has an average power output during flight of over 9 watts. The aircraft is propelled by a small propeller at the front and features movable rudder and elevator surfaces for flight control. It is controlled manually by an operator who can control throttle, rudder, and elevators, using a remote control device.

A successor to the Wasp is the Hornet. This aircraft, also manufactured by AeroVironment, uses a hydrogen fuel cell for power instead of the lithium-ion battery of the Wasp. The Hornet is of similar size to the Wasp, with a wingspan of 15 inches, and weighs 6 ounces. The fuel cell works by storing hydrogen in a dry pellet form and allowing it to react with oxygen collected from the airflow over the wing to produce electricity. The ground controller is able to vary the amount of hydrogen generated in the vehicle in addition to the usual flight controls.

Future enhancements for the Wasp and Hornet include the addition of an autopilot function to make flight control easier and a color video camera as a payload.

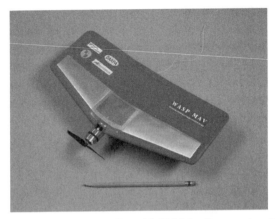

Figure 5–9   Wasp Micro Air Vehicle. (*Source*: AeroVironment)

Background

Although the original DARPA program for the MAV (Figure 5–9) focused on flight at small scales and on multi-functional materials, the latest DARPA program extends this, building on the lessons learned by conducting experiments and demonstrations in various military field trials. It will also explore the pros and cons of electric, diesel, and hybrid MAV designs.

On August 19, 2002, the Wasp achieved a world record for MAV endurance by flying for 1 hour and 47 minutes. This broke the previous record of 30 minutes set in 2000 by AeroVironment's Black Widow aircraft.

The Hornet set another record on March 21, 2003, when it completed the first fuel-cell-powered flight of a UAV. During the day, the Hornet was flown three times for a total endurance of 15 minutes.

Facts

Program: MAV Advanced Concept Technology
Type: Further develop and integrate MAV technologies into militarily useful and affordable backpackable systems suitable for dismounted soldier, Marine, and Special Forces missions
Contractors: AeroVironment

Service: DARPA, TTO
Started: FY 2004

Wasp

Contractor: AeroVironment
Endurance: 1 hour 47 minutes (August 19, 2002)
Control: Radio controlled
Wingspan: 13 inches
Total Weight: 6 ounces
Power: Lithium–ion battery
Average Power Output: 9 watts

Hornet

Contractor: AeroVironment/Lynntech (fuel cell)
Endurance: 15 minutes (3 flights on March 21, 2003)
Control: Radio controlled
Wingspan: 16 inches
Total Weight: 6 ounces
Power: Hydrogen fuel cell
Average Power Output: 10 watts

X-43A Hypersonic Flight

The X-43 is an experimental hypersonic flight research program being conducted by the NASA Dryden Flight Research Center, Edwards, California, and the NASA Langley Research Center, Hampton, Virginia. It is a multi-year NASA and industry program that aims to demonstrate hypersonic flight using air-breathing engines instead of rocket engines. The benefit of this flight technique is that it allows increased payload capacity over conventional rocket engines and the potential for improved affordability and safety.

Features

Hypersonic flight is the ability to travel at over five times the speed of sound, or Mach 5. At this speed, because the speed of sound is 761 mph, an aircraft travels at over 3,800 mph, or over a mile per second. Over the years, many aircraft have traveled at these high Mach speeds, including the X-15 and the Space Shuttle, so the speed itself is less significant than the method of propulsion. In this case, it is the scramjet engine.

The scramjet engine works by taking in air at hypersonic speeds, then burning it with onboard hydrogen fuel and allowing the exhaust gases to power the aircraft up to higher Mach numbers. The scramjet can work only at hypersonic speeds, so the X-43 uses a B-52 together with a Pegasus-derivative launch vehicle to get it to the required speed. The B-52 takes off and flies to an altitude of 20,000 feet, where it releases the launch vehicle with the X-43 attached. The launch vehicle then boosts the X-43 to an altitude of 100,000 feet and a speed of Mach 7 or 10. The X-43 is then able to separate from the launch vehicle and engage its hypersonic scramjet engine.

The ability to travel this fast and to do so without rocket power and its accompanying requirements for heavy rocket fuel has considerable applications for the military. It includes applications for missiles and weapons systems, reconnaissance and strike aircraft, and reusable space launch vehicles. In their missile form, these hypersonic weapons could strike against distant enemy targets and arrive quickly after initial detection of the target. Their speed would also allow them to be used in a kinetic manner, using the energy from their extreme velocity to penetrate hardened bunkers. As a reconnaissance and strike aircraft, hypersonic vehicles would mean that enemy air-defense systems would be unable to react in time. Finally, as a reusable space launch vehicle, the hypersonic "air-breathing" engine would provide safer, more affordable access into space.

Background

The first flight of the X-43A (Figure 5–10) occurred on April 18, 2001, when it was part of a successful captive-carry flight. On this flight, the X-43A aircraft remained attached to its Pegasus booster rocket mounted on a B-52 launch aircraft as a dress rehearsal for the free-flight mission to come. The free-flight mission took place on June 2, 2001. Unfortunately, the flight had to be aborted before the real test of the X-43A could begin. According to NASA, "about eight seconds after ignition of the rocket, a malfunction occurred that caused the booster and the attached X-43A to go out of control." The test director decided to terminate the flight, and a signal was sent to trig-

Figure 5–10   X-43. (*Source*: NASA, Photo by Lori Losey)

ger an explosion to destroy both the booster and the X-43A. No injuries or damage occurred, other than to the test vehicles, but it was a setback to the overall program.

Today, NASA has two more X-43A aircraft that it intends to test in the near future. Boeing, one of the industry partners on the program, is also researching designs that can transition aircraft propulsion from rocket-to-ramjet-to-scramjet-to-rocket. This rocket-based combined cycle propulsion system, as it is called, would help take reusable space vehicles up to Mach 12 or 15 by transitioning through the various propulsion techniques.

Facts

Program: X-43 (formerly Hyper-X)
Type: To provide "air-breathing" hypersonic engine technologies and hypersonic aircraft design tools
Platform: Requires B-52 and Pegasus-derivative launch vehicles
Contractors: Orbital Sciences (Pegasus-derived launch vehicles), MicroCraft (unpiloted research aircraft)
Service: NASA Dryden Flight Research Center/NASA Langley Research Center
Started: 1996
Inventory: 3 X-43A vehicles

X-43A

Length: Approximately 12 feet
Weight: Approximately 2,200 pounds
Performance: Mach 7–10
First Flight: April 18, 2001 (captive-carry); June 2, 2001 (terminated)

Source: NASA

6

Ground Warfare

T o begin our look at the future of ground warfare, one of the first areas to look is the U.S. Army's plan for transformation known as the *Objective Force*. The concept of the Objective Force is a "future full spectrum force: organized, manned, equipped, and trained to be more strategically responsive, deployable, agile, versatile, lethal, survivable and sustainable across the entire spectrum of military operations from Major Theater Wars through counter-terrorism to Homeland Security."

Key parts of this transformation to the Objective Force are the Future Combat Systems (FCS) and Objective Force Warrior (OFW) programs. FCS aims to design and develop a networked system of systems comprised of 18 manned and unmanned ground and aerial vehicles and sensors connected via an advanced communications network. For the warfighter, this will provide the ability to "to see first, understand first, act first, and finish decisively as the means to tactical success."

The transformation to the Objective Force is about soldiers, as well as their vehicles and sensors. The goal of the OFW program, which is operated by the U.S. Army Soldier Systems Center in Natick, Massachusetts, is to ensure that the soldier is as advanced in capability as these systems and can essentially plug in as another part of the Objective Force or another node on the network. More formally, the goal is to "provide the future soldier and small team with combat overmatch and skip-a-generation capabilities intended to improve soldier survivability, enable greater combat lethality, and provide networking communications between soldiers and other combat platforms, such as the Future Combat Systems and Comanche helicopter."

The Soldier Systems Center (Natick) is the Army's one-stop shop for soldier support. Their responsibilities include researching, developing, fielding, and managing food, clothing, shelters, airdrop systems, and soldier support items. Their goal is to provide America's soldiers with the best equipment in the world.

In addition to the OFW, the chapter also looks out to 2025 to see how the U.S. Army Soldier Systems Center is conceptualizing the future soldier in its Future Warrior concept. Beyond these two high-profile programs, the Soldier Systems Center is also carrying out innovative research and development in areas such as modular gloves for Special Operations Forces, improved lightweight helmets for Marines, electronic tracking of rations, and new camouflage patterns beyond the simple woodland and desert variety.

Along with these transformational programs for the U.S. Army, the Defense Advanced Research Projects Agency (DARPA) is running a number of information technology initiatives that will aid in countering the threat of terrorism and helping to prevent it before it can occur. Some of these programs include Terrorism Information Awareness (TIA), Human Identification at a Distance (HumanID), and Evidence Extraction and Link Discovery (EELD).

The TIA program is the much-talked-about program (formerly Total Information Awareness) that aims to develop a prototype system and network for the detection, classification, and identification of potential foreign terrorists so that the United States can take preemptive action before events of terrorism occur. The goal is essentially to create a counter-terrorism information technology system that can be used across various U.S. government agencies, including the National Security Agency, Defense Intelligence Agency, Central Intelligence Agency, and various military branches of service. HumanID and EELD are related programs under the TIA umbrella that aim to provide TIA with advanced information-processing capabilities.

HumanID aims to develop automated biometric identification technologies to detect, recognize, and identify humans at great distances based on their gait, or manner of walking. This can augment existing biometric identification techniques, such as facial recognition, has greater range, and doesn't require a full facial view. When these various biometric techniques are all taken together, they can improve accuracy and increase the number of places where this type of technology can be applied, such as airports.

The EELD program aims to develop technologies and tools for the automated discovery, extraction, and linking of sparse evidence contained in large amounts of both classified and unclassified data sources. The goal of the program is to be able to learn about emerging threats via relationships between people and organizations and their patterns of activity that may otherwise be undetected. This program can be considered a computerized Sherlock Holmes.

Another DARPA program covered is Babylon. This program aims to develop rapid, two-way, natural language speech translation interfaces and platforms for users in combat and other field environments, such as refugee processing and medical support. Essentially a hand-held translator, the product from one of the contractors to this program, VoxTec, has already received highly favorable reviews from soldiers in the field.

Finishing off the chapter, we take a look at the Brain Machine Interface program within DARPA. This program aims to create new technologies for augmenting human performance through the ability to access codes in the brain noninvasively in real time and integrate them into peripheral device or system operations. Over the years, the program has already demonstrated many incredible firsts and is making the concept of "having thoughts that act," rather than "acting on thoughts" closer than you might think.

Future Combat Systems

The FCS program is a joint DARPA and U.S. Army program that has the goal of designing and developing a networked system of systems comprised of 18 manned and unmanned ground and aerial vehicles and sensors connected via an advanced communications network. This capability will aid the U.S. Army in achieving its vision of an Objective Force before the end of the decade. The FCS will enable the warfighter to "to see first, understand first, act first, and finish decisively as the means to tactical success."

Features

The FCS program is different from the other technologies profiled because it represents a program with many underlying technologies, rather than a technology unto itself. It is comprised of 18 technologies in the form of vehicles and sensors that are networked together to support the warfighter at the "unit-of-action" level. Several of these 18 vehicles and sensors are profiled elsewhere in the book and include the Unmanned Ground Combat Vehicle (UGCV) and Hummingbird Warrior.

The goals of the FCS program are to provide a system that is "soldier-centric, network-enabled, and knowledge-empowered." By combining the best of both manned and unmanned vehicles and sensors and making that information readily available, it can help tactical units improve their situational understanding and enable them to make more informed decisions and actions on the battlefield or even during peacekeeping and humanitarian missions. Some of the central themes of FCS include increased strategic, operational, and tactical mobility, improved lethality and survivability, and reduced logistics footprint and total cost of ownership.

In effect, it provides the strength of a present-day "heavy" force with the agility and speed of deployment of a "light" force. The FCS can be deployed anywhere in the world within 96 hours and can be placed into a C-130 or similar plane, as opposed to having to be shipped into the theater.

Background

The FCS (Figure 6–1) program is a major multi-billion-dollar program within the U.S. Army in support of its vision for the Objective Force. Initially, in May 2000, four contractors were selected for the 24-month conceptual design phase of the program, which required each contractor to produce two designs: one a system of systems of their own design and another a network-centric, distributed force, including a manned command and control element/personnel carrier, a robotic direct-fire system, a robotic non-line-of-sight system, an all-weather robotic sensor system, and other required sensors. The contractors selected for this 21-month phase included Boeing, SAIC, TEAM FoCuS Vision CONSORTIUM (including Raytheon), and Team Gladiator (including Lockheed Martin).

In March 2002, the Lead Systems Integrator (LSI) was announced by DARPA and the Army to be the team of Boeing and Science Applications International Corporation (SAIC). They were awarded a $154 million, 16-month agreement to conduct the concept and technology development (CTD) phase of the FCS program.

The system development and demonstration (SDD) phase was announced in May 2003 and included a $15 billion investment approved by the Department of Defense. During this phase, the lead

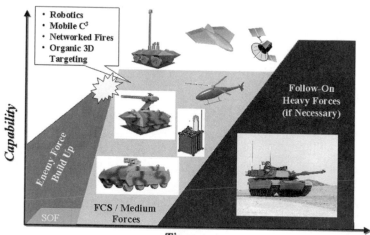

Figure 6–1 Future Combat Systems. (*Source:* DARPA)

systems integrator will work with various contractors to pull all the required technologies into a coherent system that can demonstrate live-fire and operational testing. This phase will also lead to low-rate initial production and the first unit equipped.

Facts

Program: FCS
Description: Networked, system of systems comprised of 18 manned and unmanned ground and aerial vehicles and sensors connected via an advanced communications network
Contractor: Boeing/SAIC
Service: DARPA, Tactical Technology Office (TTO)/U.S. Army
Started: FY 2000
First Unit Equipped: 2008 (expected)
Initial Operational Capability: 2010 (expected)
Cost: SDD phase $14.92 billion

Unmanned Ground Combat Vehicle

The UGCV is part of the U.S. Army's FCS program. The UGCV program is led by DARPA and the U.S. Army and is focused on developing unmanned vehicle prototypes that can carry reconnaissance, surveillance, and targeting or weapons payloads in support of network-centric warfare.

Features

By removing the need for transporting human crews in its design, the UGCV can be designed from the ground up to optimize its performance in areas such as endurance, mobility, and transportability. All these attributes help make the vehicle more effective in combat by allowing it to be easily transported to the battlefield, providing for the ability to negotiate rough terrain and even self-right itself, and to maintain high endurance for lengthy missions.

Without the requirements for a manned crew, these vehicles can carry more payload into the battlefield, which may include either equipment for reconnaissance, surveillance, and targeting or actual weapons themselves. Of course, the additional requirement due to the unmanned nature of the vehicle is that it be able to maneuver around obstacles and be easy to transport and deploy. In terms of maneuverability, if the vehicle rolls over, it must either be self-righting or be able to carry on upside down. In terms of transport and deployment, the idea is to reduce the logistics footprint of the UGCV by allowing it to be air-dropped and to conduct long-range missions.

The two current prototypes of the UGCV include one from Team Retarius that is close in size to that of the FCS "mule" vehicle and can carry up to 350 pounds, and another from Team Spinner that is close to that of the FCS Armed Reconnaissance Vehicle and can carry up to 4,500 pounds of payload. Hybrid electric power systems on both vehicles allow them to operate quietly for long periods of time. The vehicles also have low detectability, which is critical for minimizing the risk of loss of these assets to the enemy. Although they can be expendable, they are still relatively expensive and need to be both resilient and as stealthy as possible.

Background

The UGCV program (Figure 6–2) started with the selection of eight contractors in February 2001 to undertake an eight-month design effort for their UGCVs with the focus on mobility, endurance, and payload capacity. In November 2001, this team of eight contractors was selected down to four to continue with Phase IB through June 2002 with $1.5 million in funding apiece. The four contractors were SAIC, Lockheed Martin Missiles and Fire Control (Team Retarius), General Dynamics Robotic Systems, and Carnegie Mellon University. During this phase, the teams conducted hardware testing of major UGCV subsystems and refined their vehicle prototype designs.

In July 2002, Team Retarius and Team Spinner were selected for Phase II of the UGCV program, and each received $5.5 million to build a prototype vehicle during an 18-month effort. The initial prototypes were unveiled to the public in January and February 2003 and signaled the start of a period of extensive testing and refinement.

As these vehicles are tested, the FCS program will learn how their capabilities can be used to support future missions. In theory, these vehicles will be air-deployable and able to autonomously support warfighters with valuable intelligence information gathered from

Figure 6–2   Unmanned Ground Combat Vehicle from Team Retarius. (*Source:* DARPA)

deep within enemy lines. The weapons capability will also give these warfighters an unmanned combat option that can serve as a companion to the unmanned combat air vehicle (UCAV) in the air. The real test for these vehicles will be in their ability to conduct missions that challenge their mobility, endurance, and resiliency to the extremes.

Facts

Program: UGCV

Description: Vehicle prototypes for reconnaissance, surveillance, targeting, and weapons payloads in support of the Army's FCS program

Contractors: Team Retarius (Lockheed Martin Missiles and Fire Control) and Team Spinner (Carnegie Mellon University and Boeing)

Service: DARPA, TTO/U.S. Army

Weight: Reconnaissance, surveillance, and targeting, 3/4 ton; weapons, 6 tons

Payload: Reconnaissance, surveillance, and targeting, 350 pounds; weapons, 4,500 pounds

Started: FY 2001

Duration: Phase II July 2002–December 2003

First Unit Equipped: 2008 (overall FCS expected date)

Initial Operational Capability: 2010 (overall FCS expected date))

Cost: Phase II (vehicle prototypes) $11 million

Objective Force Warrior

The OFW is the Army's flagship science and technology initiative to develop and demonstrate revolutionary capabilities for Objective Force soldier systems. It is a major pillar of the Objective Force strategy and complements the FCS program. It will also provide the basis for a major upgrade to the Land Warrior System in 2010.

Features

The program is aimed at enhancing the soldier's lethality, survivability, communications, and responsiveness. To achieve this, it includes a combination of technologies, integrated in a holistic system-of-systems manner, including a head-to-toe protective system, lightweight weapons systems, networked communications, advanced power systems, and warfighter physiological status monitoring.

The head-to-toe protective system includes full-spectrum defense against chemical, biological, and other environmental threats and serves as a platform for other modular kits to be attached. The suit provides body protection against ballistic threats and incorporates a passive thermal management technique to dissipate heat away from the body during wear. The design calls for the suit to incorporate electrotextiles to supply power to the various devices that are connected. Electrotextiles are soft materials that can carry electronic components within their fabric. The suit also includes advanced headgear that incorporates a heads-up display, thermal and infrared sensors, laser eye protection, and embedded radio communications.

The communications capability provides situational awareness by enabling the sending and receiving of positional informational between the soldier, the extended team, and commanders. Communication links will also enable the soldier to access data and images from unmanned aerial vehicles, unmanned ground vehicles, and other robots and sensors. The software applications will provide personalized information to the soldier so that only pertinent information is delivered. For security purposes, they will also incorporate the required levels of authentication and authorization.

The goal of the weapons systems within the OFW is to reduce soldier weight by using new technologies such as plastic cartridges, caseless ammunition, lightweight machine guns, and even shared sensors mounted on the soldier ensemble. Because 20–40 percent of today's soldier weight is comprised of weapons and ammunitions, these new capabilities will help to significantly reduce the weight that the soldier has to carry into combat.

The power system for the computers and sensors will be disposable batteries in the short term but will move toward hybrid power sources, such as fuel cells, micro-turbine generators, and high-power rechargeable batteries over time. Vehicle-mounted recharging is a potential solution for recharging these power supplies so that many soldiers can recharge their equipment overnight or as needed. The vision of the OFW program in relation to power is to have 72-hour continuous autonomous team operations with a low-weight/-volume, self-generating/regenerating, reliable, and safe power source.

The warfighter physiological status monitoring (WPSM) is designed to monitor the soldier's vital signs using sensors embedded in the suit ensemble and help to avoid problems such as heat stress and dehydration by focusing medic resources on soldiers needing the most assistance. While medical kit availability could well be an issue, the idea is to monitor vital signs proactively in order to report up to higher levels, such as the squad level or battalion level.

The goal in terms of weight for the overall OFW system is to reduce the total physical load by 50 percent and down to a fighting weight goal of 50 pounds or less.

Background

On June 16, 2003, the Army selected Eagle Enterprise, a division of General Dynamics, to be the lead technology integrator for the OFW (Figure 6–3) Advanced Technology Demonstration (ATD). The company received $100 million for the 25-month Phase II in order to conduct preliminary and detailed design. Phase III of the program— Demonstration Build, Training, and Demonstration, will be a 15-month effort due for completion in 2006. Both of these phases are managed by the U.S. Army Natick Soldier Center.

Figure 6–3   Objective Force Warrior. (*Source:* U.S. Army Natick Soldier Center)

Facts

Program: OFW
Description: Army's flagship science and technology initiative to develop and demonstrate revolutionary capabilities for Objective Force soldier systems
Contractors: Eagle Enterprise, a division of General Dynamics
Service: U.S. Army Soldier Systems Center, Natick
Started: FY 2001
Duration: Phase II June 2003–July 2005, Phase III August 2005–October 2006
First Unit Equipped: 2008 (overall FCS expected date)
Initial Operational Capability: 2010 (overall FCS expected date))
Cost: Phase II (ATD) $100 million

Future Warrior

The Future Warrior is a soldier uniform concept demonstration program that aims to show how the future soldier may be equipped in the 2025 time frame. As a concept demonstration, its goal is to encourage dialogue and imaginations among researchers, scientists, and engineers from industry and within the U.S. Army regarding how this futuristic warrior would be equipped with emerging technology innovations.

Features

The major components of the Future Warrior include seven major subsystems. These are :

1. Headgear subsystem
2. Exoskeletal subsystem
3. Warfighter physiological monitoring subsystem
4. Micro-climate conditioning subsystem
5. Weapon subsystem
6. Power subsystem
7. Combat uniform subsystem

The Future Warrior concept takes advantage of a number of emerging technologies currently under research. These include individual strength augmentation, embedded micro-displays, high-performance nanophase composite materials, micro-turbine power generation, and electrically conductive textiles.

The headgear subsystem includes information systems providing maps, routes, situational awareness data, and communications, together with combat sensors for visual, thermal, night vision, acoustic, radar, laser threat, and combat identification. The 180-degree visor display also protects against laser and directed energy beams and provides a 360-degree situational awareness feed. The concept headgear also includes a laser rangefinder and designator that is linked wirelessly to smart munitions from the soldier's weapon. This means that rounds fired will direct themselves to where the laser is aimed.

The exoskeletal subsystem is a bit like the suit worn by Jackie Chan in the movie *The Tuxedo*. It features a lower body portion for extensive load carrying up to 200 pounds, plus an upper body portion with strength augmentation in the arms and torso of the suit. It works by using mechanically active polymers and nanostructures to augment the natural muscular movements made by the soldier. Sensors in the inner layer of the suit are used to detect intended motion, then to trigger an electrical charge in the exoskeletal system in order to activate the fibers either open or closed.

The warfighter physiological status monitoring subsystem provides information on hydration state, stress level, thermal state, sleep status, remote triage, energy balance, work load capacity, and normal baseline.

The microclimate conditioning subsystem is used to cool or warm the body by circulating cool or warm liquid around the torso within the inner layer of the combat uniform.

The weapon subsystem includes intelligent seeker munitions effective to 1 kilometer and kinetic energy projectiles effective to 300 meters.

The power subsystem consists of a 2- to 20-watt micro-turbine fueled by a liquid hydrocarbon. Ten ounces of fuel are used to power the soldier for up to six days. Backup power consists of lightweight, nanofiber battery patches that can power the soldier for up to three hours.

The combat uniform subsystem consists of three layers: a protective outer layer, a power-centric layer in the middle, and a life-critical layer next to the skin. The outer layer provides protection against chemical, biological, and ballistic threats. It also provides signature management functionality by changing the color of its camouflage, depending on the environment. The middle layer provides the power and data transmission and is also shielded against electromagnetic interference to reduce the signature emanating from the various electronic components of the system. Finally, the inner layer provides micro-climate conditioning and physiological status monitoring.

The goal of the system in terms of weight is not to add more than 15 percent of the soldier's weight as an additional burden. Although the exoskeletal subsystem may have a high weight, its impact in helping the soldier carry up to 200 pounds more than adequately compen-

Figure 6–4   Future Warrior. (*Source:* U.S. Army Natick Soldier Center)

sates. The effect for the soldier is that even for someone of 150–200 pounds in weight, the burden is only 22.5–30 pounds and much lower than the 50-pound weight goal of the OFW.

Background

The Future Warrior (Figure 6–4) concept first started in 1999 and was reintroduced on May 22, 2003, during the opening of the Institute for Soldier Nanotechnologies, a partnership between the Army and MIT. Many of the concepts that were out of bounds for the more near-term OFW were moved to the vision of the Future Warrior.

Facts

Program: Future Warrior
Description: A visionary concept of how the warrior might be equipped in the 2025 time frame

Service: U.S. Army Soldier Systems Center, Natick
Started: 1999, Redesigned in 2003
Initial Operational Capability: 2025

Terrorism Information Awareness

Terrorism Information Awareness, formerly Total Information Awareness, is a multi-year, phased development effort of the Information Awareness Office (IAO) of DARPA. It aims to develop a prototype system and network for the detection, classification, and identification of potential foreign terrorists so that the United States can take preemptive action before events of terrorism occur. The goal is to create a counter-terrorism information technology system comprised of several component programs that can achieve the following:

>> Increase the amount of information collected by an order of magnitude while still providing a scalable system.
>> Provide focused warnings within an hour of a triggering event or a threshold event.
>> Cue up appropriate analysts based on matching the event and prior patterns of activity with patterns that cover 90 percent of all previous terrorist attacks.
>> Support collaboration, analytical reasoning, and information sharing across analysts to enable effective decision-making capability based on potential future actions and the impact of current or future responses.

Features

The goal of TIA from a DARPA perspective is to create prototypes that can be used and built upon, rather than simple demonstrations with no enduring value, so that it can be rapidly transitioned into operational use. Some of the components that contribute to the TIA program include Genoa; Genoa II; Genisys; EELD; Wargaming the Asymmetric Environment (WAE); Translingual Information Detection, Extraction, and Summarization (TIDES); HumanID; Biosurveillance; Communicator; and Babylon. Several of these will be covered in subsequent sections of this book.

Technically, TIA is focused on creating a very large-scale, distributed database of information about suspected terrorists gathered from a wide array of sources, then developing appropriate techniques and algorithms for populating this database, analyzing and mining this information, determining patterns and behaviors, and converting this information into actionable intelligence.

This is a formidable challenge. Terrorists tend to leave small footprints in terms of information audit trails, so correlating very few and seemingly trivial events from a mass of information residing across many disparate and remotely distributed databases can be like looking for a needle in a haystack. The challenges are that current government systems are not well linked to one another and are, therefore, in silos; that the terrorist information footprint is purposefully small; and that correlation of this data to recognize a pattern of behavior and likely outcomes is hard to determine with accuracy. Nonetheless, there are obviously certain behaviors that would signal malicious intent. As a simple example, these may include entry into the United States, purchase of certain chemicals, renting a car, and buying airline tickets. In most cases, this pattern of behavior may be quite benign, but if the timing of these events indicates a purposeful or unconventional agenda, this may signal a warning.

Background

The name of the TIA program (Figure 6–5) was changed from Total Information Awareness to Terrorism Information Awareness, due to the misconception that the program was collecting information about civilians in a manner that raised privacy concerns. The potential privacy concerns raised by the program, as stated in DARPA's own terms in its report to Congress, include aggregation of data, unauthorized access to TIA, and unauthorized use of TIA. The TIA program addresses these potential privacy issues by putting into place an oversight board composed of senior representatives from the Department of Defense and the Intelligence Community, and chaired by the Under Secretary of Defense (Acquisition, Technology, and Logistics). The research program is also conducted using either legally obtained foreign intelligence information or artificial synthetic information that models real-world patterns of behavior so as to not create privacy concerns for civilians.

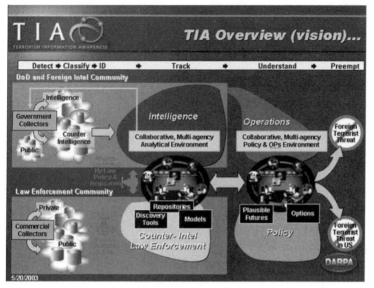

Figure 6–5 Terrorism Information Awareness. (Source: DARPA)

To date, TIA has been used by operational agencies for applications such as analyzing data from Afghanistan detainees, assessing weapons of mass destruction intelligence information related to Iraq, and aggregating large amounts of data into visual representations to discover previously unknown relationships.

Some of the organizations interested in TIA include the U.S. Army Intelligence and Security Command, National Security Agency, Defense Intelligence Agency, Central Intelligence Agency, U.S. Strategic Command, Special Operations Command, Joint Forces Command, and several others.

Facts

Program: TIA
Description: Develop a prototype system and network for the detection, classification, and identification of potential foreign terrorists so that the United States can take preemptive action before events of terrorism occur.
Service: DARPA, IAO
Started: FY 2003

Human Identification at a Distance

The Human Identification at a Distance (HumanID) program is another research project sponsored by the IAO of DARPA. The goal is to develop automated biometric identification technologies to detect, recognize, and identify humans at great distances. This technology can provide an early warning system against terrorist or criminal threats, both for protecting homeland security and for the protection of numerous sensitive facilities at home and abroad.

What is different about this program when compared with the biometric techniques in place today, such as the facial recognition systems at many of our airports, is that it aims to explore the limits of physical distance within which identification can be performed accurately and with reliability. It also combines many forms of biometric identification to provide a more accurate match, using what is termed *multi-modal fusion* to combine multiple forms of input. These forms of identification include techniques such as facial recognition, iris recognition, and gait recognition.

Features

Biometric identification works by taking a unique biological characteristic of an individual and comparing it with a known database of entries. These characteristics may include the recognition of a variety of human physical attributes, such as voice recognition, facial recognition, fingerprinting, hand geometry, and iris recognition. Typical examples in use today include fingerprint recognition and facial recognition.

Facial recognition translates a "face" into a series of numbers that can be matched in a database. The technology can be applied for one-to-many identification processes that search large databases of millions of faces for a rapid match within seconds. It can also be applied for one-to-one verification of identity processes, such as verification at automatic teller machines. One of the companies in this space, Viisage, has the world's largest installed facial recognition database of over 7 million images. Their current customers include federal government agencies, casinos, local and state police, departments of corrections, and social services departments.

An important newer technology is gait recognition, which analyzes the unique way that an individual walks. This is important because if it can be made accurate and reliable, it can provide human identification at far greater distances than facial recognition. Facial recognition is typically at distances of 25–150 feet, whereas gait recognition can be made from up to 500 feet from the subject. A multimodal fusion of several biometric techniques can often produce the best of both worlds. The gait recognition can be used to provide an identification at a distance, and the facial recognition can be used to further verify the identification as a match.

Background

Over the course of the HumanID program (Figure 6–6), DARPA has made several accomplishments and has formed several planned objectives for upcoming years. Some of the accomplishments have included performing an operational evaluation of a long-range (25–150 feet) face recognition system; developing a multi-spectral infrared and visible face recognition system; and developing a low-power millimeter wave radar system for wide field-of-view detection and narrow field-of-view gait classification.

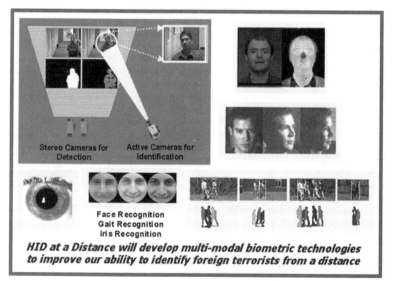

Figure 6–6 Human ID at a Distance. (*Source*: DARPA)

Plans for FY 2003 and FY 2004 include developing a multi-modal fusion algorithm for human identification; developing algorithms to locate and acquire subjects out to 500 feet; developing and demonstrating a HumanID system that operates out to 500 feet; and fusing face and gait recognition into a system that can run continuously

Facts

Program: HumanID
Description: Automated biometric identification technologies to detect, recognize, and identify humans at great distances
Techniques: Facial recognition, gait recognition
Distance: Up to 500 feet
Service: DARPA, IAO
Started: FY 2002

Evidence Extraction and Link Discovery

The EELD program aims to develop technologies and tools for the automated discovery, extraction, and linking of sparse evidence contained in large amounts of both classified and unclassified data sources. The goal of the program is to be able to learn about emerging threats via relationships between people and organizations and their patterns of activity that may otherwise be undetected.

Features

EELD works by mining unstructured textual data on computer and extracting information about relationships between individuals and organizations and learning patterns of activity. By so doing, it can discover ongoing activities and linkages that may pose a threat to national security. Examples include detecting patterns of activity and relationships based on financial transactions, communications, travel, immigration, and other activities. Input data for the EELD program typically comes from law enforcement records and other forms of legally obtained intelligence data. The three key functions of the EELD initiative are evidence extraction, link discovery, and pattern learning.

The technical challenge behind EELD is large because the evidence extracted in searching for relationships and potential threats is mostly legitimate behavior. Only when a series of relationships or activities are pieced together within a certain context of behavior do the real links and intents become apparent. Because of this, the EELD program cannot rely on already developed fraud detection algorithms because they pick up anomalous behavior and not the seemingly ordinary transactions of suspected terrorists.

Another challenge is that unstructured textual data is difficult to mine for information. A lot of the value of this information comes not from keywords but from the semantics of the text, which may be a discussion, letter, or report. Solving this challenge requires sophisticated software algorithms that can make sense of natural language text before the link discovery and pattern learning even starts.

Background

DARPA is working with a number of academic institutions and commercial enterprises, as well as other DARPA programs, to fill in all the required technical components of the EELD (Figure 6–7) program. These include the DARPA TIDES program for natural language processing; BBN, SRA International, and Syracuse University for evidence extraction; Carnegie Mellon University, Cycorp, and Alphatech for link discovery; and SRI International and USC Information Sciences Institute for pattern learning; as well as many others.

Planned accomplishments include being able to develop and demonstrate technology to work against single link-type patterns and to extend it into multiple link types (transaction types) and multiple types of entities (individuals, organizations).

Facts

Program: EELD
Description: Develop technologies and tools for the automated discovery, extraction, and linking of sparse evidence contained in large amounts of data
Service: DARPA, IAO
Started: FY 2002

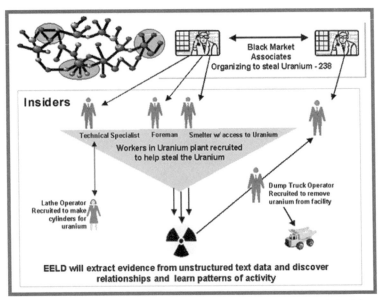

Figure 6–7   Evidence Extraction and Link Discovery. (*Source*: DARPA)

Babylon

The Babylon program aims to develop rapid, two-way, natural language speech translation interfaces and platforms for users in combat and other field environments, such as refugee processing and medical support. This two-way translation capability builds on the success of one-way translation devices already in deployment. A one-way example is the Phraselator, which was developed by Vox-Tec, a division of Marine Acoustics, Inc., and used in Afghanistan by U.S. military forces in support of Operation Enduring Freedom. It was also used during Operation Iraqi Freedom by coalition forces. The two-way translation works by translating the user's query to the respondent's language and the respondent's answer back to the user's language via an electronic, handheld device performing machine translation.

Features

Babylon focuses on language translations that are important for the military but not the primary focus of most commercial enterprises. These are often the low-population, high-terrorist-risk languages that commercial ventures do not target, due to limited market size and interest. Physically, Babylon devices are PDA-sized handhelds that have a relatively long battery life of up to 12 hours and can be easily used in the field. They are ruggedized to support harsh environments, such as water and sand, and to withstand being dropped.

One of the challenges of natural language speech translation is simply semantics—having the machine understand the intended meaning of the spoken words. One partial solution to this issue is constraining the domain or field of use of the translation to a particular task. This can help to remove some of the ambiguity from the conversation and provide more accurate translations. This is the initial focus of the Babylon program because the immediate fields of use are for applications such as refugee processing and medical support, in addition to force protection.

One-way voice-to-voice translation, such as that employed by the Phraselator from VoxTec, provides an easier technical challenge than two-way translation. Translations can be prerecorded for several hundred or even thousands of domain-specific phrases. The appropriate phrase can then be played back through a built-in speaker when the microphone picks up the English-language equivalent spoken into the device.

Background

Previous DARPA programs have focused on tasks such as one-way, phrase-based, voice-to-voice machine translation. The current Phraselator device is a result of these initiatives and the work of VoxTec. VoxTec was awarded a two-year Small Business Innovation Research (SBIR) grant from DARPA in January 2001 to develop the prototype. Over 500 Phraselators were deployed to military units in support of Operation Enduring Freedom.

The current Phraselator (Figure 6–8) supports 100–1,000 phrases per phrase module stored on Compact Flash (CF) cards. Over 20 modules have been developed for various applications and have been translated into over 40 languages. Up to 30,000 phrases can be stored on one CF card. The device is a handheld device running Windows CE on an Intel XScale PXA 255 Processor. It features a day/night touch-screen display and high-quality microphone and amplified speaker. It is powered by a rechargeable poly-lithium-ion battery or four AA batteries. In addition to speaking a phrase into the device, the user can also select from phrases displayed on screen by using a stylus to tap the screen.

Planned accomplishments for the Babylon program include building and deploying one-way speech translation systems for Pashto, Dari, Arabic, and Mandarin; developing two-way translation prototypes that are constrained to 10 domains of use; then expanding the domains of these prototypes and enhancing their robustness and ease of use in the field.

Figure 6–8   Phraselator. (*Source*: VoxTec)

Facts

Program: Babylon
Description: Develop rapid, two-way, natural language speech translation interfaces and platforms for users in the field
Contractors: VoxTec
Service: DARPA, IAO
Started: FY 2002
Duration: 3-year program

Brain Machine Interfaces

The Brain Machine Interfaces program is a DARPA program that aims to create new technologies for augmenting human performance through the ability to noninvasively access codes in the brain in real time and integrate them into peripheral device or system operations.

Features

One of the visionary concepts of the brain machine interface program is for warfighters to have "thoughts that can act" instead of "acting on thoughts." The idea is to tap into the brain to operate machines by using neuron activity to control mechanical structures in much the same way that it powers our own limbs as we move. The possibilities of being able to tap into the brain and to use it for command, control, and communications are endless. Some of the military scenarios made possible include being able to control distant robots on reconnaissance and surveillance missions, being able to communicate just by thought, being able to control exoskeletons for performance augmentation, such as those envisioned by the Future Warrior program, and much more. With a feedback loop back to the brain, the scenarios become even more powerful. Humans might be able to see in infrared and ultraviolet, sounds could be augmented and perhaps processed electronically so that speech can be heard on noisy flight decks, and if we tapped into other equally equipped animals, we could even see, hear, and smell what they do as they examine a distant cave complex.

To achieve these kinds of ambitious goals requires a unique combination of scientific disciplines, including biology, materials science, mathematics, and physics. Success with human brain machine interfaces also requires noninvasive techniques where the high-density interconnects of the brain can be read without adverse effects.

There have already been many significant accomplishments in this field of study. In late 2000, a monkey was trained to control a remote artificial arm by thought alone. In fact, this was not true mind-reading, but it achieved very similar results. The signals of the brain, picked up by implanted electrodes when the money reached for a piece of fruit, were repeatedly recorded and interpreted. When the monkey's brain executed similar tasks in later experiments, the computer was able to understand the intended action and act on the artificial arm. The tests even included sending the interpreted brain signals over the Internet to a robotic arm over 600 miles away. It is of note that even several years later, the monkeys have not suffered from the invasive techniques of the implanted electrodes.

Other developments in this area of science have included 16-element retinal implants that can help blind patients actually to distinguish light from dark and shadows. Taking this further, Johns Hopkins University and the Naval Research Laboratory are developing a nanochannel glass array with 3,200 elements that can communicate with the retina and feed images from a digital camera, either wired or wirelessly. Human clinical trials are expected within a year or so.

DARPA's most recent investment in brain machine interfaces includes a $26 million contract awarded to Duke University to continue its research in developing a deeper understanding of these interfaces and the brain itself.

Background

Brain machine interface (Figure 6–9) research has been in existence since the 1960s and has traditionally been focused on helping to aid military pilots with some of their secondary flight activities in order to help reduce their workload. In 1996, researchers at the Armstrong Laboratory at the Wright-Patterson Air Force Base were able to use EEG patterns to enable pilots to roll a flight simulator to the left or right, based on their brain waves.

The DARPA award to Duke University in 2002 also supported the launch of Duke's Center for Neuroengineering. The ongoing work at Duke includes a custom VLSI "neurochip" that can be used for decoding brain signals. This neurochip may help to restore motor function to patients who are paralyzed or affected by a neurological deficit.

As brain machine interface research becomes ever more sophisticated, the future challenges for researchers in this field are many. First, noninvasive techniques need to be developed that can work at the right level of resolution in terms of detecting the complexity of human thought as expressed by these neural cells. Second, a feedback mechanism needs to be developed so that a closed loop is created between the brain and the peripheral device. The other challenge is to be able to perform the complex calculations and pattern matching required to understand the intended meaning of more complex patterns of motor or sensory activity.

Facts

Program: Brain Machine Interface
Description: Create new technologies for augmenting human performance through the ability to noninvasively access codes in the brain in real time and integrate them into peripheral device or system operations
Service: DARPA, Defense Sciences Office (DSO)

Figure 6–9   Brain Machine Interface. (*Source*: DARPA)

7

Munitions

A s the Army's transformation toward the Objective Force starts to network together soldiers and systems via the Objective Force Warrior and Future Combat Systems initiatives, the traditional view of munitions is changing, as well. The requirements for munitions have changed considerably due to ever-changing threats and the needs of the public and our politicians in calling for greater discretion in their use. Today's requirements are for more specialized missions and for more responsive, agile, versatile, and lethal capabilities, while minimizing collateral damage to civilians and noncombatants.

The Bunker Buster, Blackout Bomb, Massive Ordnance Air Blast (MOAB), Joint Standoff Weapon (JSOW), and Joint Direct Attack Munition (JDAM) have begun the transformation toward specialized mission capability and all-weather, precision-guided targeting. The Patriot Advanced Capability PAC-3 and the Tactical Tomahawk have also started the transformation toward better air defense against ballistic missiles and improved loiter and surveillance capabilities prior to committing costly weapons to their intended targets. The latest Patriot provides us with enhanced accuracy in striking down ballistic missiles, and the latest Tomahawk provides us with greater versatility in the selection of our targets, even during flight.

Beyond these impressive present-day capabilities are a number of innovative programs designed to move the needle even further in terms of meeting future battlefield requirements for mission type and flexibility. Today's enemy may use hardened underground bunkers for protection, may have prior warning of incoming attacks, and may use rapidly moving vehicles in order to evade a direct hit.

The Affordable Moving Target Surface Engagement (AMSTE) program aims to develop and demonstrate the ability to target moving surface threats from long range, to engage them rapidly with precision standoff weapons, and to do so economically. It uses a system-of-systems approach to combine various assets on the battlefield, including sensors, communications, and weaponry for rapid engagement of moving targets and a desired accuracy of within 10 meters. Recent tests of this program have proven highly successful and have coupled the collective power of the Joint Surveillance Target Attack Radar System (Joint STARS) and Global Hawk for detection and tracking with an F/A-18 fighter and a JSOW for target engagement.

The Self-Healing Minefield program is interesting because it uses a networked series of mines intelligently to close gaps in the minefield as they are breached. The mines gain the benefits of mobility and communications in order to hop into the gaps left by exploded mines. This transformational approach toward modern minefields can help to maintain and enhance their effectiveness in hindering an enemy's progress while minimizing or removing the need for use of anti-personnel mines.

The Airborne Laser (ABL) may seem like something out of science fiction but is actually a real-life program. It consists of a heavily modified Boeing 747-700F aircraft plus battle management, command, control, communications, and intelligence (BM/C4I) capability, a Lockheed Martin-supplied beam control and fire control system, and a Northrop Grumman megawatt-class Chemical Oxygen Iodine Laser (COIL). The program is designed to counter the threat of theater ballistic missiles and will have a lethal range of hundreds of kilometers from its vantage point in the sky.

Munitions are also being developed for nonlethal effects, either to subdue crowds or combatants or for specialized missions, such as electronic warfare. Electromagnetic pulse (EMP) has been known about since the 1940s, but today it is even more of a threat. As our society and our military become ever more dependent on computers and electronics, the specter of EMP warfare is one that demands constant vigilance.

Affordable Moving Surface Target Engagement

The AMSTE is a program of the Information Exploitation Office (IXO) of the Defense Advanced Research Projects Agency (DARPA). The goal of the program is to develop and demonstrate the ability to target moving surface threats from long range, to engage them rapidly with precision standoff weapons, and to do so economically.

Features

As today's weapons systems become increasingly capable of engaging and destroying fixed and stationary targets, an approach adopted by the enemy is to use mobility as a technique for survival. This mobility strategy can be applied to better protect a variety of systems, including ground weapons, surface-to-air missiles, small-scale biological and chemical weapons facilities, and even fleeing enemy officials.

Although today's weapons systems can indeed engage these forms of mobile targets, the techniques used are often highly expensive or have the potential for high collateral damage. Either sophisticated seeker systems are used to home in on the enemy target vehicle or cluster munitions are used, which are indiscriminate and may have a wider than necessary kill area.

The AMSTE program uses a system-of-systems philosophy to combine sensors, communications, and weaponry in support of affordable, precision engagement of moving targets either on land or at sea. The goal in terms of precision is within 10 meters of the moving target, regardless of the weather and regardless of the target dynamics. For example, the program aims to be able to engage a moving vehicle, whether it is moving in a predictable manner or in a move-stop-move scenario that is perhaps indicative of traffic congestion or evasive action. Additional requirements include the ability to track the target continuously from initial nomination through to engagement, to update the weapons while in flight, and to operate from tactically significant standoff distances.

Technically, AMSTE uses multiple Ground Moving Target Indication (GMTI) radar sensors to track the target accurately, as well as precision-guided munitions and tactical communications networks. The specific platforms, sensors, and weapons can vary as long as there is an integrated system of surveillance and precision strike. As an example, a Northrop Grumman test in September 2002 used GMTI radars on board a Joint STARS and on board a surrogate Global Hawk for the surveillance part of the system, coupled with a JSOW fired from an F/A-18 aircraft for a precision strike against a moving tank. The AMSTE concept also supports precision munitions fired from ground weapons in addition to aircraft.

Background

The first field exercise for AMSTE (Figure 7–1) was conducted in fiscal year 2001 with a live weapon fired against a moving target. Over the past several years, the DARPA objectives for AMSTE have increased the complexity of the test scenarios by increasing a number of variables, such as target behavior, terrain type, number of vehicles, and tracking time. As these variables are modified, the situation becomes closer to real-life situations and becomes a lot more complex for the overall system to deal with. For the fiscal year 2003 campaign for AMSTE, the goal is to demonstrate 10-meter accuracy under unscripted target behavior, hilly terrain, lengthy tracking time, and with many vehicles nearby to confuse the target situation.

Although a single moving target may be considered tactical for many operations, its significance for modern warfare and enemy asymmetries cannot be underestimated. AMSTE is an important program that will enable the U.S. military to be more effective against tactical targets, such as surface-to-air missiles, as well as more strategic targets of opportunity, such as high-ranking enemy officials.

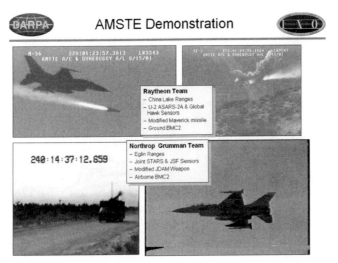

Figure 7–1   Affordable Moving Surface Target Engagement. (*Source:* DARPA)

Facts

Program: AMSTE

Description: Targeting of moving surface threats from long range to engage them rapidly with precision standoff weapons

Contractors: Northrop Grumman, Raytheon

Service: DARPA, IXO

Started: FY 2001

Status: Ongoing

Self-Healing Minefield

The Self-Healing Minefield is a program of the Advanced Technology Office (ATO) of DARPA. The self-healing minefield provides the capability of maneuver denial for enemy vehicles without the need for incorporating anti-personnel landmines. It operates via a network of mines that can communicate with one another and can physically move in order to close gaps in the minefield. In this manner, it maintains its effectiveness through a more intelligent, dynamic system, as opposed to having to rely on enhanced lethality.

Features

The key feature of the self-healing minefield is that it converts a static munition into a smart network of munitions that can act autonomously as an entire system in order to maintain its integrity and provide enhanced maneuver denial. When a breach occurs, the mines in this network are able to know where the breach is located, relative to the rest of the minefield. Nearby mines can physically move themselves by jumping to fill in the void in the network. The technical additions to the mines to achieve this capability include a communications system for mine-to-mine information sharing on status and location, as well as a mobility component to enable the mines to move themselves and literally hop from place to place, even in harsh, rugged terrain.

The mobility component is either one-sided or two-sided and is comprised of thrusters that can propel the mine up to 9 meters horizontally. Like traditional mines, the self-healing mines are 12 centimeters in diameter, 7.5 centimeters high, and weigh less than 2 kilograms. The communications system consists of two frequency-hop spread-spectrum radios, an orientation sensor, optional Global Positioning System (GPS), a processor, and an acoustic communication subsystem. GPS is optional because it is not necessary for the mines to know their exact or absolute position. Rather, they just need to know their position relative to one another, which does not necessarily require the use of GPS for position determination.

The self-healing minefield is an example of a transformational approach to an age-old technique in ground warfare. By adding mobility and communications, the single mines become a more capable, networked system that can further deter an enemy and hinder its progress.

Background

The self-healing minefield program (Figure 7–2) began in 1998 and is now formally completed as a DARPA research program. In 2002, a network of 10 mines was used to demonstrate that the system could detect a breach and respond to the breach by moving multiple mines in response. According to DARPA, the U.S. Army is looking at moving this system into its portfolio of weapon systems. A tactically significant number of mines in the self-healing network for military operations is on the order of 50–100.

If the concept of the intelligent minefield is taken a little further than the self-healing functionality, one can imagine mines that move forward and engage the enemy, mines that actively seek out their targets, such as tanks and other armored vehicles, and mines that are self-arranging in predetermined patterns in order to streamline initial deployment on the battlefield.

Facts

Program: Self-Healing Minefield
Description: Maneuver denial for enemy vehicles without the need for incorporating anti-personnel landmines
Service: DARPA, ATO
Started: 1998
Status: Complete

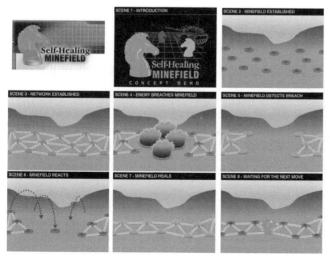

Figure 7–2 Self-Healing Minefield. (*Source*: DARPA)

Airborne Laser

The ABL is a U.S. Air Force and Missile Defense Agency (MDA) program designed to provide an ABL weapon capable of detecting, tracking, and destroying hostile theater ballistic missiles during the boost phase of flights. Team ABL consists of Boeing, Lockheed Martin, and Northrop Grumman working together to develop, integrate, and test the system. The major components include a Boeing-supplied 747-700F aircraft and battle management, command, control, communications and intelligence (BM/C4I) capability, a Lockheed Martin-supplied beam control and fire control system, and a Northrop Grumman megawatt-class COIL.

Features

The ABL program is designed to counter the threat of theater ballistic missiles and to help protect the United States, its forces abroad, and its allies. It is part of a broader strategy within the MDA that consists of a layered defense system to protect against these missiles in all phases of their flight: the boost phase, cruise phase, and terminal phase.

The threat faced by the United States and its allies is that ballistic missiles are possessed by over 30 nations worldwide that have thousands of these missiles in each of their arsenals. Several countries are also known to have developed or to be in the process of developing nuclear, biological, and chemical capabilities for these missiles.

The ABL consists of a heavily modified Boeing 747-400F freighter with a weapons-class COIL and other detection and tracking lasers and computer systems on board. The aircraft has a distinctive hump on the top of the fuselage containing a kilowatt-class active laser ranger for finding the missile, plus a 12,000-pound rotating turret assembly on the aircraft's nose containing a 1.5-meter telescope. The telescope is used to focus the other two laser beams as well as the main weapons-grade beam on the target for tracking and destruction. There are a total of four types of lasers used for these various operations from initial detection to kill. During missions, the aircraft will be capable of flying above the clouds and autonomously detecting, tracking, and destroying ballistic missiles shortly after their launch.

Refueling capability helps to ensure that the aircraft can handle long flights to problem areas around the globe and remain on station as necessary.

The technical challenges for the ABL are many. First, the aircraft must be a stable aircraft that can stay aloft for hours. The sensors must be able to locate ballistic missiles rapidly and maintain locks on their tracks. The computer systems must be able to keep track of dozens of missiles and prioritize the most dangerous ones. The optical system that guides the laser must be able to compensate for atmospheric effects between the laser and its target. The laser must also be able to maintain its aim on a missile that is moving at Mach 6 or more, and it must be powerful enough to be effective from hundreds of miles away.

Many of the components that make up this complex system of systems have already been tested and have demonstrated their capabilities. The first ABL aircraft, YAL-1A, made its first flight on July 18, 2002. During MDA tests in December 2002 over the Pacific Ocean, the ABL's infrared trackers were able to detect a Minuteman booster rocket and hold a lock until the rocket's engine burned out 500 kilometers later. The battle management system was flight tested in late summer and early fall of 2002, and the first COIL module for the YAL-1A tested at 118 percent of anticipated power during a test at Northrop Grumman's facility in January 2002.

The YAL-1A aircraft is currently in a hangar at Edwards Air Force Base's Birk Flight Test Facility. The YAL-1A designation means prototype Attack Laser, Model 1A. The aircraft is grounded while the lasers and optical components of the ABL are installed and tested. The MDA expects to have the YAL-1A ready to conduct tests representative of real ballistic missile threats by December 2004.

Background

Several of the technologies that comprise the ABL system (Figure 7–3) have a long heritage. The COIL laser was invented at the Air Force Research Laboratory's Directed Energy Directorate at Kirkland Air Force Base, New Mexico in 1977.

The ABL program office was created in 1993, and in November 1996, the Air Force awarded a $1.1 billion contract to Boeing

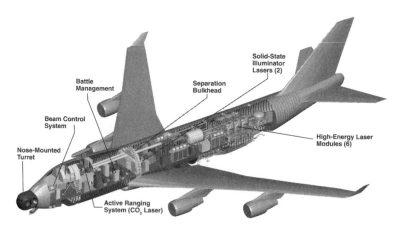

Figure 7–3   Airborne Laser. (*Source*: Boeing)

Defense Group, TRW Space and Electronics Group (now Northrop Grumman), and Lockheed Martin Missiles & Space.

In January 2000, Boeing undertook what was the largest military modification of a commercial aircraft ever made when it extensively modified a commercial 747-400F at its facility in Wichita, Kansas. The modifications included the addition of sheets of titanium to the plane's undercarriage to protect the aircraft from the laser exhaust heat, plus a 12,000-pound turret attached to the front of the aircraft to hold the 1.5-meter telescope through which the laser beam would fire.

Facts

Program: ABL
Description: ABL weapon capable of detecting, tracking, and destroying hostile theater ballistic missiles during the boost phase of their flights
Platform: Boeing 747-400F
Contractors: Boeing, Lockheed Martin, Northrop Grumman
Service: U.S. Air Force, MDA
Started: 1992
Initial Flight: July 18, 2002
Operational Altitude: 40,000 feet

Lethal Range: Classified (but "hundreds of kilometers")
Shots: Minimum of 20 (varies according to type of target and level of atmospheric disturbance)
Cost per Shot: Less than $10,000
Crew: 6 (including pilot and copilot, plus a mission crew of commander, airborne surveillance officer, weapon system operator, and special equipment operator)
Planned Inventory: 7
Status: Ongoing

Electromagnetic Pulse

Electromagnetic pulse is the name typically given to a high-altitude nuclear explosion that creates a high-intensity, short-duration, radiating electromagnetic field that can span continent-sized areas. EMP can also be generated by non-nuclear, radio frequency devices and can originate on land as well as in space. The threat for the military and for non-military alike is that EMP has a devastating effect on electronics. Although it does not cause human harm, the EMP pulse has a peak magnitude of tens of thousands of volts per meter and can induce currents of up to 5,000 amps in equipment cabling and related components. Any electronics, such as computers and telecommunications equipment, not specially hardened against this EMP, are vulnerable and can be instantly rendered inoperable.

Features

Originally considered a Cold War threat, EMP poses a continued threat to national security for a number of reasons. First, its nonlethal effect could be devastating to a recipient nation in terms of damages to critical infrastructure, such as power lines, telephones lines, and computer systems, but it could not warrant a nuclear or any other such massive response in retaliation. In addition, as the military transforms itself toward network-centric warfare with systems such as the Force XXI Battle Command Brigade and Below (FBCB2) and the Tactical Internet, it becomes ever more susceptible to these kinds of attacks. Third, the capability for creating such a weapon rests with many of the large nuclear powers that possess both the nuclear weapons and the ballistic capability to launch and detonate the weapon in space. A more likely threat is that of non-nuclear EMP, which can be triggered from devices ranging in size from a suitcase to something that could be placed in a van. The effects of these smaller weapons would be more localized but would still be capable of wiping out critical electrical infrastructure for many tens of kilometers.

The threat from space is most significant because an EMP pulse radiates outward in all directions, with an effective range of up to 2,000 kilometers. This means that if a device is set off in space at 400–500 kilometers over Kansas, it would affect all parts of the continental United States. The signal extends all the way to the horizon as seen from the point of explosion and has a declining intensity as distance increases.

The United States and its allies are countering the threat of EMP by ensuring that critical military equipment and installations are hardened against it by using techniques for EMP protection (EMPP). These techniques typically employ the use of metallic shielding to protect internal electronics from external fields. The test scenarios required ensuring that platforms such as the M1A1 Abrams main battle tank is EMP hardened and ensuring that munitions are not accidentally triggered when they experience these kinds of electromagnetic signals. One of the testing centers for this kind of work within the United States is the White Sands Missile Range, which has specialized facilities for testing several different kinds of electromagnetic effects, including a 50' x 50' x 50' test volume for EMP simulations of exoatmospheric warhead detonations.

Background

The existence of EMP (Figure 7–4) was known in the 1940s when the first nuclear weapons were being developed and tested. The actual effects of EMP were first discovered in the early 1960s when American and Soviet scientists were conducting tests on hydrogen bombs in space. One of the notable tests that confirmed these effects, "Starfish Prime," was part of a series of tests codenamed "Fishbowl" and conducted by the United States over the Pacific Ocean in July 1962. The test, which was over 650 miles up in space, caused street lights to go out and burglar alarms to go off in the Hawaiian islands over 800 miles away. Due to these effects and the risks of continued tests, the

Figure 7–4 A Trident missle undergoes an electromagnetic pulse simulation test. (*Source:* Defense Threat Reduction Agency)

United States and the Soviet Union signed the Atmospheric Test Ban Treaty in 1963.

Facts

Description: EMP
Effects: Potentially damaging currents and voltages in unprotected electronic circuits
Electric Field: 50 kilovolts per meter
Rise Time: 10 nanoseconds
Decay Time: 200 nanoseconds (to half peak)
Effective Radius: 2,000 kilometers
Current: Up to 5,000 amps
Frequencies: A few hundred Hz to 1 GHz

8

Naval Warfare

T he Navy's vision for transformation is called *Sea Power 21*. It is comprised of three fundamental concepts: Sea Shield, Sea Strike, and Sea Basing, all tied together and enabled by what is termed *FORCEnet*. This vision is to "enhance America's ability to project offense, project defense, and project sovereignty around the globe."

Sea Strike is the naval concept for "projecting dominant and decisive offensive power from the sea in support of joint objectives." This includes the establishment of transformational capabilities in four areas:

1. Persistent intelligence, surveillance, and reconnaissance (ISR)
2. Time-sensitive strike
3. Information operations
4. Ship-to-objective maneuver

Sea Shield is the concept for exploiting "control of the seas and forward-deployed defensive capabilities to defeat area-denial strategies, enabling joint forces to project and sustain power." It includes theater air and missile defense, littoral sea control, and homeland defense.

Sea Basing is the concept for "sustainable global projection of American power from the high seas at the operational level of war." It provides allied forces with forward-deployed bases such as aircraft carriers from which to launch operations without the concerns of flyover rights or permissions for basing troops in foreign countries.

Finally, FORCEnet is the Navy's "operational construct and architectural framework for naval warfare in the information age which integrates warriors, weapons, sensors, networks, command and control, and platforms into a networked, distributed combat force, scalable across the spectrum of conflict from seabed to space and sea to land." FORCEnet effectively implements network-centric warfare for the Navy in much the same way that the Objective Force and Future Combat Systems will do for the Army.

These transformational objectives require a transformation of the Navy to meet the needs of today's battlefield and tomorrow's. This is particularly true in the area of littoral combat—being able to engage the enemy in the shallow regions of the ocean near the shoreline.

This chapter takes a look at several of the transformational initiatives currently underway within the fleet. These include the new CVN 21 future aircraft carrier, the DD(X) land attack destroyer, the CG(X) cruiser, and the Littoral Combat Ship (LCS). The LCS is currently the Navy's number-one budget priority with the goal of creating a new class of warship that is smaller, faster, networked, agile, and affordable. With a modular design, it will support a variety of specialized missions to help assure access and to defend against threats from enemy surface ships, mines, and submarines operating in the littoral regions of the world. It will utilize specialized mission modules and accompanying Navy specialists to perform highly focused tasks and return to their bases. According to Admiral Vern Clark, Chief of Naval Operations, "Our most transformational effort and number one budget priority, the Littoral Combat Ship, will be the first navy ship to separate capability from hull form and provide a robust, affordable, focused-mission ship."*

The chapter finishes the look at the future Navy with an examination of two undersea vessels: the Virginia-class submarine and the Long-Term Mine Reconnaissance System (LMRS). The Virginia class is the world's most sophisticated submarine, optimized for operation in the littorals and featuring advanced technologies in the areas of firepower, maneuverability, and stealth. The LMRS provides the Navy with greater ability to detect mines by using this system of systems to autonomously perform missions that can cover over 400 square nautical miles in just 40 hours.

CVN 21 Future Aircraft Carrier

The CVN 21 is the Navy's next-generation aircraft carrier and is scheduled to begin construction in 2007 with delivery planned for 2014. As the future centerpiece of the Navy Carrier Strike group, the CVN 21 includes a number of innovations, including an enhanced flight deck with increased sortie rates, improved weapons movement, a redesigned island, a new nuclear power plant, allowance for future technologies, and reduced manning.

Features

The CVN 21 will have a new nuclear propulsion plant that requires fewer operators and provides increased electrical power for elsewhere on the carrier. The electrical distribution system will also be more efficient and will support the replacement of steam systems with electrical auxiliaries.

The flight deck redesign includes a new electromagnetic aircraft-launching system that replaces the steam-driven catapult launchers of current carriers. This change in technology will reduce crew work-

---

*. Statement of Admiral Vern Clark, U.S. Navy Chief of Naval Operations before the Senate Appropriations Subcommitter for Defense, April 2, 2003, *http://www.chinfo.navy.mil/navpalib/cno/testimony/clark030402.txt.*

Figure 8–1   CVN 21. (*Source:* Northrop Grumman)

load, enhance safety, and reduce long-term operating costs of the carrier's 50-year life expectancy.

Future aircraft to be part of the carrier include the Joint Strike Fighter (JSF), the F/A-18E/F, and the Unmanned Combat Aerial Vehicle (UCAV). It is anticipated that the various redesigns on the CVN 21 will allow for a crew reduction of about 800 personnel.

Background

On July 10, 2003, the U.S. Navy awarded Northrop Grumman a contract to support the future aircraft carrier program, CVN 21 (Figure 8–1). The $107.6 million contract enabled the company to continue presystem development and design efforts. The total U.S. Navy budget for the CVN 21 in fiscal year 2004 is approximately $1.5 billion for research and development plus advanced procurement.

Facts

Type: Centerpiece of Navy Carrier Strike group
Contractor: Northrop Grumman
Aircraft: JSF, F/A-18E/F, UCAV
Armaments: Integrated Warfare System (IWS)
Launching System: Electromagnetic
Crew: 800 less than typical carrier

Life Expectancy: 50 years
Construction Begins: 2007
Delivery: 2014
Service: U.S. Navy

Source: Northrop Grumman

DD(X) Land Attack Destroyer

The DD(X) Land Attack Destroyer is a multi-mission surface combatant that is the centerpiece of the U.S. Navy's future family of ships for what is known as the Surface Combatant Navy. The DD(X) is also the platform whereby transformational technologies for the rest of the surface fleet, including the future CG(X) cruiser and LCS, as well as the existing Aegis cruisers and destroyers, can be developed and tested both on land and at sea. In this regard, it is both a new class of ship in itself and a technology platform and proving ground for the rest of the future fleet.

Features

The mission of the DD(X) includes the ability to bring offensive, precision firepower to support forces ashore. The DD(X) is designed for the littoral areas, meaning the near shore, and includes advances in combat systems, hull form, propulsion, stealth, survivability, manning, and quality of life.

Some of areas currently being designed, manufactured, and tested include 10 specific engineering development models:

1. Advanced gun system (AGS) and munitions
2. Integrated power system (IPS)
3. Dual-band radar (DBR) suite
4. Total ship computing environment (TSCE)
5. Peripheral vertical launch (PVL) system
6. Integrated deckhouse and apertures
7. Autonomic fire suppression system (AFSS)
8. Infrared mockups
9. Hull form scale model
10. Integrated undersea warfare (IUW) system

The Advanced Gun System (AGS) includes support for increased range, improved lethality, an unmanned magazine, and increased sustainability in support of forces ashore. It also includes a long-range land attack projectile (LRLAP) that uses GPS for in-flight guidance. The Autonomic Fire Suppression System (AFSS) not only helps to put out fires but also helps to reduce the crew size. It features fully automated and unmanned response to both accidental and combat-induced fires. The dual-band radar (DBR) features the ability to detect hostile targets amid considerable land and sea clutter typical of littoral regions. The integrated deckhouse and apertures are designed to provide protection against electromagnetic fields nuclear, biological, and chemical (NBC) contaminants, and conventional warheads, and to support low-radar cross-section and infrared signatures for low observability. The integrated power system (IPS) uses permanent magnet synchronous motors (PMMs) to reduce acoustic noise, reduce operating and support costs, and allow more flexibility in ship design. The integrated undersea warfare (IUW) capability aims to provide in-stride mine avoidance and in situ environmental adaptation (the latter is assumed to mean some form of dynamic camouflage adaptation based on surroundings). The PVLS provides the ability to house land attack missiles and anti-air weapons to meet deep strike requirements and to provide flexibility in ship design by allowing these components to be placed anywhere on deck. The total ship computing environment (TSCE) supports network-centric warfare and command and control of all sensors, weapons, and ship control systems. It is built on an open architecture to support future enhancements. The TSCE also provides a common operational picture (COP) by combining both on- and off-board data. Finally, the hull form is designed to minimize radar cross-section while meeting requirements for basic seakeeping, such as maneuverability and stability.

Background

The DD(X) program originated back in 1991 when Navy planners first put together operational requirements for the next-generation surface combatant. The initial phases of the program included a system concept design (Phase I) and an initial systems design (Phase II). Both of these phases involved two competing teams, a "blue team"

Figure 8–2   DD(X) Land Attack Destroyer. (*Source*: Northrop Grumman)

led by Bath Iron Works with Lockheed Martin as the systems integrator and a "gold team" led by Ingalls Shipbuilding with Raytheon as the systems integrator.

In May 2001, the program, which was then called DD 21, was suspended pending the upcoming Quadrennial Defense Review (QDR). In November 2001, after the QDR and the events of September 11, the program was renamed DD(X) and was restructured to "focus on technology development and maturation, including robust land-based and sea-based testing of prototype technologies that could be leveraged across multiple ship classes."

On April 29, 2002, Northrop Grumman was awarded a $2.9 billion contract over four years to complete the system design for the DD(X) (Figure 8–2). The total U.S. Navy budget for the DD(X) in fiscal year 2004 is approximately $1.1 billion for research and development, with another $15 billion budgeted for the following five years.

Facts

Type: Multi-mission surface combatant/technology platform for Surface Combatant Navy
Contractor: Northrop Grumman
Length: 600 feet
Beam: 79.1 feet
Draft: 27.6 feet

Speed: 30.3 knots
Displacement: 14,064 LT
Weapons: 80 AVLS cells, 2 AGS 155-mm guns with 600 rounds, 2 40-mm close in guns, torpedoes
Hull: Wave-piercing tumblehome
Superstructure: Composite structure
Aviation: 1 MH60R and 3 VTUAVs
Boats: 2 7m RHIBs
Sensors: Dual Band Radar, Acoustic Sensor Suite, EO/IR System, ES/ELINT
Integrated Power System: 2 MT 30, 2 Small gas turbine gensets, 2 36 MW Permanent Magnet Motors
Crew: N/A
Life Expectancy: N/A
Construction Begins: FY 03–FY 06 (Testing of Engineering Development Models)
Delivery: N/A
Service: U.S. Navy

Source: U.S. Navy (Naval Sea Systems Command), Northrop Grumman

CG(X) Cruiser

The CG(X) cruiser is part of the family of ships within the future Surface Combatant Navy. It is the air dominance cruiser contingent of the surface combatant ships and will share many features in common with the DD(X) destroyer, including the hull form, propulsion plant, and basic combat systems. The DD(X) program will provide the technology and engineering baseline that contributes transformational technologies to the CG(X).

Features

The CG(X) cruiser is a multi-mission ship that is set to replace the Ticonderoga-class Aegis cruisers currently in service. Its mission will include having faster and longer-range missiles to support self-defense against incoming air attacks as well as to provide broader defense capabilities to detect, track, and destroy ballistic missiles outside the atmosphere. The advanced radar design on the CG(X) will include higher capabilities for detecting low-radar cross-section missiles at extended ranges.

The many changes leveraged from the DD(X), such as hull form, propulsion, and basic combat systems, will help the CG(X) to reduce operating and support costs and crew size. It will differ by using next-generation air and missile defense systems and advanced radars. Another difference is that it may substitute the Advanced Gun System (AGS) on the DD(X) with extra vertical launch systems (VLS).

Background

Because the CG(X) (Figure 8–3) will build on the innovations being designed for the DD(X) destroyer, there is limited information available about the detailed design of the CG(X) and the detailed plans for the fleet. At this stage in the program, there is less definition than the DD(X), and the requirements for the CG(X) are still under some degree of flux. Some information on the cost per ship can be gathered, however, by studying the cost estimates from the Congressional Budget Office in its March 2003 report, "Transforming the Navy's Surface Combatant Force." The study came up with cost estimates for the surface combatants, including the CG(X), based on top-level descriptions from Navy briefings and press reports. The estimate for the first CG(X) to be produced is $3.2 billion. This is $500 million higher than the first DD(X) to be produced and is based on the Congressional Budget Office's estimates for differences between the ships in four main areas. These four areas:

1. The cost of the next-generation Aegis system

2. Construction costs for installing this weapon system

3. An increase to 200 VLS cells in the CG(X), compared with the expected 128 cells of the DD(X)

4. An extra amount for anticipated change orders

The Congressional Budget Office's estimate for the cost of future CG(X) cruisers, beyond the first ship, is $2.2 billion.

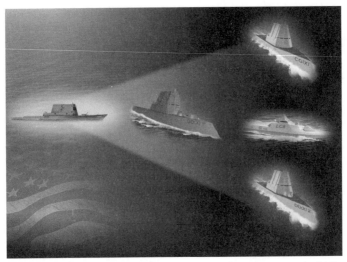

Figure 8–3   Transition from DD(X) into other programs, including CG(X). (*Source:* Northrop Grumman)

Facts

Type: Multi-mission surface combatant/air dominance cruiser
Contractor: None announced
Crew: Reduced manned
Life Expectancy: N/A
Construction Begins: N/A
Delivery: N/A
Status: Concept stage
Service: U.S. Navy

Source: U.S. Navy (Naval Sea Systems Command)

Littoral Combat Ship

The LCS is part of the family of ships within the future Surface Combatant Navy, along with the DD(X) destroyer and the CG(X) cruiser. The LCS is a small, fast, and highly maneuverable, focused mission ship that is designed for warfighting in the littorals. As a relatively low-cost, high-production, modular ship, its missions include anti-surface warfare, anti-submarine warfare, and countering other asymmetric threats in the littorals where its shallow draft, speed, and specialized equipment provide it with an advantage over the other ships in the fleet.

Features

The LCS will be smaller and have a shallower draft than the DD(X) and CG(X), and will be capable of focused missions in the littorals to help assure access and to defend against threats from enemy surface ships, mines, and submarines. A modular architecture allows various modules to be placed on the ship based on mission objectives. These modules may include necessary equipment and weapons to support anti-surface warfare against small boats, mine countermeasures, littoral anti-submarine warfare, intelligence, surveillance and reconnaissance, homeland defense, special operations, and logistics support. It is envisioned that specialty crew detachments would accompany these modules, then rotate back to their bases when the specific mission is completed. Modules may include anything that can be placed in a container, including unmanned aerial vehicles, helicopters, underwater vehicles, and other sensors and weapons systems deemed vital to a particular mission. The design of the mission modules also calls for modules to be rapidly reconfigurable in order to support changes to the mission or changes to the type of threat encountered.

In addition to the modularity of the LCS, the ship will also be equipped with network-centric technologies to allow it to operate as part of the larger, surface combatant force. Innovations from the DD(X) program will be leveraged to provide it with the latest in weapons, sensors, computer systems, hull form, propulsion, smart control systems, self-defense, and optimal manning.

Background

In November 2002, the Navy's Naval Sea Systems Command awarded six $500,000 contracts to perform 90-day concept studies related to the LCS (Figure 8–4). The awards were made to Bath Iron Works, Gibbs & Cox, John J. McMullen Associates, Lockheed Martin, Northrop Grumman, and Textron Systems. The three specific

Figure 8–4   Littoral Combat Ship. (*Source*: Lockheed Martin)

threats to be covered within the ship design were diesel submarines in the littorals, fast and armed small craft, and mines.

Later, in July 2003, three companies were awarded a firm-fixed-price contract for the performance of the "Flight 0" LCS preliminary design. The contractors included General Dynamics-Bath Iron Works ($8,900,000); Lockheed Martin Naval Electronics & Surveillance Systems-Surface Systems ($9,993,359); and Raytheon Company, Integrated Defense Systems ($9,996,124). As part of this work, the contractors will perform preliminary design efforts to refine their proposed LCS concepts. The work is expected to be completed in 2004.

Facts

Type: Surface combatant/focused-mission ship
Description: Networked, agile, and high-speed surface combatant with versatile warfighting capabilities optimized for littoral missions
Contractor: General Dynamics-Bath Iron Works, Lockheed Martin Naval Electronics & Surveillance Systems-Surface Systems, Raytheon Company-Integrated Defense Systems

Attributes:

>> Innovative hull form and propulsion system supporting economical loiter speeds, sustained Battle Group transit speeds and high speed sprints

>> Signature-management technologies to minimize infra-red, acoustic, magnetic, radar and wake emissions

>> State-of-the-art Damage Control Technology and Self-Defense Systems

>> Mission manned

Displacement: 1,000–4,000 tons
Draft: Less than 20 feet
Speed: 40–50 knots
Crew: Reduced manned
Life Expectancy: N/A
Construction Begins: FY 2005
Delivery: 2007 (First ship in the water)
Service: U.S. Navy

Source: U.S. Navy (Naval Sea Systems Command)

Virginia-Class Submarine

The Virginia-class submarines are the U.S. Navy's newest attack submarines and the most advanced submarines in the world. They are optimized for operation in the littorals (the shallow coastal regions of the ocean near the shore) and feature advanced technologies in the areas of firepower, maneuverability, and stealth.

Features

The Virginia-class submarine is 377 feet long, 34 feet in diameter, and can travel at a speed of more than 25 knots. In terms of endurance, it can remain submerged for up to three months at a time. Typical missions for the Virginia class will include countering various threats from surface ships, mines, and diesel submarines; conducting undetected surveillance and reconnaissance; and the insertion and extraction of Special Operations Forces.

Some of the innovations on board the Virginia-class submarines include a new type of periscope, a modular design, and enhanced command, control, communications, computers, intelligence, surveillance, and reconnaissance (C4ISR) capabilities. The new periscope is comprised of a photonics mast that contains several high-resolution color cameras and can send images to screen displays in the control room of the ship. The mast also contains a laser range finder that can help in calling periscope ranges. The modular design of the Virginia class gives the submarine a basic layout comprising the nuclear power plant, ship control functions, and self-defense mechanisms. The rest of the structure is available for various modular payloads according to mission type. For example, the torpedo tubes support launch and recovery of the LMRS and other forms of unmanned underwater vehicle (UUV). The redesign has also helped to reduce 15 crew watch-standers from the submarines' complement, compared with the crew required for a Seawolf-class submarine. The Virginia-class acoustic sensor suite includes a high-frequency sonar optimized for detection of diesel-electric and advanced air-independent propulsion (AIP) submarines, mines, and other hazards.

Background

The Virginia class (Figure 8–5) will help to replace the aging fleet of Los Angeles-class submarines and provide greater affordability than the current Seawolf class.

In September 1998, the U.S. Navy awarded a $4.2 billion contract for the team of General Dynamics' Electric Boat and Northrop Grumman Newport News Shipbuilding to begin construction of the first four ships in the Virginia class. These first four ships are scheduled to be delivered to the Navy between 2004 and 2007.

The keel-laying ceremony for the second Virginia-class submarine, *Texas* (SSN 775), took place on July 12, 2002, with the keel being authenticated by First Lady Laura Bush. Initial operational capability for the Virginia class is expected in 2006.

Facts

General Characteristics, Virginia Class

Builders: General Dynamics Electric Boat and Northrop Grumman Newport News Shipbuilding
Powerplant: 1 nuclear reactor, 1 shaft

Length: 377 feet (114.91 meters)
Beam: 34 feet (10.36 meters)
Displacement: Approximately 7,800 tons (7,925.18 metric tons)
Speed: 25+ knots (28+ mph, 46.3+ kph)
Depth: In excess of 800 feet
Cost: About $1.65 billion each (based on FY 1995 dollars and 30-ship class)
Ships:
>> *Virginia* (SSN 774), under construction; delivery in 2004
>> *Texas* (SSN 775), under construction; delivery in 2005
>> *Hawaii* (SSN 776), under construction; delivery in 2007
>> *North Carolina* (SSN 777), named December 11, 2000; delivery in 2006
Crew: 134 officers and enlisted
Payload: 38 weapons, including VLS; Special Operations Forces
Armament: Tomahawk land attack missiles, 12 VLS tubes, Mk-48 advanced capability torpedoes, 4 21-inch torpedo tubes, Mk-60 CAPTOR mines, advanced mobile mines, and UUVs
Countermeasures: Internal (reloadable), 14 external (non-reloadable)
Sonars: Spherical active/passive array, lightweight wide aperture arrays, TB-29 and future towed arrays, high-frequency sail and chin arrays

Source: U.S. Navy

Figure 8–5 Virginia-class submarine. (*Source*: Northrop Grumman)

Long-Term Mine Reconnaissance System

The LMRS is a submarine-based mine reconnaissance system that incorporates a UUV that is launched and retrieved through submarine torpedo tubes.

Features

The LMRS comprises several elements in addition to the actual UUV itself. The system built by Boeing for the U.S. Navy comprises two 20-foot-long, 21-inch-diameter, torpedo-shaped UUVs, a 60-foot robotic recovery arm, onboard handling equipment, support electronics, a shore-based depot, and a specialized van for vehicle transportation.

The LMRS is fully autonomous and untethered, meaning that it can be sent on missions for several hours while the host submarine conducts other missions of its own. It is also designed for full launch, recovery, and maintenance from Los Angeles- and Virginia-class submarines, using existing torpedo tubes as the launch technique. Four support personnel install, maintain, and utilize the system during operations. A typical mission is 40 hours, with each UUV alternated three times for a total of six separate sorties. During this time, the LMRS can cover a search area of 400 square nautical miles in its search for enemy mines.

The components of the LMRS UUV include a propulsion section, ballast and trim section, forward and aft electronics, side-look sonar (SLS) section, and forward-looking sonar at the front of the UUV.

Planned upgrades for the LMRS include the incorporation of synthetic aperture sonar (SAS), precision underwater mapping, and improved acoustic communications.

Background

The LMRS (Figure 8–6) is a five-year, over $100 million program that was started in November 1999. The previous program, the Near-Term Mine Reconnaissance System (NMRS), completed testing in May 1999. Both programs were part of the Navy's UUV master plan.

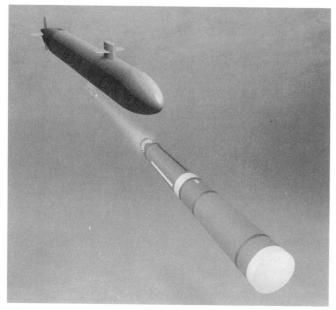

Figure 8–6   Long-Term Mine Reconnaissance System. (*Source*: U.S. Navy)

Boeing has been the prime contractor for the LMRS program and delivered the first system for testing to the U.S. Navy in November 2002. In October 2002, the Office of Naval Research announced that the SAS had been rapidly transitioned into the LMRS system. The SAS demonstrated four times the range and 36 times the resolution of the side-looking sonar and was, therefore, transitioned in ahead of the planned schedule. Initial operational capability for the LMRS is expected to be 2004.

Facts

Type: Submarine-based mine reconnaissance system
Contractor: Boeing
Platform: Los Angeles- and Virginia-class submarines
Length: 20 feet
Diameter: 21 inches
Support Personnel: 4
Service: U.S. Navy
Initial Operational Capability: 2004

Source: U.S. Navy (Naval Sea Systems Command)

Glossary

Aerodynamic Missile—(DOD, NATO) A missile which uses aerodynamic forces to maintain its flight path. See also ballistic missile; guided missile.

AFB—Air Force Base.

Altimeter—An instrument that measures height above ground.

AMRAAM—Advanced medium-range air-to-air missile.

ASROC—Anti-Submarine ROCket.

Asymmetric Warfare—Warfare targeted at the vulnerabilities of an enemy.

Autonomous Flight—Self-guided flight that requires no human intervention or control.

Avionics—Aviation electronics.

Ballistic Missile—(DOD, NATO) Any missile which does not rely upon aerodynamic surfaces to produce lift and consequently follows a ballistic trajectory when thrust is terminated. See also aerodynamic missile; guided missile.

Ballistic Trajectory—(DOD, NATO) The trajectory traced after the propulsive force is terminated and the body is acted upon only by gravity and aerodynamic drag.

Boost Phase—(DOD) That portion of the flight of a ballistic missile or space vehicle during which the booster and sustainer engines operate. See also midcourse phase; reentry phase; terminal phase.

C4ISR—Command, control, communications, computers, intelligence, surveillance, and reconnaissance.

CBR—Chemical, biological, and radiological.

CBRNE—Chemical, biological, radiological, nuclear, and high-yield explosives.

CBU—Cluster Bomb Unit.

CBU-87/B Combined Effects Munition—All-purpose, air-delivered, 1,000-pound cluster bomb.

CBU-89 Gator Mine—Air-delivered, 1,000-pound cluster bomb containing anti-tank and anti-personnel mines.

CBU-97—1,000-pound bomb with sensor-fused submunitions for anti-armor.

Chaff—(DOD) Radar confusion reflectors, consisting of thin, narrow metallic strips of various lengths and frequency responses, which are used to reflect echoes for confusion purposes. Causes enemy radar guided missiles to lock on to it instead of the real aircraft, ship, or other platform.

Circular Error Probable—(DOD) An indicator of the delivery accuracy of a weapon system, used as a factor in determining probable damage to a target. It is the radius of a circle within which half of a missile's projectiles are expected to fall. Also called CEP.

Cluster Bomb Unit—(DOD, NATO) An aircraft store composed of a dispenser and submunitions. Also called CBU.

Cold War—(DOD) A state of international tension wherein political, economic, technological, sociological, psychological, paramilitary, and military measures short of overt armed conflict involving regular military forces are employed to achieve national objectives.

Collateral Damage—(DOD) Unintentional or incidental injury or damage to persons or objects that would not be lawful military targets in the circumstances ruling at the time. Such damage is not unlawful so long as it is not excessive in light of the overall military advantage anticipated from the attack.

Command and Control—(DOD) The exercise of authority and direction by a properly designated commander over assigned and attached forces in the accomplishment of the mission. Command and control functions are performed through an arrangement of personnel, equipment, communications, facilities, and procedures employed by a commander in planning, directing, coordinating, and controlling forces and operations in the accomplishment of the mission. Also called C2.

Conventional Weapon—(DOD, NATO) A weapon that is neither nuclear, biological, nor chemical.

Cruise Missile—(DOD) Guided missile, the major portion of whose flight path to its target is conducted at approximately constant velocity; depends on the dynamic reaction of air for lift and upon propulsion forces to balance drag.

Decoy—(DOD) An imitation in any sense of a person, object, or phenomenon that is intended to deceive enemy surveillance devices or mislead enemy evaluation. Also called dummy.

Deterrence—(DOD) The prevention from action by fear of the consequences. Deterrence is a state of mind brought about by the existence of a credible threat of unacceptable counteraction.

Doppler Radar—(DOD) A radar system that differentiates between fixed and moving targets by detecting the apparent change in frequency of the reflected wave due to motion of target or the observer.

Electromagnetic Jamming—(DOD) The deliberate radiation, reradiation, or reflection of electromagnetic energy for the purpose of preventing or reducing an enemy's effective use of the electromagnetic spectrum, and with the intent of degrading or neutralizing the enemy's combat capability.

Electronic Warfare—(DOD) Any military action involving the use of electromagnetic and directed energy to control the electromagnetic spectrum or to attack the enemy. Also called EW. The three major subdivisions within electronic warfare are: electronic attack, electronic protection, and electronic warfare support.

FBCB2—Force XXI Battle Command Brigade and Below.

Fire Control—(DOD, NATO) The control of all operations in connection with the application of fire on a target.

Fire Control Radar—(DOD, NATO) Radar used to provide target information inputs to a weapon fire control system.

Force XXI Battle Command Brigade and Below—The main digital command and control system for the U.S. Army at the Brigade and below level. It provides on-the-move, real-time, and near-real-time battle command information and is a key component of the Army Battle Command System (ABCS). Also called FBCB2.

Forward Area—(DOD) An area in proximity to combat.

Friendly Fire—(DOD) In casualty reporting, a casualty circumstance applicable to persons killed or wounded in action mistakenly or accidentally by friendly forces actively engaged with the enemy, who are directing fire at a hostile force or what is thought to be a hostile force.

GBU—Guided Bomb Unit.

GBU-27—Air-delivered, 2,000-pound laser-guided bomb.

General-Purpose Bombs—Free-fall, nonguided bomb.

Global Positioning System—(DOD) A satellite constellation that provides highly accurate position, velocity, and time navigation information to users. Also called GPS.

GMTI—Ground Moving Target Indicator.

GPMG—General-Purpose Machine Gun.

GPS—Global Positioning System.

Guided Missile—(DOD) An unmanned vehicle moving above the surface of the Earth whose trajectory or flight path is capable of being altered by an external or internal mechanism. See also aerodynamic missile; ballistic missile.

ICBM—Intercontinental Ballistic Missile.

Inertial Guidance—(DOD) A guidance system designed to project a missile over a predetermined path, wherein the path of the missile is adjusted after launching by devices wholly within the missile and independent of outside information. The system measures and converts accelerations experienced to distance traveled in a certain direction.

Initial Operational Capability—(DOD) The first attainment of the capability to employ effectively a weapon, item of equipment, or system of approved specific characteristics that is manned or operated by an adequately trained, equipped, and supported military unit or force. Also called IOC.

INS—Inertial Navigation System.

Interdiction—(DOD) An action to divert, disrupt, delay, or destroy the enemy's surface military potential before it can be used effectively against friendly forces.

IOC—Initial Operational Capability.

JASSM—Joint Air-to-Surface Standoff Missile.

JDAM—Joint Direct Attack Munitions.

JSGPM—Joint Service General-Purpose Mask.

JSLIST—Joint Service Lightweight Integrated Suit Technology.

JSOW—Joint Standoff Weapon.

Laser Illuminator—(DOD) A device for enhancing the illumination in a zone of action by irradiating with a laser beam.

Laser Rangefinder—(DOD, NATO) A device which uses laser energy for determining the distance from the device to a place or object.

Laser Seeker—(DOD, NATO) A device based on a direction sensitive receiver which detects the energy reflected from a laser designated target and defines the direction of the target relative to the receiver.

Laser Target Designator—(DOD) A device that emits a beam of laser energy which is used to mark a specific place or object. Also called LTD.

Materiel—(DOD) All items (including ships, tanks, self-propelled weapons, aircraft, etc., and related spares, repair parts, and support equipment, but excluding real property, installations, and utilities) necessary to equip, operate, maintain, and support military activities without distinction as to its application for administrative or combat purposes.

Mbps—Megabytes per second.

MCBIP—Marine Corps Combat Identification Program.

Midcourse Phase—(DOD) That portion of the trajectory of a ballistic missile between the boost phase and the reentry phase. See also ballistic trajectory; boost phase; reentry phase; terminal phase.

Mk-62 Naval Mine—Naval mine dropped from an aircraft and adapted from the Mk-82 general-purpose bomb.

Mk-82 General-Purpose Bomb—Free fall, nonguided, general-purpose 500-pound bomb.

Mk-83 General-Purpose Bomb—Free fall, nonguided, general-purpose 1,000-pound bomb.

Mk-84 General-Purpose Bomb—Free fall, nonguided, general-purpose 2,000-pound bomb.

Moving Target Indicator—(DOD, NATO) A radar presentation which shows only targets that are in motion. Signals from stationary targets are subtracted out of the return signal by the output of a suitable memory circuit.

MSL—Mean Sea Level.

Munition—(DOD, NATO) A complete device charged with explosives, propellants, pyrotechnics, initiating composition, or nuclear, biological, or chemical material for use in military operations, including demolitions. Certain suitably modified munitions can be used for training, ceremonial, or nonoperational purposes. Also called ammunition. (*Note:* In common usage, "munitions" [plural] can be military weapons, ammunition, and equipment.)

Nautical Mile—(DOD) A measure of distance equal to one minute of arc on the Earth's surface. The United States has adopted the international nautical mile equal to 1,852 meters or 6,076.11549 feet. Also called nm.

NBC—Nuclear, biological, or chemical.

Objective Force—U.S. Army concept for future full-spectrum force: organized, manned, equipped, and trained to be more strategically responsive, deployable, agile, versatile, lethal, survivable, and sustainable across the entire spectrum of military operations from Major Theater Wars through counter-terrorism to Homeland Security.

Operation Desert Fox—"To strike military and security targets in Iraq that contribute to Iraq's ability to produce, store, maintain, and deliver weapons of mass destruction." (*Source*: *http:// www.defenselink.mil/specilaists/desert_fox.*)

Operation Allied Force—"Our military objective is to degrade and damage the military and security structure that President Milosevic (Yugoslav President) has used to depopulate and destroy the Albanian majority in Kosovo." (*Source*: Prepared statement of William S. Cohen, Secretary of Defense, to the Senate Armed Services Committee on April 15, 1999.)

Operation Enduring Freedom—The military phase of the war against terrorism that began on October 7, 2001.

Operation Iraqi Freedom—"The multinational coalition effort to liberate the Iraqi people, eliminate Iraq's weapons of mass destruction, and end the regime of Saddam Hussein." (From DOD)

Operation Joint Endeavor— U.S. and Allied peacekeeping operation in Bosnia between December 1995 and December 1996.

Operation Just Cause—U.S. military operation between December 1989 and January 1990 to protect U.S. interests and neutralize Panamanian Defense Forces and command and control in Panama.

Operation Southern Watch—U.S. and coalition enforcement of the no-fly zone over Southern Iraq.

Operational Requirements Document—(DOD) A formatted statement containing performance and related operational parameters for the proposed concept or system. Prepared by the user or user's representative at each milestone beginning with Milestone I, Concept

Demonstration Approval of the Requirements Generation Process. Also called ORD.

Ordnance—(DOD) Explosives, chemicals, pyrotechnics, and similar stores, e.g., bombs, guns and ammunition, flares, smoke, or napalm.

Overpressure—(DOD, NATO) The pressure resulting from the blast wave of an explosion. It is referred to as "positive" when it exceeds atmospheric pressure and "negative" during the passage of the wave when resulting pressures are less than atmospheric pressure.

Payload—(DOD, NATO) 1. The sum of the weight of passengers and cargo that an aircraft can carry. 2. The warhead, its container, and activating devices in a military missile. 3. The satellite or research vehicle of a space probe or research missile. 4. The load (expressed in tons of cargo or equipment, gallons of liquid, or number of passengers) which the vehicle is designed to transport under specified conditions of operation, in addition to its unladen weight.

Phased-Array Radar— An electronic scanning radar as opposed to a conventional mechanical radar. Supports increased data rates, instantaneous beam positioning, multi-mode operation and multi-target capability.

Precision-Guided Munitions—(DOD) A weapon that uses a seeker to detect electromagnetic energy reflected from a target or reference point and, through processing, provides guidance commands to a control system that guides the weapon to the target. Also called PGM. See also munitions.

Radar—(DOD) A radio detection device that provides information on range, azimuth, and/or elevation of objects.

Radar Altimeter—An altimeter that uses radar signals for measuring height above ground.

Radar Clutter—(DOD, NATO) Unwanted signals, echoes, or images on the face of the display tube that interfere with observation of desired signals.

RAF—Royal Air Force.

Reentry Phase—(DOD) That portion of the trajectory of a ballistic missile or space vehicle where there is a significant interaction of the vehicle and the Earth's atmosphere. See also boost phase; midcourse phase; terminal phase.

RF—Radio Frequency.

SAR—Synthetic Aperture Radar.

Sensor-Fuzed Weapons—Bombs with infrared sensors for attacking armored targets.

SLBM—Submarine-Launched Ballistic Missile.

Sortie—(DOD, NATO) In air operations, an operational flight by one aircraft.

Standoff—Ability to engage the enemy from a distance.

Submunition—(DOD, NATO) Any munition that, to perform its task, separates from a parent munition.

Subsonic—(DOD) Of or pertaining to speeds less than the speed of sound.

Supersonic—(DOD) Of or pertaining to speed in excess of the speed of sound.

Tactical Internet—Command, control, communications, and computers (C4) network providing the backbone for information to be distributed from the Army Battle Command and Control Systems (ABCS) and the Force XXI Battle Command Brigade and Below (FBCB2).

Terminal Phase—(DOD) That portion of the trajectory of a ballistic missile between reentry into the atmosphere or the end of the midcourse phase and impact or arrival in the vicinity of the target. See also boost phase; midcourse phase; reentry phase.

Theatre—(DOD) The geographical area outside the continental United States for which a commander of a combatant command has been assigned responsibility.

Transformation—"Transformation is the process of changing form, nature or function. Within the United States military, transformation requires changing the form, or structure of our military forces; the nature of our military culture and doctrine supporting those forces; and streamlining our warfighting functions to more effectively meet the complexities of the new threats challenging our nation in the new millennium." (*Source:* United States Joint Forces Command)

TSSAM —Tri-Service Standoff Attack Missile.

Turbojet—(DOD) A jet engine whose air is supplied by a turbine-driven compressor, the turbine being activated by exhaust gases.

V/STOL—Vertical and/or short takeoff and landing aircraft.

Vertical Replenishment—(DOD, NATO) The use of a helicopter for the transfer of materiel to or from a ship. Also called VERTREP.

WCMD—Wind-Corrected Munitions Dispenser.

WMD—Weapons of mass destruction.

Note: Items marked DOD or NATO prior to the definition are from *The DOD Dictionary of Military Terms*, available at *http://www.dtic.mil/doctrine/jel/doddict/*.

The DOD Dictionary and the Joint Acronyms and Abbreviations master data base are managed by the Joint Doctrine Division, J-7, Joint Staff.

References and Web Sites

AeroVironment Inc, *www.aerovironment.com*

Alvis Vickers, Ltd., *www.alvisvickers.co.uk*

Boeing, *www.boeing.com*

British Army, *http://www.army.mod.uk*

Crownhill Fort, *http://www.crownhillfort.co.uk*

Defense Advanced Research Projects Agency, *www.darpa.mil*

Department of Defense, *http://www.defenselink.mil*

Federation of American Scientists, *www.fas.org*

Fleet Air Arm Museum, *http://www.fleetairarm.com*

Fort Hood, *http://www.hood.army.mil*

Frontier Systems Inc, *www.recce.com*

Lockheed Martin, *www.lockheedmartin.com*

Naval Sea Systems Command, *http://www.navsea.navy.mil*

Northrop Grumman, *www.northropgrumman.com*

Raytheon, *www.raytheon.com*

Royal Air Force, *http://www.raf.mod.uk*

Royal Navy, *http://www.royal-navy.mod.uk*

Soldier Systems Center (Natick), *http://www.natick.army.mil*

The Tank Museum, Bovington, *http://www.tankmuseum.co.uk*

U.S. Air Force, *www.af.mil*

U.S. Army, *www.army.mil*

U.S. Coast Guard, *http://www.uscg.mil/USCG.shtm*

U.S. Navy, *www.navy.mil*

U.S. Marine Corps, *www.usmc.mil*

United Defense, L.P., *http://www.uniteddefense.com*

United States Air Force Museum, *http://www.wpafb.af.mil/museum*

VoxTec, *www.voxtec.com*

Index

A

ABCS. *See* Army Battle Command System

ABL. *See* Airborne Laser

Abrams, General Creighton W., 58

Aegis Weapons System
 background, 125–26
 Cold War, 125
 facts on, 126–27
 features, 124–25
 overview, 124

Affordable Moving Surface Target Engagement (AMSTE), 152, 212
 background, 214
 facts on, 215
 features, 213–14
 GMTI radars, 214
 overview, 213

AGM-154 Joint Standoff Weapon
 background, 102
 facts on, 102–3
 features, 101–2
 overview, 101

AGM-114B/K/M/N Hellfire
 background, 94–95
 facts on, 96
 features, 94
 Operation Desert Shield, 95
 Operation Desert Storm, 95
 Operation Iraqi Freedom, 95
 Operation Just Cause, 95
 overview, 94

AH-64D Apache Longbow
 background, 27–28
 facts on, 28
 features, 26–27
 Operation Desert Storm, 27–28
 Operation Iraqi Freedom, 27
 overview, 26

AIM-9 Sidewinder
  background, 97
  facts on, 97–98
  features, 96–97
  overview, 96
Air warfare (battlefield for today)
  AH-64D Apache Longbow, 26–28
  AV-8B Harrier II Plus (Harrier Jump
    Jet), 17–20
  B-2 Spirit, 12–15
  B-52 Stratofortress, 15–17
  B-1B Lancer, 10–12
  Defense Satellite Communications
    System, 39–41
  E-3 Sentry (AWACS), 29–31
  E-8C Joint STARS, 31–34
  Evolved Expendable Launch Vehicle
    (EELV), 50–53
  F-117A Nighthawk, 20–22
  Ground-Based Electro-Optical Deep
    Space Surveillance, 48–50
  Merlin HM Mk-1 Helicopter, 23–25
  Military Strategic and Tactical Relay
    System, 42–44
  Navstar Global Positioning System, 9,
    44–46
  overview, 7–9
  PAVE PAWS Radar System, 46–48
  RQ-1 Predator, 34–37
  RQ-4A Global Hawk, 37–39
  U.S. Air Force, 8–9
Air warfare (battlefield of tomorrow)
  F-35 Joint Strike Fighter, 154–58
  F-22 Raptor, 154, 158–61
  Future Combat System (FCS), 154
  global engagement, 153
  Hummingbird Warrior, 175–77
  Micro Air Vehicle (MAV), 176–79
  Organic Air Vehicle (OAV), 172–75
  overview, 153–55
  RAH-66 Comanche, 154, 161–64
  Unmanned Combat Armed Rotorcraft
    (UCAR), 170–71
  V-22 Osprey, 164–66
  X-43 experimental hypersonic flight
    research program, 155
  X-43A Hypersonic Flight, 179–82

X-45A Unmanned Combat Air Vehi-
  cle (UCAV), 167–70
Airborne Laser (ABL), 212–13
  background, 219–20
  facts on, 220–21
  features, 218–19
  overview, 218
  YAL-1A, 219
Aircraft carrier
  CVN 21 Future Aircraft Carrier, 227–28
  Nimitz-Class Aircraft Carrier, 121–24
AMSTE. See Affordable Moving Surface
  Target Engagement
Apache Longbow. See AH-64D Apache
  Longbow
Arleigh Burke-Class Destroyers
  background, 131
  facts on, 131–34
  features, 130–31
  overview, 130
  USS Arleigh Burke, 131
Army Battle Command System (ABCS)
  Force XXI Battle Command Brigade
    and Below (FBCB2), 76
  Tactical Internet, 79
Atmospheric Test Ban Treaty, 223
Attack Submarines (SSN)
  background, 135–36
  facts on, 137–39
  features, 134–35
  overview, 134
  USS Cheyenne, 136
  USS Connecticut, 136
  USS Los Angeles, 135
  USS Louisville, 135–36
  USS Seawolf, 136
  USS Virginia, 136
AV-8B Harrier II Plus (Harrier Jump Jet)
  background, 18–19
  facts on, 19–20
  features, 18
  Operation Allied Force, 19
  Operation Desert Storm, 19
  Operation Enduring Freedom, 19
  Operation Southern Watch, 19
  overview, 17–18
AWACS. See E-3 Sentry

B

B-2 Spirit
  background, 13–14
  facts on, 14–15
  features, 13
  Operation Allied Force, 13, 14
  Operation Enduring Freedom, 13, 14
  Operation Iraqi Freedom, 13, 14
  overview, 12–13
B-52 Stratofortress
  background, 16
  facts on, 16–17
  features, 16
  Gulf War, 16
  Operation Desert Storm, 15
  Operation Enduring Freedom, 15
  Operation Iraqi Freedom, 15
  overview, 15
B-1B Lancer
  background, 11–12
  Dyess AFB, 11
  facts on, 12
  features, 10–11
  Operation Allied Force, 10
  Operation Desert Fox, 10
  Operation Iraqi Freedom, 10
  overview, 10
Babylon
  background, 205–6
  facts on, 207
  features, 205
  overview, 204–5
Battlefield Combat Identification System
    (BCIS), 74–76
Battlefield (for today)
  air warfare, 7–53
  Department of Defense, 5
  ground warfare, 55–81
  munitions, 83–117
  naval warfare, 119–46
  overview, 1–6
  Quadrennial Defense Review of 2001,
    5
  technological transformations, 1–6
  transformation of military, 1–6
Battlefield (of tomorrow)

Affordable Moving Surface Target
    Engagement (AMSTE), 152
  air warfare, 153–82
  Defense Advanced Research Projects
    Agency (DARPA), 149–51
  Future Combat Systems (FCS) initia-
    tive, 148–49
  ground warfare, 183–209
  Joint Strike Fighter, 151–52
  munitions, 211–23
  naval warfare, 225–41
  overview, 147–52
  technology, 148–52
  Terrorism Information Awareness
    (TIA), 152
  trends, 148–49
BCIS (Battlefield Combat Identification
    System), 74–76
BFVS. See Bradley Fighting Vehicle Sys-
    tem
Biometric identification, 200
Blitzkrieg, 3–4
BLU-114/B "Blackout Bomb"
  background, 88–89
  facts on, 89
  features, 88
  Operation Allied Force, 88, 89
  Operation Iraqi Freedom, 88, 89
  overview, 88
BLU-82/B "Daisy Cutter"
  background, 90–91
  facts on, 91
  features, 90
  Gulf War, 90–91
  Operation Enduring Freedom, 90–91
  overview, 90
  Vietnam War, 90
Bradley Fighting Vehicle System (BFVS)
  background, 61
  facts on, 61–62
  features, 60–61
  overview, 60
Brain Machine Interfaces
  background, 208–9
  facts on, 209
  features, 207–8
  overview, 207

Bunker Buster. *See* GBU-28/GBU-37 "Bunker Buster"

C

CG(X) Cruiser
    background, 233
    facts on, 233–34
    features, 232–33
    overview, 232
Challenger 2 Main Battle Tank
    background, 63–64
    facts on, 64–65
    features, 63
    Operation Iraqi Freedom, 62, 64
    overview, 62–63
    tanks, 62–65
Cold War, 125
Comanche. *See* RAH-66 Comanche
CVN 21 Future Aircraft Carrier
    background, 228
    facts on, 228
    features, 227
    overview, 227

D

Daisy Cutter. *See* BLU-82/B "Daisy Cutter"
DARPA. *See* Defense Advanced Research Projects Agency
DD(X) Land Attack Destroyer
    background, 230–31
    facts on, 231–32
    features, 229–30
    overview, 229
Defense Advanced Research Projects Agency (DARPA), 149–51, 184–85
Defense Satellite Communications System (DSCS)
    background, 40
    facts on, 40–41
    features, 40
    overview, 39
"Dunking" sonar, 23

E

E-3 Sentry (AWACS)
    background, 30
    E-8C Joint STARS compared, 32
    facts on, 30–31
    features, 29–30
    Operation Desert Storm, 30
    overview, 29
E-8C Joint STARS
    background, 33
    E-3 Sentry (AWACS) compared, 32
    facts on, 33–34
    features, 32–33
    overview, 32
EELD. *See* Evidence Extraction and Link Discovery
EELV. *See* Evolved Expendable Launch Vehicle
Electromagnetic pulse (EMP), 213
    background, 222–23
    facts on, 223
    features, 221–22
    overview, 221
Evidence Extraction and Link Discovery (EELD), 184–85
    background, 203
    facts on, 203
    features, 202–3
    overview, 202
Evolved Expendable Launch Vehicle (EELV)
    background, 51–52
    facts on, 52
    features, 51
    overview, 50–51
Experimental Test Site, 49

F

F-35 Joint Strike Fighter, 154
    background, 157
    facts on, 157–58
    features, 156–57
    overview, 155–56
F-22 Raptor, 154
    background, 160

facts on, 161
features, 159–60
overview, 158–59
F-117A Nighthawk
  background, 21–22
  facts on, 22
  features, 20–21
  Operation Allied Force, 20
  Operation Desert Storm, 20, 21
  Operation Just Cause, 20
  overview, 20
Facial recognition, 200–201
FBCB2. *See* Force XXI Battle Command
  Brigade and Below
FCS. *See* Future Combat Systems
Fleet Ballistic Missile Submarines (SSBN)
  background, 140
  facts on, 141–42
  features, 139–40
  Ohio-class submarines, 140
  overview, 139
  USS *George Washington*, 140
  USS *Louisiana*, 140
Force XXI Battle Command Brigade and
  Below (FBCB2)
  Army Battle Command System
    (ABCS), 76
  background, 78
  facts on, 78
  features, 77–78
  overview, 76–77
FORCEnet, 226
Friendly fire, 74, 100
Future Combat Systems (FCS), 148–49,
  154
  background, 187–88
  facts on, 188
  features, 186
  overview, 186
Future Warrior
  background, 196
  facts on, 196–97
  features, 194–96
  overview, 194

G

Gait recognition, 201
GBU-28/GBU-37 "Bunker Buster"
  background, 86–87
  facts on, 87
  features, 86
  Gulf War, 86
  Operation Iraqi Freedom, 87
  overview, 86
GEODSS. *See* Ground-Based Electro-
  Optical Deep Space Surveillance
Global engagement, 153
Global Hawk. *See* RQ-4A Global Hawk
GMTI radars, 214
GPS. *See* Navstar Global Positioning Sys-
  tem
Ground-Based Electro-Optical Deep
  Space Surveillance
  background, 49
  facts on, 49–50
  features, 49
  overview, 48–49
Ground warfare (battlefield for today)
  Bradley Fighting Vehicle System
    (BFVS), 60–62
  Challenger 2 Main Battle Tank, 62–65
  Force XXI Battle Command Brigade
    and Below (FBCB2), 56–57, 76–
    78
  Joint Service Lightweight Integrated
    Suit Technology, 70–72
  M40/42 Chemical Biological Protec-
    tive Masks, 72–74
  M1A1 Abrams, 57–60
  M2A3 Bradley Fighting Vehicle Sys-
    tem, 60–62
  M3A3 Bradley Fighting Vehicle Sys-
    tem, 60–62
  Marine Corps Combat Identification
    Program, 74–76
  Night Vision Goggles (AN/PVS-7),
    67–69
  overview, 55–57
  soldiers' equipment, 55–57
  Tactical Internet, 56–57, 79–81
  Warrior Fighting Vehicle, 65–67

Ground warfare (battlefield of tomor-
row)
Babylon, 204–6
Brain Machine Interfaces, 207–9
Defense Advanced Research Projects
Agency (DARPA), 184–85
Evidence Extraction and Link Discov-
ery (EELD), 184–85, 202–4
Future Combat Systems (FCS), 186–
88
Future Warrior, 194–97
Human Identification at a Distance
(HumanID), 184–85, 200–202
Objective Force, 183–84
Objective Force Warrior (OFW), 191–
93
overview, 183–85
Terrorism Information Awareness
(TIA), 184–85, 197–200
Unmanned Ground Combat Vehicle
(UGCV), 188–90
Guided-Missile Submarines (SSGN)
background, 142–43
facts on, 143–44
features, 142
overview, 142
Gulf War
BLU-82/B "Daisy Cutter," 90–91
GBU-28/GBU-37 "Bunker Buster," 86
M1A1 Abrams, 58
Marine Corps Combat Identification
Program, 74

H

Harrier Jump Jet. See AV-8B Harrier II
Plus
Hellfire. See AGM-114B/K/M/N Hellfire
High-Altitude Endurance UAV program,
38
"Hit-to-kill" approach, 104
Hornet, 178
Human Identification at a Distance
(HumanID), 184–85
background, 201
biometric identification, 200

facial recognition, 200–201
facts on, 201–2
features, 200–201
gait recognition, 201
overview, 200
Hummingbird Warrior
background, 176
facts on, 176–77
features, 175–76
OAV compared, 175
overview, 175
Hypersonic flight. See X-43A Hypersonic
Flight

I

Identification program. See Human Identification at a Distance
Independent (tank), 3

J

Joint Direct Attack Munition (JDAM)
background, 99–100
facts on, 100–101
features, 99
friendly fire, 100
Operation Allied Force, 99
Operation Iraqi Freedom, 99
overview, 98
Joint Service Lightweight Integrated Suit
Technology
background, 71
facts on, 72
features, 70–71
Operation Iraqi Freedom, 70
overview, 70
Joint Standoff Weapon. See AGM-154
Joint Standoff Weapon
Joint STARS. See E-8C Joint STARS
JSF. See F-35 Joint Strike Fighter
JSLIST. See Joint Service Lightweight
Integrated Suit Technology

L

Language translation, 204–6
Laser, airborne. *See* Airborne Laser
Laser-guided bombs, 84–85
LCS. *See* Littoral Combat Ship
LG-118A Peacekeeper
   background, 113–14
   facts on, 114–15
   features, 113
   overview, 113
LGM-30 Minuteman III
   background, 110–11
   facts on, 111–12
   features, 110
   overview, 109–10
Littoral Combat Ship (LCS)
   background, 235
   facts on, 236–37
   features, 234–35
   overview, 234
Long-Term Mine Reconnaissance System
   (LMRS)
   background, 240–41
   facts on, 241
   features, 240
   overview, 240

M

M40/42 Chemical Biological Protective
   Masks
   background, 73
   facts on, 74
   features, 72–73
   overview, 72
M1A1 Abrams
   background, 58
   facts on, 58–60
   features, 57–58
   Gulf War, 58
   overview, 57
   tanks, 57–60
M2A3 Bradley Fighting Vehicle System,
   60–62
M3A3 Bradley Fighting Vehicle System,
   60–62

Marine Corps Combat Identification Program
   background, 75
   facts on, 75–76
   features, 74–75
   Gulf War, 74
   Operation Iraqi Freedom, 74
   overview, 74
Masks. *See* M40/42 Chemical Biological
   Protective Masks
Massive Ordnance Air Blast Bomb
   (MOAB)
   background, 92–93
   facts on, 93
   features, 92
   Operation Iraqi Freedom, 92–93
   overview, 92
MAV. *See* Micro Air Vehicle
Mazar-e-Sharif, 2
Merlin HM Mk-1 Helicopter
   background, 24
   facts on, 25
   features, 23–24
   overview, 23
Micro Air Vehicle (MAV)
   background, 178
   facts on, 178–79
   features, 177
   Hornet, 179
   overview, 176
   Wasp, 178
Military Strategic and Tactical Relay System (Milstar)
   background, 43
   facts on, 43–44
   features, 42
   overview, 42
Minuteman III. *See* LGM-30 Minuteman
   III
MOAB. *See* Massive Ordnance Air Blast
   Bomb
Moncrieff, Colin Scott, 2
Moncrieff counterweight disappearing
   gun, 2, 3
Munitions (battlefield for today)
   AGM-154 Joint Standoff Weapon,
   101–3

AGM-114B/K/M/N Hellfire, 94–96
AIM-9 Sidewinder, 96–98
blackout bomb, 85
BLU-114/B "Blackout Bomb," 88–89
BLU-82/B "Daisy Cutter," 90–91
GBU-28/GBU-37 "Bunker Buster,"
    86–87
Gulf War, 83–84
Hellfire missile, 85
Joint Direct Attack Munition
    (JDAM), 98–101
laser-guided bombs (LGBs), 83–84
LG-118A Peacekeeper, 113–15
LGM-30 Minuteman III, 109–12
Massive Ordnance Air Blast Bomb
    (MOAB), 84, 92–93
Operation Allied Force, 85
Operation Iraqi Freedom, 84, 85
overview, 83–85
Patriot Advanced Capability-3 (PAC-
    3), 85, 104–6
Tactical Tomahawk, 85
Tomahawk Cruise Missile, 85, 106–9
Trident Fleet Ballistic Missile, 115–17
Munitions (battlefield of tomorrow)
    Affordable Moving Surface Target
        Engagement (AMSTE), 212–15
    Airborne Laser (ABL), 212–13, 218–
        21
    electromagnetic pulse (EMP), 213,
        221–23
    overview, 211–13
    Self-Healing Minefield, 212, 215–17

N

Naval warfare (battlefield for today)
    Aegis Weapons System, 124–27
    Arleigh Burke-Class Destroyers, 130–
        34
    Attack Submarines (SSN), 134–39
    Fleet Ballistic Missile Submarines
        (SSBN), 139–42
    Guided-Missile Submarines (SSGN),
        142–44
    Nimitz-Class Aircraft Carrier, 121–24

overview, 119–20
    Sea Shadow (IX 529), 144–46
    Ticonderoga-Class Cruisers, 127–30
Naval warfare (battlefield of tomorrow)
    CG(X) Cruiser, 232–34
    CVN 21 Future Aircraft Carrier, 227–
        28
    DD(X) Land Attack Destroyer, 229–
        32
    FORCEnet, 226
    Littoral Combat Ship (LCS), 234–37
    Long-Term Mine Reconnaissance Sys-
        tem (LMRS), 240–41
    overview, 225–27
    Sea Basing, 226
    Sea Power 21, 225–26
    Sea Shield, 225–26
    Sea Strike, 225
    transformational objectives, 226–27
    Virginia-Class Submarine, 237–39
Navstar Global Positioning System
    background, 45
    facts on, 45–46
    features, 44–45
    overview, 44
Night Vision Goggles (AN/PVS-7)
    background, 68–69
    facts on, 69
    features, 67–68
    Operation Iraqi Freedom, 67
    overview, 67
Nighthawk. See F-117A Nighthawk
Nimitz-Class Aircraft Carrier
    background, 122–24
    facts on, 123–24
    features, 121–22
    overview, 121
    USS Ronald Reagan, 121–22, 123

O

Objective Force, 183–84
Objective Force Warrior (OFW), 191–93
    background, 192
    facts on, 193
    features, 191–92

overview, 191
Ohio-class submarines, 140
Operation Allied Force
    BLU-114/B "Blackout Bomb," 88, 89
    Joint Direct Attack Munition
        (JDAM), 99
    Tomahawk Cruise Missile, 106
Operation Desert Fox, 106
Operation Desert Shield, 95
Operation Desert Storm
    AGM-114B/K/M/N Hellfire, 95
    Defense Satellite Communications
        System, 40
    E-8C Joint STARS, 33
    Patriot Advanced Capability-3 (PAC-
        3), 105
    Tomahawk Cruise Missile, 106
    Warrior Fighting Vehicle, 65
Operation Enduring Freedom
    BLU-82/B "Daisy Cutter," 90–91
    E-8C Joint STARS, 33
    RQ-4A Global Hawk, 38
Operation Iraqi Freedom
    AGM-114B/K/M/N Hellfire, 95
    BLU-114/B "Blackout Bomb," 88, 89
    Challenger 2 Main Battle Tank, 62, 64
    E-8C Joint STARS, 33
    GBU-28/GBU-37 "Bunker Buster," 87
    Joint Direct Attack Munition
        (JDAM), 99
    Joint Service Lightweight Integrated
        Suit Technology, 70
    Marine Corps Combat Identification
        Program, 74
    Massive Ordnance Air Blast Bomb
        (MOAB), 92–93
    Night Vision Goggles (AN/PVS-7), 67
    RQ-1 Predator, 36
    Tomahawk Cruise Missile, 108
Operation Joint Endeavor, 33
Operation Just Cause, 95
Organic Air Vehicle (OAV)
    background, 173
    facts on, 174–75
    features, 172–73
    Hummingbird Warrior compared,
        175

overview, 172
Osprey. See V-22 Osprey

P

Patriot Advanced Capability-3 (PAC-3)
    background, 105
    facts on, 105–6
    features, 104–5
    "hit-to-kill" approach, 104
    Operation Desert Storm, 105
    overview, 104
PAVE PAWS Radar System
    background, 47
    facts on, 47–48
    features, 47
    overview, 46
Peacekeeper. See LG-118A Peacekeeper
Phraselator, 204–6
Predator. See RQ-1 Predator

Q

Quadrennial Defense Review of 2001, 5

R

RAH-66 Comanche, 154
    background, 163
    facts on, 163–64
    features, 162–63
    overview, 161–62
Raptor. See F-22 Raptor
RQ-1 Predator
    background, 35–36
    facts on, 36–37
    features, 35
    overview, 34
RQ-4A Global Hawk
    background, 38
    facts on, 38–39
    features, 37–38
    overview, 37
Rumsfeld, Donald, 2

S

Scramjet engine, 180
Sea Basing, 226
Sea Power 21, 225–26
Sea Shadow (IX 529)
   background, 145
   facts on, 146
   features, 144–45
   overview, 144
Sea Shield, 225–26
Sea Strike, 225
Self-Healing Minefield, 212
   background, 216–17
   facts on, 217
   features, 216
   overview, 215–16
Sidewinder. *See* AIM-9 Sidewinder
SSBN. *See* Fleet Ballistic Missile Submarines
SSGN. *See* Guided-Missile Submarines
Submarines
   Attack Submarines, 134–39
   Fleet Ballistic Missile Submarines, 139–42
   Guided-Missile Submarines, 142–43
   Virginia-Class Submarine, 237–39

T

Tactical Internet
   Army Battle Command System (ABCS), 79
   background, 81
   facts on, 81
   features, 80
   overview, 79
Tactical Tomahawk, 106–7
Technology
   future issues, 148–52
   present issues, 1–6
Terrorism Information Awareness (TIA), 152, 184–85
   background, 198–99
   facts on, 199–200
   features, 197–98
   overview, 197

TIA. *See* Terrorism Information Awareness
Ticonderoga-Class Cruisers
   background, 128
   facts on, 128–30
   features, 127
   overview, 127
Tomahawk Cruise Missile
   background, 108
   facts on, 108–9
   features, 107
   Operation Allied Force, 106
   Operation Desert Fox, 106
   Operation Desert Storm, 106
   Operation Iraqi Freedom, 108
   overview, 106
   Tactical Tomahawk, 106–7
Trends, future, 148–49
Trident Fleet Ballistic Missile
   background, 116
   facts on, 116–17
   features, 115
   overview, 115

U

UCAR. *See* Unmanned Combat Armed Rotorcraft
UCAV program, 168–69
UGCV. *See* Unmanned Ground Combat Vehicle
Unmanned Combat Armed Rotorcraft (UCAR)
   background, 171
   facts on, 172
   features, 170–71
   overview, 170
Unmanned Ground Combat Vehicle (UGCV)
   background, 189–90
   facts on, 190
   features, 188–89
   overview, 188
USS *Arleigh Burke*, 131
USS *Cheyenne*, 136
USS *Connecticut*, 136

USS *George Washington*, 140
USS *Los Angeles*, 135
USS *Louisiana*, 140
USS *Louisville*, 135–36
USS *Ronald Reagan*, 121–22, 123
USS *Seawolf*, 136
USS *Virginia*, 136

V

V-22 Osprey
    background, 165–66
    facts on, 166
    features, 165
    overview, 164
Vietnam War, 90
Virginia-Class Submarine
    background, 238
    facts on, 239
    features, 237–38
    overview, 237

W

Warrior Fighting Vehicle
    background, 66
    facts on, 67
    features, 65
    Operation Desert Storm, 65
    overview, 65
Wasp, 177–78

X

X-43 experimental hypersonic flight
    research program, 155
X-43A Hypersonic Flight
    background, 180–81
    facts on, 182
    features, 180
    overview, 179–80
    scramjet engine, 180
X-45A Unmanned Combat Air Vehicle
    background, 168–69
    facts on, 169–70
    features, 167–68
    overview, 167

Y

YAL-1A, 219

8 reasons why you should read the Financial Times for 4 weeks RISK-FREE!

To help you stay current with significant developments in the world economy ... and to assist you to make informed business decisions — the Financial Times brings you:

 Fast, meaningful overviews of international affairs ... plus daily briefings on major world news.

 Perceptive coverage of economic, business, financial and political developments with special focus on emerging markets.

 More international business news than any other publication.

 Sophisticated financial analysis and commentary on world market activity plus stock quotes from over 30 countries.

❺ Reports on international companies and a section on global investing.

❻ Specialized pages on management, marketing, advertising and technological innovations from all parts of the world.

❼ Highly valued single-topic special reports (over 200 annually) on countries, industries, investment opportunities, technology and more.

❽ The Saturday Weekend FT section — a globetrotter's guide to leisure-time activities around the world: the arts, fine dining, travel, sports and more.

FT **FINANCIAL TIMES**
World business newspaper

The *Financial Times* delivers a world of business news.

Use the Risk-Free Trial Voucher below!

To stay ahead in today's business world you need to be well-informed on a daily basis. And not just on the national level. You need a news source that closely monitors the entire world of business, and then delivers it in a concise, quick-read format.

With the *Financial Times* you get the major stories from every region of the world. Reports found nowhere else. You get business, management, politics, economics, technology and more.

Now you can try the *Financial Times* for 4 weeks, absolutely risk free. And better yet, if you wish to continue receiving the *Financial Times* you'll get great savings off the regular subscription rate. Just use the voucher below.